SERIAL
KILLERS

A shocking history

SERIAL
KILLERS

A shocking history

igloo

Published in 2011
by Igloo Books Ltd
Cottage Farm
Sywell
NN6 0BJ

www.igloo-books.com

A copy of the British Library Cataloguing-in-Publication
Data is available from the British Library

10 9 8 7 6 5 4 3 2 1

ISBN 978-0-85734-792-3

Printed and manufactured in China

Contents

Contents

Introduction

Murder, and the minds of people who commit this kind of crime, are compelling subjects. But there is one kind of murder that stands out from all others. This type of murder is perpetrated by a killer who becomes addicted to the thrill of committing the crime.

A single brutal slaying does not satisfy a psychopath; he or she must strike again and again. This kind of murderer is known as a serial killer. It is their chilling, real-life stories that fascinate the most.

But it is not only the murders that are interesting. Our natural curiosity is heightened because, in most cases, serial killers present ordinary faces to the world. We could bump into them any day, in a store, on a train…or in a street in the middle of the night.

Serial killers make up our worst nightmares because any of these psychopaths could live next door, displaying an ordinary face, yet capable of sickening deeds.

There are exceptions—no one would consider Charles Manson and his 'Family' of followers as the people next door. But, more usual is the case of Wayne Gacy: family man, pillar of the community, children's party host. This part-time children's clown killed 33 people in an horrific manner. And a handsome charmer like John Haigh would have been a perfect guest at any dinner table—if you didn't know that he kept an acid bath in which to dissolve the bodies of his victims.

Whereas a mass murderer tends to strike just once, and can even recoil at the horror of the crime they have committed, a serial killer's bloodlust is rarely satisfied. The thrill of getting away with one murder simply leads to the next.

There is nothing new about serial killing. Jack the Ripper, in Victorian London, could never have known that many years later, he would be labeled a serial killer. His victim count was not high and his reign of terror was short, yet the nature of his crimes earned him the title. Herman Mudgett, who disposed of as many as 200 people in 19th century Chicago, is known as America's first serial killer.

These are just two examples of the manic murderers portrayed here in the history of crime.

1ST PAGE: Serial killer Ted Bundy is led into the Pitkin County courthouse, in Aspen, Colorado, in 1977.

2ND PAGE: Aileen Wuornos leaves courtroom 4A in the Marion County Judicial Center in Ocala, Florida, in February 2001.

ABOVE: Albert De Salvo, the Boston Strangler, prays in the chapel at Walpole State Prison, Massachusetts, in the early 1970s.

Beverley Allitt

Beverley Allitt suffered from the rare syndrome Münchausen's Disease by Proxy, a psychological disorder in which those affected feign illness or trauma to draw sympathy from others. She had visited doctors no fewer than 50 times since adolescence with phantom ailments, including pregnancy, a stomach ulcer, and a brain tumor. The freak Münchausen's condition can also have a much more perilous side effect—causing sufferers to harm others deliberately so they can care for them later. This was an especially dangerous trait in the case of Beverley Allitt—because she was a nurse.

Child-Killing Nurse Showed No Mercy, No Remorse

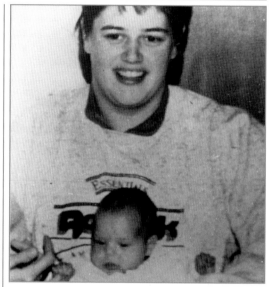

ABOVE: Mentally disturbed Beverley Allitt pretended to care for babies and young children, but she was in fact a callous murderer.

Since childhood, Allitt had always wanted to be an 'angel of mercy'. At the age of 17, she took a pre-nursing training course and got her first job at the Grantham and Kesteven General Hospital, Lincolnshire, as a trainee nurse on the pediatric ward, looking after sick children. But the children on Ward Four just got sicker and sicker.

Eight-week-old Liam Taylor was her first murder victim. He died of a massive heart attack on February 23, 1991, just two days after being admitted with a chest infection. Ten days later, Timothy Hardwick, a mentally and physically handicapped 11-year-old, died after being treated by Allitt for an epileptic fit, within three hours of being admitted. The following month, five-week-old Becky Phillips died after suffering convulsions at home hours after being released from hospital. She too had been under the care of Nurse Allitt on Ward Four. Finally, Claire Peck, aged just 15 months, died on April 22 after routine treatment for asthma.

Baby Claire was the last of Allitt's victims to die, although nine other children under Allitt's 'care' had contracted life-threatening conditions. Following Claire's death, the hospital authorities realized that the odds of so many children falling seriously ill on one ward was beyond coincidence and police were called in. Their first convincing evidence that a killer was responsible came after tests on one of Ward Four's tiny

survivors, frail five-month-old Paul Crampton, revealed that he had an abnormally high level of insulin in his blood. He could only have been injected with the drug while in hospital.

A lengthy police and medical investigation had at first failed to find the cause of the series of mystery deaths but, once blood tests had been carried out on other victims, a simple check of staff rotas showed that the common factor was Beverley Allitt. She had administered to the children lethal and near-lethal overdoses of both insulin and potassium chloride. She had also tried to suffocate some of them.

At her trial at Nottingham Crown Court in May 1993, a jury heard how, in her twisted mind, she believed she was doing no wrong in killing without mercy. The plain, overweight, frumpy 24-year-old was found guilty of murdering four children, attempting to murder another three and causing grievous bodily harm to a further six. For the families of the young victims, the jury's verdict ended two years of torment. However, Allitt herself showed not a shred of emotion as she was sentenced to serve life, four times over, in a prison for the criminally insane.

RIGHT: Allitt pictured at home. The nurse injected her multiple victims with lethal doses of insulin and potassium chloride.

Nathaniel Bar-Jonah

Although never charged with murder, 210lb (5.7kg) chef Nathaniel Bar-Jonah, a convicted felon and child sex attacker, was suspected of molesting, killing, and cannibalizing as many as 54 children. Born David Paul Brown in Worcester, Massachusetts, in February 1957, he might have been one of America's most notorious criminals—but it may never be known whether or not the frightening murder toll was real or the figment of his sick imagination.

A Sick Fantasy—
Or Did He Kill 54?

In 1974, David Brown received one year of probation for impersonating a policeman and sexually assaulting an eight-year-old boy. In 1977, he was convicted of kidnapping and attempted murder by strangling two boys as they left a movie theater. He was sentenced to 20 years' imprisonment.

While incarcerated, he changed his name to Nathaniel Bar-Jonah, as he wished people to think he was Jewish— 'so he could feel persecution', according to psychiatrists.

Shortly after his 1991 release, he was charged with assaulting another Massachusetts boy. A judge released him on the condition that he move in with his mother in Great Falls, Montana. Once there, he continued to prey on children, sexually assaulting a 14-year-old boy from Great Falls while hanging the boy's eight-year-old cousin from a kitchen ceiling. Both survived.

After more spells in prison and one in a mental institution, he was arrested again in 1999 for impersonating a police officer outside an elementary school and carrying gun and pepper spray. Police searched Bar-Jonah's home, uncovering thousands of newspaper pictures of children aged between five and 17, among them some he had been convicted of abducting previously. They also found cannibalistic coded recipe journals featuring dishes called 'barbecued kid', 'little boy stew', and 'lunch on the patio with roasted child'.

More disturbingly, bone fragments identified as belonging to an unknown young male were discovered under his house. Hair from another was found in a meat grinder in his kitchen.

Among the pictures of children found in the house was that of 10-year-old Zachary Ramsey, who had gone missing in 1997 on his return from school. Within days of the child's disappearance, Bar-Jonah had a barbeque for neighbors, where several of the guests complained of 'strange-tasting' meat. He had told them it was venison. Little did the guests know they may have helped Bar-Jonah dispose of the little boy.

There was a mass of evidence that pointed to Bar-Jonah being Zachary's killer—not least his telling the boy's mother, Rachel, that he had 'hunted, killed, butchered and wrapped the meat' of her son. Despite this, she insisted that she did not think Bar-Jonah had anything to do with Zachary's disappearance and believed the child still to be alive. This deep-held belief was confirmed by a psychic she visited. The child's remains have never been found.

The trial for the sexual abuse and attempted murder of the Great Falls boys finally got underway in Montana in 2002. The jury found Bar-Jonah guilty of kidnapping and sexual assault and gave him the maximum sentence of 130 years' imprisonment.

Suffering from severe diabetes, Bar-Jonah was found dead from a heart attack in his cell on April 13, 2008, the true scale of his sick crimes still unknown.

Sawney Beane

No one knows the truth about the strange saga of Sawney Beane. The facts about this ancient case of multiple murders are lost in the mists of time, and it is acknowledged that much of the story may be myth more than legend. However, it amply proves that 'serial killers' have been with us through the ages. And it is perhaps illuminating to look back to a time when, although the term had not yet been coined, there were villains whose murderous tally stacked up, not into single figures nor even into the teens, but into the hundreds.

Curse Of The Cave-Dwelling Cannibals

Sawney Beane, reputedly born around 1380, was the vagabond son of a road-mender and ditch digger who lived near Edinburgh, Scotland. Too feckless to follow his father's trade, he seduced a local girl and was driven out of town. Beane and his mistress fled to Galloway, on the west coast of Scotland, where they lived in a cave and raised a family on the proceeds of sheep stealing and robbing travelers.

However, unlike other historic outlaws of the highway, such as Robin Hood and Dick Turpin, there was nothing romantic about the way of life of the Beanes. For robbery soon turned to murder and murder to cannibalism. Such human monsters are a rare and usually solitary breed but the Beane clan worked as an entire family team. They lived in a deep, tortuous cave system that was accessible only at low tide. The sea flooded some 220 yards (200m) into the cave entrance before the family's hideout was reached.

Over 25 years the evil clan founded by Sawney (sometimes known as 'Sandy') Beane grew, through exclusively incestuous unions, to eight sons, six daughters, 18 grandsons and 14 granddaughters. Together they made an entire coastal area unsafe for both man and beast. They hunted in packs, like wild animals, attacking groups of up to six travelers on foot or two riders on horseback. Anyone caught would be robbed, slaughtered, and eaten as the most effective means of disposing of their victims and feeding the family. The number of their victims is unknown but, according to folklore, probably exceeded 100; some histories say over 1,000.

The story passed down anecdotally over the years is that when grim tales of the cave dwellers at last reached King James I of Scotland in 1435, he raised a special force to track down and capture the Beanes. It arrived on the Galloway coast just as the Beanes made a fatal blunder. While a group of them were attacking a man and his wife, they were surprised by a party of horsemen and fled, leaving the woman's disemboweled body on the roadside. The royal forces were not far distant and took up the pursuit, using tracker dogs to follow the trail of the fugitives to their subterranean lair.

Although undoubtedly exaggerated over the years, the scene the royal force found within the caves was likened to a human abattoir. Legend has it that hung from the cave roof or laid out on racks were male and female corpses, both whole and dismembered, some fresh, some smoked, some dried, some pickled, and some salted. There were also animal carcasses, stolen saddles, bundles of clothes, provisions, and valuables.

The bestial Beanes, all 48 of them, were shackled and taken to Leith, near Edinburgh, where they were summarily tried and, without exception, condemned to death. Sawney Beane had his hands, feet, and penis severed. The other male members of the clan then suffered the same dismemberment and all were left to bleed to death. As they did so, they were made to watch their womenfolk being tossed alive into three great fires.

RIGHT: An artist's impression of the beastly Sawney Beane outside his family's gruesome cave dwelling.

Bender Family

The Bender family attracted victims like the flies that buzzed around the dingy Wayside Inn they ran on a dusty Kansas trail. Any passing stranger who appeared to have some money would be invited to their dinner table within the dirty 16ft by 20ft (5x6m) cabin. Many did not live to enjoy their meal, instead ending up being murdered in the most horrific manner.

Unwary Wayfarers Slain By Trapdoor Tricksters

No one knows when the Benders' murderous reign began, but the end came after Dr William York left his brother's house at Fort Scott, Kansas, on March 9, 1873, to ride home to the town of Independence. He did not arrive, so his brother, a colonel in the US Cavalry, set out to scour the trail. Colonel York's first call was at the Wayside Inn, at the hamlet of Cherryvale, where the Benders offered him food and shelter.

The colonel knew his brother had intended breaking his journey there, and that night he too got to know the unsavory owners. There was old man Bender, a 60-year-old surly East European immigrant, his shrewish wife aged 50, a half-witted son and an ugly, unmarried daughter. They all denied any knowledge of

Dr York, blaming bandits or Indians for the brother's disappearance. But because of the colonel's persistent inquiries, they panicked and, hurriedly packing their belongings onto a cart, they fled.

On May 9, another search party on the trail of Dr York found the Wayside Inn abandoned and found several animals, including a small flock of sheep, either dead or dying from hunger and thirst. They also noticed that recent rains had revealed a freshly dug grave. It contained the body of Dr York, his skull smashed and his throat cut from ear to ear.

Further digging revealed the remains of no fewer than seven other victims. All of them had been killed in the same way apart from a small girl. Judging from her position, it was apparent she had been thrown into the shallow grave while still alive. Later, another child's body was unearthed, dreadfully decomposed but probably that of a girl of about eight.

Meanwhile, other members of the search party were investigating the source of a foul smell that permeated the cabin. Beneath a trapdoor in the floor they found

ABOVE: The Bender family's humble log cabin, inside which they murdered and robbed at will.

ABOVE LEFT AND RIGHT: Sketched portraits of the evil Bender family, who lured unsuspecting travelers to their deaths.

a roughly-dug pit, its floor and walls stained with blood—and the modus operandi of the ghastly Benders gradually became clear.

The family would invite a guest to join them for dinner, always taking great care to ensure he or she was seated with their backs to a curtained-off sleeping area. One of the family would be waiting behind the curtain to smash the victim's skull with a heavy hammer and finish him or her off with a knife to the throat. After searching the body for valuables, it would be dropped through a trapdoor into the revolting cellar below. Then after nightfall, it would be buried in a shallow grave.

Following these grisly discoveries, posses were formed to hunt down the Benders but they were never discovered—at least, officially. Legend has it that one of the several local vigilante patrols caught up with the Benders and local lawmen allowed rough and instant justice to be meted out to them.

David Berkowitz

His weapon was a .44 revolver, and at first the New York tabloids tagged him 'the .44-Caliber Killer'. But from the moment when police found a seemingly deranged note at the scene of one particularly senseless double murder, the killer became known for his bizarre nickname: 'Son of Sam'.

Sick Taunts Of The Killer Called 'Son of Sam'

The first of a series of callously teasing letters was left by the killer after shooting student Valentina Suriani and boyfriend Alexander Esau as they sat in their car in the Bronx in April 1977. Detectives did not know what to make of the rambling missive, in which the gunman complained that he was 'deeply hurt' that the media were referring to him as a woman-hater. He wrote…

I am not. But I am a monster. I am the Son of Sam. I am a little brat. Sam loves to drink blood. "Go out and kill," commands father Sam…I am on a different wavelength to everybody else—programed to kill. However, to stop me you must kill me. Attention all police: Shoot me first—shoot to kill or else. Keep out of my way or you will die! I am the monster—

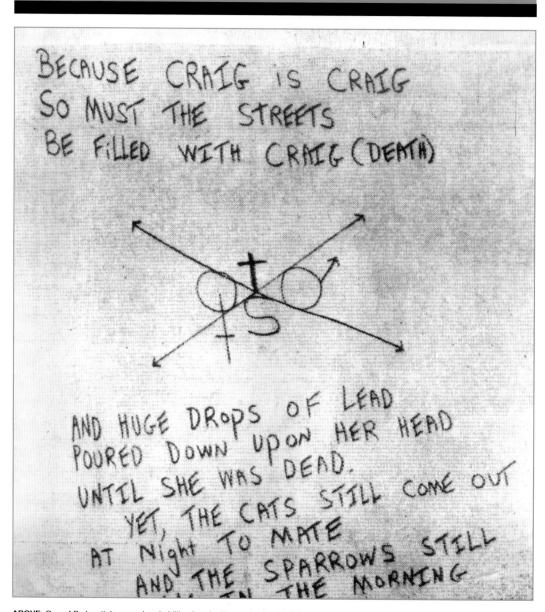

ABOVE: One of Berkowitz's crazed and chilling handwritten notes in which he appears to describe hammering a victim to death.

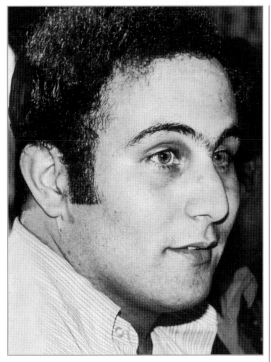

ABOVE: A portrait of convicted New York City serial killer David Berkowitz, known as the 'Son of Sam'.

"Beelzebub, the Chubby Behemoth". I love to hunt. Prowling the streets looking for fair game—tasty meat. I live for the hunt—my life. I don't belong on earth. I'll be back! I'll be back! Yours in murder—Mr Monster.'

This 'Son of Sam', this 'Mr Monster' was a plump, chubby-cheeked, 33-year-old bachelor named David Berkowitz. Born illegitimately to a Brooklyn showgirl on June 1, 1953, he was raised by caring, adoptive parents who ran a hardware store in the Bronx. He was deeply affected in his early teens by the death of his doting adoptive mother, Pearl Berkowitz, complaining that her death from cancer was caused by 'evil forces… as part of a master-plan to break me down'. When he was 18, his adoptive father remarried David left home and enlisted in the Army.

ABOVE: One of Berkowitz's bizarre notes. One line reads: 'I am possessed', another, 'I am going to have a nervous breakdown'.

During three years' service in Korea, he converted from Judaism to fundamentalist Christianity and, once back in the United States, spent his off-duty hours preaching from street corners in Louisville, Kentucky, where he was stationed. In 1974 he returned to the Bronx where, after a spell as a security guard, he joined the US Mail, sorting letters.

It was while working as a mailman that Berkowitz brought fear to the streets of New York for almost exactly one year, from July 29, 1976, to August 1, 1977. He killed six women and viciously wounded another seven. And throughout his mad campaign of carnage, he taunted police with a series of letters bragging about his deeds. Ironically, in his role as a postal worker, Berkowitz may well have handled the mailbags that contained his own letters as 'Son of Sam'.

Berkowitz's first killing seemed wholly random. He laid in wait as a car pulled up in a quiet street in the Bronx and 18-year-old Donna Lauria stepped out, said goodbye to her friend Jody Valente, who remained in the car, and turned to head into her parents' apartment.

Berkowitz ran from the shadows, pulled his .44 caliber gun from a paper bag, crouched down and fired three shots. Donna died and Jody was wounded.

The killer struck again on October 23, and once again the targets were two young people in a parked car, this time in the borough of Queens. Detective's daughter Rosemary Keenan, 18, escaped the bullets but her 20-year-old friend, Carl Denaro, was shot in the head and survived.

A month later, two young women sitting on the steps of their Queens home were less lucky. The gunman walked up and wounded both Joanne Lomino and Donna DeMasi, the latter being permanently paralyzed by a bullet to her spine. In January 1977, two bullets shattered the window of a car parked in Queens, one hitting John Diel but the other missing his girlfriend Christine Freund. In the same area in March, student Virginia Voskerichian died with a bullet to the face. Because the bullets all came from the same pistol, a 300-strong '.44 Killer' Task Force was organized, but were hampered by apparent lack of motive.

ABOVE: Flanked by lawyers and warders, Berkowitz holds a news conference at Attica prison, New York State, in June 1980.

I am so glad sb. has been apprehended but I wish that someone would help me.

final desperation

ABOVE: Another of Berkowitz's scrawlings, this time after his arrest. He confesses that he is 'not well'.

As his notoriety grew, and the 'Son of Sam' note was found at the scene of the Bronx double murder in April 1977, Berkowitz began sending letters to the rival tabloid *New York Post* and *New York Daily News*. Journalist Jimmy Breslin adopted the very risky tactic of replying in his column on the *News*. One letter from the killer warned him: 'Mr Breslin, sir, don't think that because you haven't heard from (me) for a while that I went to sleep. No, rather, I am still here. Like a spirit roaming the night. Thirsty, hungry, seldom stopping to rest.'

On July 29, 1977, the anniversary of his first attack, Breslin asked 'Son of Sam' in his column: 'Will you kill again?' The very next night, Berkowitz shot dead 20-year-old Stacy Moskowitz and blinded her date, Robert Violante, as they sat in their car in a Brooklyn street.

Berkowitz was finally caught thanks to a $35 parking ticket, issued near the scene of the shooting. A computer trace of the summons showed that it had been slapped on a Ford Galaxie, license plate 561XLB, owned by David Berkowitz. Task Force detectives caught up with it parked outside the killer's apartment—with a rifle protruding from a bag on the back seat and an arsenal of weapons in the trunk. In the glovebox was a letter addressed to police, promising more attacks, including a massacre at a Long Island nightclub where Berkowitz planned to 'go out in a blaze of glory'.

When an unsuspecting Berkowitz emerged from his apartment and stepped into his car, he found 15 guns trained at his head. He had no time to draw the .44 he was carrying in a brown paper bag. 'Okay, you've got me,' he said. 'What took you so long?'

On the evidence of his maniacal letters, Berkowitz could have entered a defense of insanity. Instead, he pleaded guilty to all charges and, on August 23, 1977, he was sentenced to 365 years' imprisonment.

'Bible John' and Peter Tobin

In an interview with a police psychiatrist following his arrest in 2006, murderer Peter Tobin admitted that he had killed as many as 50 women. When questioned about this, he replied: 'Prove it.' Proving it has been tantalizingly difficult. For if police theories are correct, Tobin's crimes stretch back more than 40 years—to a time when a serial killer known only as 'Bible John' stalked the streets of Glasgow.

The Baffling Case Of Elusive 'Bible John'

Are Peter Tobin and 'Bible John' one and the same? The evidence and the similarities have convinced many, many, including retired Scottish cops who were on the original case in the 1960s when the unidentified killer strangled three young women.

His first victim was Patricia Docker, 29, found dead in a doorway on February 23, 1968, after spending the previous evening at a Glasgow dance hall. On August 16, 1969, Jemima McDonald, 32, was found dead in derelict apartments. She too had been out to a ballroom where she had met a young man. On October 30, Helen Puttock, 29, was murdered after leaving the same ballroom with a man and her body was found dumped at a bus stop. All the women had been strangled, all had had their handbags stolen, and all were menstruating at the time of their deaths.

Witnesses described the man Helen had danced with on the night she died. He had given his name as 'John', had seemed a 'nice guy' but weirdly quoted Biblical texts and condemned dancehalls as 'dens of iniquity'. The press gave him the nickname 'Bible John'.

Police then lost track of the killer—until 2006 when retired detective superintendent Joe Jackson, who

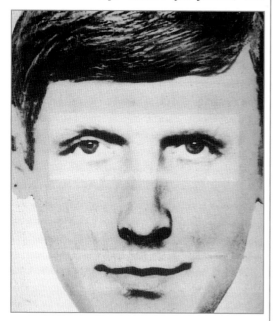

ABOVE: A Photofit of 'Bible John', whom Scottish police first sought in the 1960s after he strangled three young women.

BELOW: Tobin is taken from Linlithgow Sheriff Court, after a hearing in connection with the Vicky Hamilton murder on November 15, 2007.

had been on the 'Bible John' case in the Sixties, was watching TV when he finally glimpsed his suspect.

A 23-year-old Polish student called Angelika Kluk had been murdered, her mutilated body hidden under the floor of a Glasgow church. Now the likely killer had come to light—a drifter, odd-job man and religious crank called Peter Tobin. Jackson's reaction: 'I said to myself, this guy fits the bill. It's as good as we're going to get.'

Tobin, born in Renfrewshire in 1946, had been sent to reform school at the age of seven, had unsuccessfully married three times and had spent a lifetime in and out of prison, including a 10-year term for a double rape in 1993. He would have been 21 at the time of the 'Bible John' slayings.

Tobin's conviction in 2007 for the murder of student Angelika Kluk the previous year allowed the media to point to him as the likely face of 'Bible John'. Indeed, the similarity was striking between a 1969 police drawing of 'Bible John' and Tobin's police mugshot from the same era.

The investigation then moved to southern England, where Tobin was found to have buried the body of 15-year-old Scottish schoolgirl Vicky Hamilton, missing since 1991. Her remains were found at a house in Margate, Kent, where Tobin had previously lived. The skeletal remains of another missing young girl were also found under the patio of the house in Margate.

Already sentenced to life for murdering Angelika Kluk, Tobin, 62, was given a second term in 2008 for Vicky Hamilton's killing and told he could expect to die in jail. Meanwhile, investigations continued over other unsolved cases dating back to the 1960s.

David and Catherine Birnie

To label David and Catherine Birnie as the 'Bonnie and Clyde' of serial killers is unfair on Bonnie and Clyde. The American outlaws killed for cash; the sick Australian duo killed for thrills.

Predators Who Became Partners In Pure Evil

The couple, both born in Perth, Western Australia, in 1951, first met at the age of 12 and were lovers at just 14. Both were from dysfunctional families and both turned to petty crime in their teens.

Quitting school at 15, David became an apprentice jockey but was reported for physically harming the horses. In and out of jail for thefts and assaults, his worst early offense was breaking into an elderly lady's house naked and raping her.

Catherine Harrison, as she was then, also spent some of her teens in prison but, thanks to the encouragement of a parole officer, seemed to be settling down when, at 21, she wed and went on to have seven children.

David Birnie also married in his early 20s and had a baby daughter but in the mid-1980s tracked Catherine down and persuaded her to abandon her husband. She changed her last name to match Birnie's and together the pair began to indulge their sexual fantasies of rape and murder.

On October 6, 1986, student Mary Neilson knocked on the door of their shabby bungalow on Moorhouse Street, in the Perth suburb of Willagee, to buy cheap tires which Birnie had secured through his job at a car wreckers yard. Mary, 22, was forced into a bedroom at knifepoint and raped as Catherine watched. They then drove her to nearby Glen Eagle State Forest where Birnie raped her again before strangling her.

Two weeks later, another body joined Mary's in her shallow grave. The Birnies picked up 15-year-old hitch-hiker Susannah Candy and kept her prisoner for several days, raping her repeatedly before Catherine strangled her.

On November 1, bar manager Noelene Patterson, aged 31, was 'rescued' after running out of gasoline and was taken back to Moorhouse Street, where the Birnies chained her to a bed and repeatedly raped her over three days. They killed her after forcing sleeping pills down her throat and she was buried beside the others.

Three days later, Denise Brown, a 21-year-old computer operator, suffered a similar fate after being picked up at a bus stop. She suffered horribly as attempts to stab her to death failed and she sat up in her shallow grave. David Birnie finished her off with an ax.

The Birnies' murderous rampage ended when a weeping 17-year-old ran naked into a grocery store on November 10 after escaping from the Birnies' house while left briefly unchained. David and Catherine Birnie admitted all charges of rape and murder, and in March 1987 were each sentenced to life imprisonment. While in jail, they exchanged 2,600 letters.

David Birnie hanged himself in his cell in October 2005, the day before he was due in court for raping a fellow prisoner. Catherine Birnie remained incarcerated without hope of freedom after her case was reviewed in March 2009—and her papers marked: 'Never to be released.'

Lawrence Bittaker and Roy Norris

There were clear indicators of murderous intent in the early life of Lawrence Sigmund Bittaker. Born in 1940, he dropped out of school at 17 after several brushes with police and juvenile authorities. Thereafter he was in and out of institutions for two decades. In 1961 he found himself being psychiatrically evaluated while in prison in California, where he was found to be 'paranoid' and 'borderline psychotic', with little control over his impulses. Despite this, he was released within two years.

Teenage Girls Were Strangled With Wire Coat Hangers

In jail again in the Seventies, psychiatrists warned that Bittaker was 'more than likely' to commit new crimes upon his release. Another psychiatrist dubbed him a 'sophisticated psychopath' whose prospects for successful parole were 'guarded at best'. Again the warnings were ignored and Bittaker was released in 1978.

By then, it was too late for the five teenage girls he went on to rape, torture, and murder. His killing spree, committed with his accomplice Roy Norris, lasted between June and October 1979 and briefly brought terror to the Los Angeles suburbs.

Roy Norris, born in 1948, was also a school dropout. He joined the Navy and served in Vietnam, but was discharged with psychological problems. He was arrested for attempted rape in San Diego in 1969, and while out on bail was rearrested twice for

ABOVE: Lawrence Bittaker (pictured) and his accomplice Roy Norris murdered five young women in a cargo van over five months in 1979.

further sex attacks.

Confined to a state hospital as a mentally disordered sex offender, he was freed on probation in 1975, his release papers describing him as someone who would bring 'no further danger to others'. Only three months later he raped a 27-year-old woman and was jailed in California Men's Colony, San Luis Obispo, where he met and befriended Bittaker.

In January 1979, Norris was out of jail again and teamed up with Bittaker in Los Angeles. By October, they snuffed out five young, innocent lives. They abducted the girls in a windowless cargo van with side sliding door which they labeled 'Murder Mack'.

On June 24, while patrolling the coastline of Greater LA, they pounced on 16-year-old Cindy Schaeffer, bundled her into the van, taped her mouth, and bound her arms and legs. Both men raped the girl, then Bittaker strangled her with a wire coat hanger tightened with pliers. They dumped her body in a mountain canyon.

The following month, they picked up hitch-hiker Andrea Hall, 18, and subjected her to multiple rape before Bittaker stabbed her with an ice pick in both ears and, when she wouldn't die fast enough, strangled her. He threw her body over a cliff.

On September 3, the killers spotted two girls on a bus stop bench and offered them a ride. Jackie Gilliam, 15, and Leah Lamp, 13, were kept alive for two days, constantly raped and tortured while the evil pair tape-recorded their victims. Finally, Bittaker stabbed Jackie in both ears with the ice pick and each man took turns finishing her off by strangulation. Norris then battered Leah with a sledgehammer. The bodies were thrown over a cliff.

Their last victim was 16-year-old Lynette Ledford, who suffered a similar fate, eventually being strangled with wire and pliers. Her body was found the following day, November 1, on a lawn in Hermosa Beach.

The couple were apprehended because Norris boasted about the killings to an old prison friend who tipped off the police. Norris testified against his accomplice for a jail sentence that would have him eligible for parole in 2010.

Bittaker was sentenced to death in 1981. He was still on Death Row over a quarter of a century later— answering female fan mail under his favored nickname: 'Pliers' Bittaker.

Robert Black

At his trial, Robert Black was described by prosecutors as 'every parent's worst nightmare'. A Scottish child molester and killer, he had a disturbed childhood himself, being fostered and spending his schooldays as a loner prone to outbreaks of mindless violence. His classroom nickname was 'Smelly Robbie'.

Every Parent's Worst Nightmare

His foster mother died in 1958 when Robert was just 11, and he was sent to a children's home near Falkirk, close to his birthplace. He lasted there a year before a fumbled attempt at rape of a local girl caused him to be packed off to a stricter establishment. There he was regularly abused by a male member of staff, and from that time onward, Black associated sex with dominance and submission.

At 15, he left the home and got a job as a delivery boy in Glasgow. He later admitted that, while on his rounds, he molested as many as 40 girls. Seemingly, none of the attacks was reported. Even more astonishing was that, at the age of 17, he got away with what may well have been judged a murder attempt.

He approached a seven-year-old girl in a park, led her to a deserted building, throttled her until she passed out and then sexually assaulted her. He left her unconscious and she was later found wandering the streets confused, crying, and bleeding. Brought to court, he was given no more than a 'good behavior' order after a psychiatric report declared that this was 'an isolated incident'.

Tragically, a chance to stop Robert Black from progressing to full-scale murders had been lost. It would take more than a quarter of a century before the evil pervert was caught and caged. By then, as a burly lorry driver, he had kidnapped, raped, and murdered at least three girls and was a suspect in a string of unsolved child murders across Britain and in Europe.

Black was finally caught in the village of Stow, south of Edinburgh, in July 1990 after being spotted bundling a six-year-old girl into his van. A sharp-eyed postman jotted down the license plate and called police. The girl was found bound and gagged in the back.

Detectives spent four years piecing together the evidence to convict him of murder. They used work records from his job delivering advertising posters to connect him with the scene of each abduction on the relevant day, and later at the sites where the bodies were found.

Eleven-year-old Susan Maxwell was snatched by the scruffy-looking van driver from near her home in the Scottish Borders in 1982. The following year, Caroline Hogg, aged five, was taken from a fairground near her Edinburgh home. Sarah Harper, aged 10, from Morley, near Leeds, was abducted in 1986.

At Newcastle upon Tyne Crown Court on May 20, 1994, Black, then aged 47, was given 10 life sentences, with an order that he serve at least 35 years in prison, for the three proven murders and the abduction of a 15-year-old girl. But police said he could be responsible for 16 further unsolved murders in Britain, France, and Germany.

Wayne Boden

Wayne Boden was a serial killer who earned the nickname the 'Vampire Rapist' because of his penchant for biting his victims. It was a trait that led to his conviction on the grounds of dental evidence—one of the first such of its kind in North America and several years ahead of another, more notorious serial killer, Ted Bundy (see page 29). Boden had one other kink: he had a fascination for vampires and, after strangling his victims and raping them, he would bite their breasts to drink their blood.

'Vampire Rapist' Bit His Victims' Breasts

The gory modus operandi of the Canadian serial killer caused a two-year reign of terror, first in Montreal and then in Calgary, where Boden carried out his murders between October 1969 and May 1971. His first victim was Shirley Audette whose body was found dumped at the rear of an apartment complex in downtown Montreal. Although she was fully clothed, she had been raped and strangled and had savage bite marks on her breasts. Boden lived next door but was not

suspected. It was a missed opportunity to put an early stop to the killer, particularly as a former boyfriend of Shirley told police he believed she had a new man in her life and was 'getting into something dangerous'.

The following month, jewelry store clerk Marielle Archambault happily left work at closing time with a young man whom she introduced to her colleagues as 'Bill'. When she failed to report for work the following morning, Archambault's boss went to her apartment and had it unlocked by the landlady. They found Marielle's fully-clad body on the couch, her pantyhose and bra ripped, her breasts covered with teeth marks.

'Bill' waited two months before striking again. In January 1970, the boyfriend of Jean Way, 24, arrived at her apartment on a date but got no answer. This was probably because the 'Vampire Rapist' was in her bedroom at the time, hovering over her dead body. When the boyfriend returned later, he found the door unlocked and Jean lying on the bed. She had been strangled and her breasts bitten.

In the cases of two of these murders, there was little sign of a struggle. The girls actually seemed serene in death—one even having a faint smile on her lips. Detectives surmised that the killer had an attraction for girls who wanted and accepted 'rough sex'. These masochistic tendencies may have led the 'Vampire Rapist' to lose control during frenzied and ferocious sex, and asphyxiate the girls before abusing their bodies.

Jean Way's murder was the last in Montreal. 'Bill' had disappeared from that city—only to turn up in another one 2,500 miles (4,000km) away. In May 1971, Calgary schoolteacher Elizabeth Porteous was found murdered in her apartment. On this occasion, the victim had clearly put up a fierce fight for her life before being raped and strangled and her breasts mutilated with bite marks.

From Elizabeth's work colleagues, detectives discovered that she had a new boyfriend named 'Bill' who drove a distinctive blue Mercedes. It was the car in which Jean Way had been seen on the day of her murder. That, plus the clue of a broken cufflink found under Elizabeth's body, led police to Boden.

The clinching evidence came from orthodontists who matched a cast of Boden's teeth to bite marks on his victims. The 'Vampire Rapist' was sentenced in Calgary to life imprisonment for Elizabeth's murder, then returned to Montreal to receive three further life sentences. He died in 2006 of skin cancer, aged 57.

William Bonin

It is an indictment of North America's crime-ridden highways that 'Freeway Killer' William Bonin shared his nickname with two other serial killers. By his murder tally, however, Bonin stands out—having raped and murdered as many as 36 young men and boys, 14 for which he was convicted and eventually executed.

'Freeway Killer' Who Raped and Murdered Teenage Boys

Bonin was born in Connecticut in 1947, the son of a gambling alcoholic. His mother doted on him and often removed him from his father's frequent rages by having him stay with his grandfather, a convicted child molester. His childhood experiences were to influence him toward a life of sadism and, ultimately, slaughter.

At the age of only eight, he was caught stealing license plates. His first criminal conviction was when he was 10 and was followed by repeated stays in detention centers, where he was sexually abused by older boys. By his teens, back home with his mother, Bonin began molesting younger children. After high school, he joined the US Air Force and served in Vietnam as a gunner, earning a Good Conduct Medal. After a brief marriage ended in divorce, he moved to California.

As a 22-year-old, working as a truck driver and living in Downey, California, he was convicted of his first sex crimes: kidnapping and abusing young boys in four separate attacks. He was diagnosed as mentally disturbed and sent to Atascadero State Hospital, from where he was released in May 1974, with psychiatrists declaring he was no longer a danger.

But in 1979 he began a killing spree that targeted homosexual young men, usually young male prostitutes and sometimes hitch-hikers, whom he would pick up in his van as he cruised around the Los Angeles area.

up in early 1980, the youngest victim being 12-year-old James McCabe, who had been abducted, raped, and killed.

Butts later said that, although he had been sickened by his first killing, he went on to actively enjoy raping, torturing, and murdering. He told police: 'After the first one, I couldn't do anything about it. Bonin had a hypnotic way about him.'

Extraordinarily, Butts was not Bonin's only accomplice. He also recruited two mentally subnormal 19-year-olds, James Munro and Gregory Miley, and a fourth accomplice, who was aged only 15. It was Bonin's attempt to involve a fourth teenager into his killing games that led to his arrest. The horrified 18-year-old tipped off police who set up a surveillance of Bonin.

On the night of June 11, 1980, they caught him in the act of assaulting a 15-year-old boy in the back of his van. Rounded up by police, all four of Bonin's accomplices gave evidence against him to avoid the death sentence. Butts hanged himself in his cell and the others served jail terms.

Bonin confessed to abducting, raping, and killing 21 boys and young men, although he was a police suspect in at least another 15 other murders. He was eventually charged with 14 of the murders. He showed no remorse and said simply: 'I couldn't stop killing. It got easier with each one we did.' In a later prison confession, he added: 'If I had not been arrested I would still be killing. I couldn't stop killing.'

Convicted on all counts, Bonin was sentenced to death by Judge William Keene in January 1982 but it was to be another 14 years before the execution was carried out. On February 23, 1996, he was taken from Death Row to the old gas chamber at San Quentin Prison and became the first person to be executed by lethal injection in California.

ABOVE: The body count of 'Freeway Killer' William Bonin may have totaled 36 young men and boys.

On many of these sorties, he teamed up with factory worker Vernon Butts, a 22-year-old weirdo who claimed to be a wizard and slept in a coffin.

Their first known murder victim was 14-year-old hitch-hiker Thomas Lundgren. The boy was kidnapped, assaulted, and strangled on May 28, 1979, and his body dumped at Malibu. Before the year was out, seven more teenagers had been killed. More bodies started turning

Werner Boost

Werner Boost, born in 1928, the illegitimate son of an East German peasant, was a child thief who originally made a living transporting refugees across the Iron Curtain. Because of subsequent events, it may well be that some of the escapees, having entrusted Boost to get them across the border, were not helped out of a miserable life in the East but out of life altogether.

Death At The Double

His murderous character became clearer, however, after Boost relocated to Düsseldorf in 1950 and became a killer who preyed on courting couples. His first known attack in the city was made with an accomplice, Franz Lorbach. In January 1953, the pair crept up to a car parked in a quiet suburban street and disturbed lawyer Bernd Serve and his 19-year-old male lover. Dr Serve was shot through the head but the lover was only beaten and robbed.

The murderous duo's next crime, in October 1955, was to earn Boost the nickname the 'Düsseldorf Double Killer'. Again accompanied by Lorbach, Boost robbed and battered to death Thear Kurmann and her boyfriend, 26-year-old baker Friedhelm Behre, after they left a restaurant. Their bodies were discovered a month later trapped in their car in a water-filled gravel pit.

Boost carried out his final double killing in February 1956. The charred bodies of Peter Falkenberg and 20-year-old secretary Hildegard Wassing were discovered in a smoldering haystack. Both had been bludgeoned and robbed, and Falkenberg had been shot through the head. The bloodstained car in which they had been attacked was also discovered.

A further attempt at double murder took place in May of that year in woodland outside the city but

LEFT: Werner Boost (pictured) and his accomplice, Franz Lorbach, carried out a string of murders in 1950s Germany.

failed because the woman's screams alerted passers-by. In the same area on June 10 a forest ranger spotted an armed man apparently tracking a young couple. Boost surrendered to the ranger, protesting his innocence of any crime.

Evidence linking him to the 'Düsseldorf Double Killer' was slim and Boost might have got away with murder if Lorbach had not buckled under police interrogation, admitting his role in the killings and naming his accomplice. Lorbach told police that Boost's favored method was to sedate the couples then rape the women before killing them. Excusing his own part in the crimes, he claimed he had been 'hypnotized' into committing them.

Boost was sentenced to life imprisonment on December 14, 1959, for the murder of Dr Serve. Lorbach was jailed for six years. Despite police suspicion, evidence linking the two men to the other murders could not be proved.

Ian Brady and Myra Hindley

Tough cops wept when they first listened to the tape. Now, when played in a hushed courtroom, hardened reporters were also reduced to tears. No one there that day in 1966 would ever forget the harrowing recording. It was of a little girl's voice, pleading for her mother and begging for mercy.

Tiny 'Moors Murders' Victim Taped Pleading For Mercy

The recording was of Lesley Ann Downey, at 10 the youngest victim of 'Moors Murderers' Ian Brady and Myra Hindley. It was made by the evil couple as the little girl was put to death, her plaintive cries accompanied by the sounds of torture and sexual assault. The only other voice was Hindley's, coldly

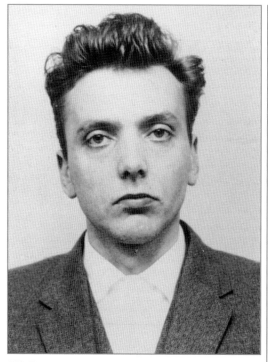

ABOVE: Ian Brady was sentenced to life imprisonment on May 7, 1966. The judge told him and his accomplice that they were 'evil beyond belief.'

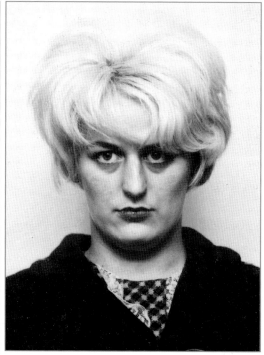

ABOVE: A portrait of 'Moors Murderer' Myra Hindley taken during her trial. While in prison, Hindley claimed to be a reformed character, but she was never released and died in 2002.

ordering the child to 'shut up' and 'be quiet'. The 16-minute tape ended with a scream.

The 'Moors Murderers' are, to an entire British generation, the epitome of evil. Between 1962 and 1965, Brady and his lover Hindley abducted, tortured, and murdered at least five, possibly eight, children or teenagers. Most of the bodies were buried on bleak Saddleworth Moor, on the hills outside Manchester.

Brady, born in 1938, the illegitimate son of a Glasgow waitress, was a teenage burglar before moving to Manchester in 1954, settling into a job as a clerk. There he encountered 19-year-old typist Myra Hindley in 1961. It was a meeting of evil minds. Brady was a sadistic fetishist who drew a willing Hindley into his perverted games. They took pictures of themselves having sex while dressed in leather, brandishing whips and acting out Nazi crimes. Soon the games turned to reality.

In July 1963, Hindley lured 16-year-old Pauline Reade onto Saddleworth Moor, where Brady raped her then hit her over the head with a shovel before cutting her throat. Four months later, 12-year-old John Kilbride was taken to the moor, held down and molested by Brady before being strangled and buried.

In June 1964, Hindley asked another 12-year-old, Keith Bennett, to carry some shopping for her, then invited him for a trip across the moor. There the boy was abused and strangled, Brady taking photographs of the body before burying it.

Ten-year-old Lesley Ann Downey disappeared while

attending a Christmas fair on December 26. She was taken to Brady's home and forced to pose nude for pornographic photographs before being killed.

In October 1965, the couple invited Hindley's brother-in-law, David Smith, to their suburban home. Brady talked openly to him about previous murders but, fearful that he might go to the police, tried to implicate him in a fresh killing. Brady lured 17-year-old Edward Evans to the house and attacked the teenager with a hatchet—having first ensured that Smith's fingerprints were on the murder weapon.

Smith pretended to play along with Brady and even helped him and Hindley clear up. Then he ran to the police. He told detectives that, after the killing, the bloodstained couple had sat around laughing and drinking wine. Brady had boasted to him: 'It's the messiest yet. It normally only takes one blow.'

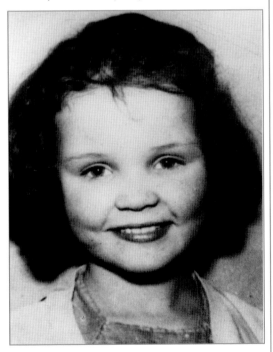

ABOVE: A family photograph of Lesley Ann Downey shortly before her death at the hands of the 'Moors Murderers'.

ABOVE: Hindley (left) was complicit in all the crimes. She is still Britain's most notorious female serial killer.

With Brady and Hindley under arrest—the latter denying any part in the killings—police searched their house. They found a photograph of Hindley posing next to John Kilbride's shallow grave on Saddleworth Moor. Other photographs showed poor Lesley Ann Downey in pornographic poses. But the most horrifying discovery was the recording made of her dying cries: 'Please take your hands off me a minute, please. Please, Mum, please. I can't tell you. I cannot breathe. Please God. Why? What are you doing with me?'

That damning tape was finally played at the trial of Brady and Hindley at Chester Assizes, which ended in May 1966 with the couple being found guilty of the murder of the little girl and of Evans. Handing down life sentences, the judge told the killers: 'You are evil beyond belief.'

While incarcerated, Brady 'confessed' to five other murders but, being diagnosed as suffering from paranoid

ABOVE: Manchester police excavated large areas of Saddleworth Moor in the hunt for bodies.

psychosis, no further charges were brought. The killer went on hunger strikes in a vain bid to end his life.

By contrast, Myra Hindley fought for her release, claiming to be a wholly reformed character. Despite controversial campaigns to free her, she ultimately became Britain's longest-serving female prisoner and, after 36 years in jail, died of heart problems in 2002.

Still reviled because of her crimes against children four decades earlier, her passing at the age of 60 still made front-page news. One typical headline read: 'At last Myra is where she belongs—HELL.'

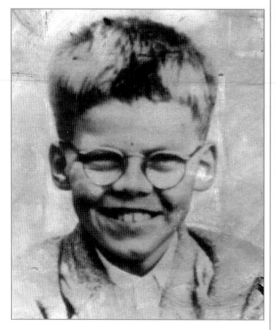

ABOVE: John Bennett was the third victim of the evil duo. Hindley lured him onto Sadddleworth Moor where Brady strangled him.

ABOVE: Police officers dig near the site where Lesley Ann Downey's body was discovered, in 1965.

ABOVE: Ian Brady in police custody prior to his court appearance for the Moors Murders for which he was later convicted.

Marquise De Brinvilliers

Marie-Madeleine-Marguerite, Marquise de Brinvilliers was the eldest of five children in the French aristocratic 17th century family d'Aubray. The daughter of Viscount Antoine Dreux d'Aubray, a civil lieutenant of Paris, she was married in 1651 at the age of 21, to a married army officer, Antoine Gobelin de Brinvilliers, a gambling womanizer who paid her little attention. As a result, she took a lover, one Chevalier Jean-Baptiste de Sainte-Croix, an army captain and friend of her father.

Libertine Who Learned The Art Of Poison

Outraged by his daughter's affair with a trusted family friend, the old man forbade her from seeing Sainte-Croix, and in 1663 had him thrown into the Bastille. On his release, however, the lovers were reunited and plotted to take revenge on d'Aubray—and at the same time ensure her inheritance. In the Bastille, Sainte-Croix had learned the art of poisoning. With the assistance of one of the royal apothecaries to the court of King Louis XIV, he obtained tasteless but lethal potions, which Marie fed to her father, who in 1666 became her victim.

With her high-spending habits, Marie's share of Viscount d'Aubray's inheritance did not last long, and when the money ran out, she turned her attention to the rest of the family. Her elder brother died in 1670, followed by her younger brother and then her sister and sister-in-law. Former lovers suffered the same fate. Marie's husband survived but was prone to mysterious illnesses. Ruthlessly, Marie perfected her poison techniques on as many as 50 people during 'mercy missions' visiting the sick in a local hospital. The marquise was finally exposed when her lover Sainte-Croix died in 1672. He left instructions that a box should be delivered to his mistress, Marie, but his wife opened it and saw a variety of poisons and incriminating papers.

Marie went on the run but was arrested in Liege. Under interrogation, she threatened: 'Half the people of quality are involved in this sort of thing, and I could ruin them if I were to talk.' The once haughty libertine was brutally tortured, her jailers mainly employing

ABOVE: An artist's impression of jailers torturing the Marquise de Brinvilliers with the 'water cure'.

what was known as 'the water cure'—in which she was forced to drink 16 pints (9 liters) of water. Tried in Paris in 1676 and found guilty, she was executed, her body and severed head being thrown onto a fire.

Many members of the French nobility breathed a sigh of relief at her death because, while confessing her own guilt, she had refused to name other aristocrats caught up in sex scandals. The dramatic and romantic mysteries surrounding the case have since inspired poet Robert Browning (*The Poisoner*) and several authors, including Alexandre Dumas (*The Marquise de Brinvilliers*) and Arthur Conan Doyle (*The Leather Funnel*).

Jerry Brudos

A detective asked Jerry Brudos a simple question: 'Do you feel some remorse, Jerry? Do you feel sorry for your victims, for the girls who died?' Brudos picked up a piece of paper, screwed it up and threw it on the floor. 'That much,' he said. 'I care about those girls as much as that piece of wadded up paper…'

Fetish Fiend Dressed Dead Bodies Like Dolls

Jerome Henry Brudos was a murdering rapist with a fetish for women's clothes and shoes. He first came to police attention when, as a 17-year-old, he forced a woman to pose for naked pictures at knifepoint. He was confined to a mental hospital for nine months with a personality disorder.

After his release, he continued stealing underwear from washing lines. By the time he was 28 and committed his first murder, Brudos had accumulated a large collection of women's attire.

That first victim was a 19-year-old encyclopedia saleswoman, Linda Slawson, who knocked on the door of the Brudos home in Portland, Oregon, one day in January 1968. With his wife and two children upstairs, Brudos, then aged 28, knocked the young woman unconscious.

He took Linda to the garage where he strangled her and abused the corpse. Brudos then sent his family out for hamburgers so he could play with her body. He dressed her up like a doll in the clothes he had been collecting over the years and photographed his handiwork. Finally, he chopped off the left foot and, with a newly fitted shoe, put it in his refrigerator. The body was disposed of in the Willamette River.

Three other murders followed. Jan Whitney, 23, was picked up at the roadside in November 1968 when her car broke down. He took her home and raped the corpse. After dressing her up, he decided to keep her and hung her from a hook in the garage ceiling. Several days later he consigned her body to the river, but not before slicing off her right breast.

Student Karen Sprinkler, 19, was abducted from a department store car park in March 1969 and taken to his home, where she was forced to pose for him. She

ABOVE: The Willamette River in Portland, Oregon, where Jerry Brudos dumped the bodies of most of his victims.

was then hanged and her body similarly abused. This time, both breasts were removed before her corpse was dumped, this time in the Long Tom River.

Linda Salee, 23, died a month later. Brudos had flashed a fake police badge at her and 'arrested' her for shoplifting. He took her back to the garage where he strangled and raped her as she expired. He kept the body for a day, violating the corpse before she too ended up in the river.

After quizzing fellow students of Karen Sprinkler, police discovered several girls had received phone calls from a man asking to meet them. A trap was set with one of the girls arranging a date with Brudos and he was arrested.

He pleaded insanity at his trial but psychiatric reports declared him sane. He was sentenced to life imprisonment at Oregon State Penitentiary.

Ted Bundy

The total number will never be known, but at least 30 and as many as 100 unfortunate women and girls were victims of Ted Bundy during his four-year killing spree. That such a savage slayer seemed on the surface to be a handsome, dapper and charming man makes his case all the more compelling. So when did this all-American boy turn into a depraved monster?

Charmer With Movie Star Looks Was Merciless Manic

LEFT: The many faces of prolific American serial killer, Ted Bundy — all of them evil.

The answer may be earlier than anyone thought. When he was three years of age, Ted's 15-year-old aunt awoke one night to find that Ted had lifted the bedclothes and had placing butcher's knives around her body. 'He just stood there and grinned,' she recalled. 'I shooed him out of the room and took the knives back to the kitchen. I remember thinking at the time that it was a very strange thing for a little kid to do.'

Young Theodore Robert was living with his grandparents at the time. Born on November 24, 1946, to an unmarried teenage mother in Philadelphia, he took on the name Bundy when she moved to Washington State in 1950 and wed hospital cook Johnnie Bundy. The bridegroom adopted Ted as his own son and he grew up with them in their Tacoma home in apparent domestic harmony.

Young Bundy became the all-American boy, joining the Boy Scouts, having a paper round and doing backyard clearance and mowing jobs for pocket money. His school grades were good and he was a high school athlete, then a student at the University of Washington. He became a campaign worker both for the Republican Party and for the Crime Commission in Washington State, where former colleagues believed he could have ended up a leading lawyer, a top politician, perhaps even a Senator.

But further clues to his character had arisen. His student reports spoke of a volatile temper. And although his undeniable charm and movie star looks won him no shortage of dates, some girlfriends recalled him as a sadistic lover who acted out weird bondage fantasies. Nevertheless, in 1971 he applied for voluntary work at a Seattle rape crisis center and, after being screened for 'maturity and balance', he was accepted as a counsellor.

It was this innocent image that Bundy played up to when he finally faced his accusers in a series of court and killed.

By mid-1974, Bundy, then aged 28, had become sufficiently emboldened to operate by daylight and even to give his real name, introducing himself with: 'Hi, I'm Ted.' In July, the killer, with his arm in a sling, wandered among a crowd of 40,000 who were swimming and sunbathing at Lake Sammamish State Park, near Seattle, approaching young girls and asking if they would help with his sailboat. One who declined nevertheless watched as the man—'really friendly, very polite, very sincere, with a nice smile'—lured another girl to his distinctive VW Beetle car. He killed two women that day, their naked bodies found in woodland months later, along with those of three other women, one a known missing person and two unidentifiable.

But the trail in Washington went cold when Bundy moved state, enrolling at the University of Utah law school in Salt Lake City. There, in October and November, four girls aged between 16 and 18 were abducted, battered, raped, and strangled. The slaughter

ABOVE: Bundy at one of many court appearances. During one, in Aspen, Colorado, he leapt from a window and escaped.

appearances starting in 1975, during which the smiling, smooth-talker tried to charm jurors into believing he had no need to kidnap and kill. As he boasted: 'Why should I want to attack women? I had all the female companionship I wanted. I must have slept with dozens and all of them went to bed with me willingly.'

Even today, the mystery remains as to the total number of murders Bundy committed: the nine murders with which he was officially attributed, the 20 to 30 to which he had confessed or the 100-plus with which some investigators credit him, the general estimate being 35.

The manner of these deaths was not gentle. Typically, Bundy would bludgeon his victims, then strangle them to death. He also engaged in rape and necrophilia. His first known victim was law student Lynda Ann Healy, 21, who vanished from her Seattle apartment on the morning of January 31, 1974, leaving only a bloodstain on her pillow as a clue to her kidnapping and murder. Over the next three months, three more students, all teenagers, and two other women had been abducted

ABOVE: Bundy stalled his execution for 10 years, but eventually went to the electric chair in February 1989.

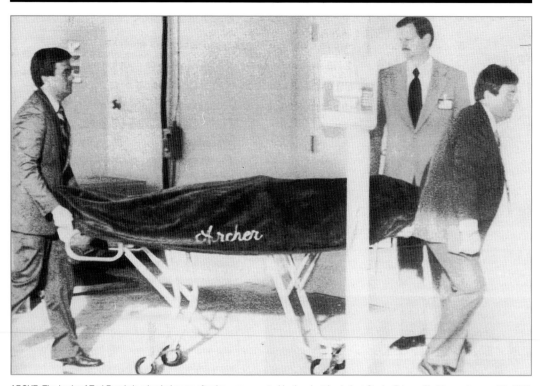

ABOVE: The body of Ted Bundy is wheeled away after he was executed in the electric chair at Starke Prison, Florida, on January 24, 1989.

spread from Utah to Colorado, where between January and April 1975 at least five women went missing.

Police finally nabbed Bundy in Salt Lake City one night in August 1975—but initially only for a traffic violation. He was driving his VW with no lights when stopped and found to be in possession of a pair of handcuffs, a crowbar, a ski mask, and a nylon stocking. Charged with possessing tools for burglary, he was put in an identity line-up and was picked out by one of his would-be victims, 18-year-old Carol Da Ronch. She'd had a lucky escape when Bundy, posing as a police officer, had handcuffed her and dragged her into his VW, from which she rolled out as it slowed at a bend.

Bundy was charged with kidnapping but after months of legal argument—during much of which, incredibly, he was allowed out on bail—he was found guilty and sentenced to between one and 15 years. He was then

moved to Colorado to stand trial for the murder of a 23-year-old student, abducted from a ski resort in January.

During a break in the court hearing at Aspen, Bundy leaped from a window and was free for eight days before recapture. He escaped a second time by cutting through a ceiling panel of his cell and stealing a police car. Driving first to Chicago, then traveling south to Florida, Bundy rented a room near the University of Florida, Tallahassee, and again went on the rampage. On January 15, 1978, he crept into a dormitory at the university and viciously battered four students, strangling two of them to death before taking bites out of the buttocks of one of them.

Bundy's last victim was his youngest. On February 8, in Lake City, Florida, 12-year-old Kimberly Leach was strangled and sexually violated. A week later, when a Pensacola policeman stopped him for driving a stolen car, the killer tried to escape but was clubbed unconscious. He was brought to trial in Miami and convicted of the Tallahassee student murders and subsequently, in 1980, of the murder of young Kimberly Leach.

Bundy stalled his execution for almost 10 years with a string of appeals but finally confessed to 30 murders, including attacks in California, Michigan, Pennsylvania, Idaho, and Vermont. He went to the electric chair in Florida's Starke Prison in January 1989.

John Bunting and accomplices

On May 21, 1999, Adelaide police reopened a missing persons investigation that led them to a disused bank vault in rural Snowtown, South Australia. What they found there was a chamber of horrors that would stun the nation. Six acid-filled plastic barrels contained the grisly, mummified remains of eight dismembered bodies. Three days later, two further bodies were found buried in a backyard in a suburb north of Adelaide. A day later, four men were arrested, and the search for justice began.

Dismembered Bodies In Chamber Of Horrors

Former abattoir worker John Justin Bunting, born in Queensland in 1966, was the ringleader of a dysfunctional group of victims of child sex abuse and incest who shared an overriding hatred for homosexuals and pedophiles. Bunting, a psychopathic killer, and himself a victim of childhood sexual abuse, enlisted the help of friends (Robert Wagner and Mark Haydon, Bunting's second wife Elizabeth Harvey and stepson James Vlassakis) to partake in various acts of abduction, torture, and disposal of bodies.

Usually based on flimsy evidence or rumor, victims were murdered if suspected of being pedophiles. Others were killed because they were obese, illiterate, mentally disabled, gay or drug addicted. Most of the victims were friends, acquaintances or family members of at least one of the group.

Although not the motive for the killings, the murderers took on the identity of their victims to claim their welfare benefits, forging their signatures to pocket $95,000 and in some cases 'inheriting' their cars.

Bunting's killing spree began in August 1992. Clinton Trezise, 22, was struck about the head with a hammer several times in Bunting's living room after being invited round for a social visit.

For the next seven years, Bunting and his accomplices took the lives of various men and women—using torture methods such as electric clamps, pliers, cigarettes, and lit sparklers inserted in the penis in order to 'cure' their victims of their crimes. The victims were forced to call their torturers 'God', 'Master', 'Chief Inspector', and 'Lord Sir'.

Among the death toll was Suzanne Allen, 47, a friend of Bunting; Elizabeth Haydon, 37, wife of one of Bunting's co-conspirators; and Thomas Trevilyan, 18, who had helped murder one victim but was later killed after discussing the crime with others. In September 1998, Bunting's stepson, James Vlassakis, was persuaded to participate in the murder of his own half-brother Troy Youde, just 21, who was killed in his house after being dragged from his bed while asleep.

David Johnson, 24, was the last to be murdered, in May 1999. He was lured to the disused bank with the promise of a low-price computer. There he was handcuffed and made to give his bank details. Two of the killers left to confirm the details were correct and Bunting strangled Johnson before they returned.

In the final stages of a complex, year-long missing persons investigation, police entered the former Snowtown branch of the State Bank of South Australia after a tip-off from neighbors. The discovery there of the eight dismembered bodies horrified hardened cops. Days later, two more bodies were uncovered at Bunting's former house and were linked to the same killers. Bunting, Haydon, Wagner, and Vlassakis were arrested and charged with murder.

After 11 months of shocking evidence in South Australia's longest and most complex criminal trial, the jury returned a guilty verdict against John Bunting and Robert Wagner. The jury found Bunting killed 11 people while his accomplice, Wagner, a bisexual muscleman, murdered seven. They were each sentenced to life imprisonment on each count, to be served cumulatively. The presiding judge, Justice Brian Martin, said the men were 'in the business of killing for pleasure' and were 'incapable of true rehabilitation'.

In a separate trial in the Adelaide Supreme Court, 22-year-old James Vlassakis, pleaded guilty to four counts of murder and was handed a life sentence with a 26-year non-parole period.

The proceedings against Mark Haydon continued into September 2005, when murder charges against him were dropped in return for guilty pleas to charges of assisting in the killings, including that of his wife, Elizabeth.

The convictions proved what South Australians first gathered four years previously: that a group of sadistic killers had operated unchecked in their midst for most of the previous decade. Finally, their reign of terror had been brought to an end.

Angelo Buono and Kenneth Bianchi

Kenneth Bianchi, born to an alcoholic prostitute who gave him up at birth, was deeply troubled from a young age. His adoptive mother described him as 'a compulsive liar who had risen from the cradle dissembling'. After a brief marriage to his high school sweetheart, he drifted from New York State to California, where in 1977 he teamed up with his older cousin Angelo Buono Jr.—and together they became known as the Hillside Stranglers.

Raped, Tortured, And Slain By The 'Hillside Stranglers'

Buono was an ugly man, both physically and mentally. He was coarse, ignorant, and sadistic but, incredibly, was popular with women and gave himself the nickname 'Italian Stallion'. Also from Rochester, New York, he had moved to California with his divorced mother and, like Bianchi, he briefly married a young girlfriend before walking out on her and their baby.

Between brief spells in jail for theft, Buono again wed and fathered several further children in and out of wedlock before his wife divorced him after he handcuffed her, put a gun to her stomach and threatened to kill her.

Buono worked as a car upholsterer, carrying out his business from his home at Glendale, in the San Fernando Valley. It was there that younger cousin Bianchi joined him and the couple, then aged 42 and 26, regularly invited prostitutes to the house. It would be these who would become their first victims.

The body of a 21-year-old Hollywood girl was found on a hillside on Chevy Chase Drive on October had been involved. The evidence was sperm samples taken from the teenager's body. As further corpses turned up, police also realized that the killers were experimenting with forms of torture. After being abused by both men, the girls would be strangled. But other methods of killing, such as lethal injection, electric shock, and carbon monoxide poisoning, were also tried by the killers.

During one week in November, Bianchi and Buono disposed of five bodies, the youngest being of schoolgirls aged 12 and 14. Two more teenagers and

ABOVE: Kenneth Bianchi and his older cousin stripped, raped, and sometimes sodomized their victims.

6, 1977. Twelve days later, the body of a 19-year-old was dumped near the Forest Lawn Cemetery. And on October 31, a girl aged just 15 was found dead on a hillside in Glendale.

A pattern had emerged. The girls had been stripped naked, violently raped, and sometimes sodomized. They were then carefully cleaned by the killers so as to leave no clues. Finally they were dumped by roadsides where they were certain to be discovered, often displayed in lascivious postures.

After the third murder, police knew that two men

ABOVE: The self styled 'Italian Stallion', Angelo Buono committed his first murder in October 1977

ABOVE: Bianchi takes the stand during his trial. His claim of insanity saved him from the death penalty.

were killed before the end of the year, and a 20-year-old died the following February.

The deadly duo lured their victims by cruising around Los Angeles in Buono's car pretending to be plain-clothes cops, stopping to flash fake badges at unsuspecting victims. Ordered into their 'unmarked police car', the girls were driven to Buono's home to be tortured and murdered. But in the spring of 1978, to the bafflement of Los Angeles police, the killings suddenly stopped.

The reason was that the killers had fallen out, and Bianchi had left California to live with his girlfriend and baby son in Bellingham, Washington State. There, Bianchi took a job as a security guard, and in January 1979 he lured two girl students into a house he was guarding and strangled them. But without the aid of his partner, he left many clues and police arrested him the next day. The nature of the crime and several documents in his possession linked him with the Hillside Strangler cases.

At his trial for the two Bellingham murders, Bianchi pleaded insanity, claiming that he suffered from 'multi personality disorder', and the evidence of six Washington State psychiatrists saved him from the death penalty. With a life sentence, he was moved to California to give evidence against Buono for the Los Angeles killings.

The inadmissibility of 'insane' Bianchi's testimony delayed the start of Buono's trial until November 1981 and, along with the lack of forensic evidence, caused it to last nearly two years. Buono denied all charges and blamed the murders on his cousin. On October 31, 1983, he was found guilty on two counts—but the jury's recommendation meant that he too evaded the death sentence in favor of life in prison, where he died

of a heart condition in 2002.

At the close of his trial, it became clear that Judge Ronald George would have preferred Buono's death to have been administered more swiftly. He complained to the jury: 'Angelo Buono and Kenneth Bianchi subjected various of their murder victims to the administration of lethal gas, electrocution, strangulation by rope, and lethal hypodermic injection. Yet the two defendants are destined to spend their lives in prison, housed, fed, and clothed at taxpayer expense, better cared for than some of the destitute law-abiding members of our community.'

William Burke and William Hare

In the early 19th century, the frontiers of medicine were advancing at an inexorable rate. Yet there was one vital ingredient lacking in this exploration of the human body—and that was a supply of the bodies themselves. At that time, it was unheard of for anyone to donate their body for research, so a supply of corpses had to be provided for dissection and the fresher the better. William Burke and William Hare were the men to fulfill this service, and by their nefarious trade became Scotland's most celebrated and gruesome serial murderers.

Unholy Duo Who Went Into The 'Body Business'

The Irish-born pair came together when Burke, who had deserted his wife and young family, came to stay at Hare's cheap Edinburgh lodging house in 1827. They went into the 'body business' together soon afterward upon the death of a boarder known as Old Donald, who succumbed to a long illness, owing £4 in rent. To recoup his loss, landlord Hare hit upon the plan of selling the corpse to one of the city's doctors. They removed Old Donald's body from the coffin that lay in the backyard, wrapped it in sacking and presented

themselves at the door of Number 10 Surgeons' Square, the Edinburgh establishment of the brilliant anatomist Dr Robert Knox. The price was struck at seven pounds and 10 shillings, and all sides left well satisfied with the night's work.

It was easy money but the pair realized they would have difficulty in continually restocking the merchandise they required for their new unholy trade. Churchyards were now well guarded at night because of previous raids by grave robbers, and many tombs even had iron bars around them. The only solution was to 'create' new corpses.

The first of a further 16 victims was an old man called Joe the Mumper, who fell ill of a high fever and was too weak to offer resistance as Burke and Hare laid a pillow over his face and held him down until he suffocated. His body fetched £10 at Surgeons' Square. The second victim was dispatched in what became the hallmark of Burke and Hare's murder technique. A boarder, whose name they did not even know, was confined to his bed with jaundice. While the man was asleep, Burke held his mouth and nose until there was no sign of breathing.

Third to die was an old woman tramp whom Hare met in a city bar, lured to the lodging house and suffocated. In the spring of 1828, the killers saw off two more boarders, both destitute women. Then came the murder of a prostitute, Mary Paterson. The sight of her naked body, barely six hours into death, aroused great excitement among the medical students, one of whom claimed to recognize her. Mary's shapely figure and good looks were even remarked upon in the popular newspapers. Dr Knox gladly reveled in the publicity and, rather than take the body straight onto the dissecting table, he had it preserved in whiskey for three months, allowing it to become almost a tourist attraction.

Burke and Hare became increasingly audacious. On one occasion, Burke encountered a drunken woman being escorted along the street by a policeman. He intervened, convinced the officer that he was a Good Samaritan and had the hapless wretch released into his care. Not surprisingly, she was delivered to Surgeons' Square that very night.

In June 1828, the partners committed their vilest crime. Burke was stopped in the street and asked for directions by a woman leading by the hand a young boy who was deaf and dumb. Burke led her to his home where he and Hare killed her before also disposing of her son. Burke took the boy over his knee and, as he later told police, 'broke his back' while the terrified youngster stared piteously into his face. The two victims were then stuffed into a barrel and sold for £16 the pair.

In the end, Burke and Hare were trapped by their over-confidence and carelessness. In October 1828, a female boarder turned up the corner of her straw mattress and was horrified to discover the body of a naked crone, her face horribly bloodstained. She went

ABOVE LEFT: Notorious Scottish murderer William Burke, as he appeared in court. Burke, with his accomplice William Hare, murdered nine people, selling the bodies to medical schools for dissection.

ABOVE RIGHT: William Hare was an accomplice of William Burke and Robert Knox. Burke was hanged for his crimes but Hare gave evidence and was released with Robert Knox.

ABOVE: An angry mob pursues Helen MacDougal, mistress of serial killer William Burke, through the streets of Edinburgh, circa 1829.

ABOVE: Crowds gather to watch the execution of William Burke at the Lawnmarket, Edinburgh, on January 28, 1829.

to the police and the killers were arrested. Hare, given an offer of immunity by turning King's Evidence, immediately denounced his former partner.

The trial of William Burke began on Christmas Eve 1828 and continued without pause until the last guilty verdict was returned on Christmas morning. The court's sentence was that he be hanged and his body be used for medical science. A crowd of thousands, among them the poet Walter Scott, watched him die on the gallows on January 28, 1829.

Burke's body was then removed to the medical rooms, where guests were admitted in batches of 50 to watch it being dissected. The following day, the general public was admitted, thousands of curious strangers filing past his remains. The body was then salted and put into barrels for use in future experiments.

Only Burke suffered the full weight of the law but the other players in the vile pantomime did not enjoy their freedom. The infamous Dr Knox continued to deny complicity in the crimes but found his medical career in ruins. He died in disgrace in December 1862. The wives of Burke and Hare, who assisted the pair in their vile trade, suffered public hatred wherever they went. And Hare himself, having turned against his accomplice to obtain his own freedom, moved away from Edinburgh and lived out a miserable existence in the slums of London, eventually dying a poverty-stricken blind beggar.

David Carpenter

The so-called 'Trailside Killings' in the San Francisco Bay Area began in August 1979 with the murder of 44-year-old Edda Kane, who had been hiking in Mount Tamalpais State Park. She was raped and then shot through the back of the head while kneeling.

Stuttering Psycho Known As The 'Trailside Killer'

Seven months later, 23-year-old Barbara Schwartz was stabbed while on her knees. Then came Anne Alderson, a 26-year-old jogger, found dead in the park with three bullets in her head. She, too, had been in the kneeling position at the time of her death.

ABOVE: Mount Tamalpais State Park, where David Carpenter carried out the 'Trailside Killings'.

The killer went into overdrive in late 1980. Hiker Shawna May, 25, was shot and placed in a shallow grave in Point Reyes Park. Nearby was the body of another missing person, Diane O'Connell, 22, also shot in the head. On the same day, November 29, two more bodies were found in Point Reyes: Cynthia Moreland, 18, and Richard Towers, 19, had been killed on the same October weekend as Alderson.

The discovery of four bodies in one day caused a howl of outrage in the media and spread fear across the Bay Area, where jogging, hiking, and other healthy outdoor activities were a way of life. However, police had few leads to follow. No one had seen the mysterious 'Trailside Killer' and survived.

Then, in March 1981, hitch-hikers Ellen Hansen and Gene Blake were threatened at gunpoint in a park near Santa Cruz. She was shot dead, but her boyfriend managed to crawl away, bleeding profusely from his wounds. Blake's description allowed police to release a composite picture of the killer.

The net was closing in on the 'Trailside Killer'—but not before he had claimed a final victim. In May, Heather Skaggs, 20, was found dead in Big Basin Redwood State Park. Bullets used to kill her matched those fired at Gene Blake and Ellen Hansen. But now there were further clues. Heather had worked in the same print store as a known sex offender, David Carpenter, she had last been seen near his home—and work colleagues said they believed Carpenter had tried to date her.

The trail clearly led to the man who should have been a suspect from the start. Carpenter was a psycho with a pronounced stutter who, in 1960 at the age of 30, had been arrested and sentenced to 14 years in prison for attacking a woman with a hammer and knife. Freed early, he re-offended in 1970 and spent seven years in jail for kidnapping. In between his two prison terms, he had been a principal suspect in California's mysterious 'Zodiac murders' (see page 219) but was ultimately cleared.

Indeed, one other murder victim may have preceded the uproar over the 'Trailside Killings'. Anna Menjivas, who had been a friend of Carpenter's, disappeared from her home in 1979 and was found dead in Mount Tamalpais Park, the area of the next three murders. Yet police failed to link her death to Carpenter until after his arrest.

On July 6, 1984, Carpenter was found guilty in Los Angeles of the murders of Heather Skaggs and Ellen Hansen. He was sentenced to death in the gas chamber of San Quentin. At a second trial in San Diego, Carpenter was convicted of five more murders and two rapes and again sentenced to death, but a string of appeals meant he languished indefinitely on Death Row.

Andrei Chikatilo

Crazed cannibal Andrei Chikatilo was questioned several times during his 12 years of slaughter and released on every occasion. The mild-mannered former schoolteacher convinced detectives that he was a faithful husband, proud father, and studious academic.

'Rostov Ripper' Killed And Ate More Than 50

A **university graduate,** Chikatilo completed his military service and in 1963, at the age of 27, he met and married Fayina, a pit worker's daughter. They had a son and a daughter as Chikatilo continued his home studies, gaining a degree in literature and taking a job as a teacher. For reasons no one then guessed, he gave up the post in 1981 and started work as a supply clerk, a humble job but one that involved much travel.

This gave him greater scope for his perverted pleasures, for Chikatilo was already a killer. Although living in an apartment in Rostov-on-Don, Russia, he had also bought a dilapidated shack outside the town, to which he regularly brought back prostitutes for sex. In December 1978, he lured a nine-year-old girl there and, following a failed attempt at rape, brutally stabbed her to death.

It transpired from his wife's later evidence that Chikatilo could not have sex in any normal way. He needed to instil terror before he could perform adequately. He would rape his victims only after working himself into a frenzy as he stabbed and mutilated them.

He went on to kill at least 53 people around Rostov and as far afield as St Petersburg and Tashkent, Uzbekistan. He would hang around bus stops and railroad stations, stalking his victims, mainly targeting prostitutes, tramps or runaways, whom he lured with the promise of gifts or a meal.

Most of his victims were raped after death and then mutilated, with various organs cut out or bitten off. He would often consume their flesh. His oldest victim was a 44-year-old prostitute and his youngest a seven-year-old boy. There was also a mother and her 11-year-old daughter, who vanished after he took them on a picnic.

'I paid no attention to age or sex,' he later told police, adding: 'Eating my victims is the ultimate sacrifice they can make for me. They are literally giving themselves to me.'

Chikatilo avoided capture because of police blunders. He was arrested after his very first murder when neighbors reported strange happenings at his shack. During the 12-year hunt for the so-called 'Rostov Ripper', he was questioned by police on at

ABOVE: Andrei Chikatilo behind the bars of an iron cage during his trial in Rostov in 1992.

least eight further occasions, on one of them being kept in custody for 10 days. They even closed the case briefly when inquiries switched to another suspect—who, bizarrely, confessed to murder and was executed.

The killings did in fact cease for three months. That was because Chikatilo had been sent to prison, not for any violent crime but on an old charge of stealing linoleum. After his release, he slaughtered eight people in a single month.

Chikatilo was finally arrested outside a cafe in November 1990. He admitted murdering 11 boys and 42 girls but police believe there may have been more. He went on trial chained in an iron cage within the Rostov courtroom where, in October 1992, he was sentenced to death. He was executed with a bullet in the back of the neck on February 14, 1994.

ABOVE: Chikatilo relished cannibalism. He once said that eating his victims is 'the ultimate sacrifice they can make for me'.

John Reginald Christie

In the annals of British crime, few addresses are more enduringly spine-chilling than 10 Rillington Place, in London's Notting Hill district. Now trendily upgraded, the area was, in the postwar years, distinctly shabby and seedy. It is a description that could equally have applied to one of the occupants: the balding, bespectacled John Reginald Halliday Christie.

The Chilling Secret of 10 Rillington Place

Christie committed at least six and possibly eight murders in his rented ground-floor apartment there, hiding the corpses around the house as a gruesome legacy for the next tenant to find. One body was of a woman for whose death her husband was wrongly sent the gallows.

Born in Halifax, Yorkshire, in 1898, Christie was a weakly youth who nevertheless enlisted in World War One and suffered eye and throat injuries in a mustard gas attack. He returned home with a small disability pension, married a local girl and went to work for the Post Office.

This was where his life of crime began, for he was caught stealing postal orders and was sent to jail, the first of several spells behind bars for what were, at first, petty offenses. When wife Ethel discovered he was also visiting prostitutes, Christie moved alone to London, where he served three further jail terms for theft and attacking a woman.

After a nine-year separation, he wrote to Ethel seeking a reconciliation, and in 1938 they moved into 10 Rillington Place. Extraordinarily, World War Two

BELOW: Austrian refugee Ruth Fuerst, who was murdered by Christie in 1943 and buried in his backyard.

saw him back into uniform as a police special constable, no checks having been made for previous convictions. Under that guise of authority and respectability, he began murdering women.

In 1943, he picked up a 17-year-old Austrian refugee, took her back to Rillington Place while his wife was absent and strangled her with a rope. Under cover of darkness, he buried her body in the small communal ackyard, where it lay undisturbed for a decade.

After losing his police post the following year, Christie worked at various clerking jobs, in one of which he chatted up a 31-year-old co-worker and invited her to his home. There, he raped and strangled her with a stocking and buried her alongside his first victim.

In 1948 truck driver Timothy Evans, his wife Beryl, and their baby Geraldine moved into the apartment

ABOVE: John Christie was first jailed for stealing postal orders, but his criminal activities soon escalated to murder by strangulation.

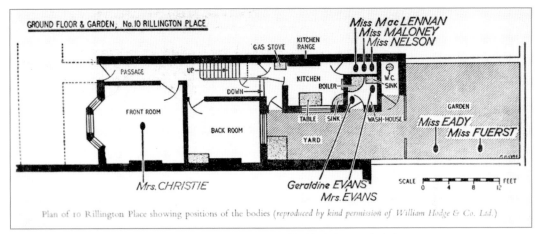

Plan of 10 Rillington Place showing positions of the bodies (*reproduced by kind permission of William Hodge & Co. Ltd.*)

ABOVE: A plan of Christie's apartment of evil, showing the locations in which his victims were buried.

BELOW: Christie's 'murder room', situated at the rear of his ground-floor apartment.

above Christie's. A year later, Beryl and 14-month-old Geraldine were murdered. Inexplicably, Evans, who was of subnormal intelligence, went to the police to confess to killing his wife—but when they raided the house and also found his daughter's body, he changed his story, blaming his neighbor. Christie gave evidence against Evans, sealing his fate. He was hanged on March 9, 1950.

Christie's next victim was his wife. In 1952 he strangled Ethel in bed and buried her under the floorboards. That left him free to bring prostitutes to the apartment, three of whom he murdered and stuffed into cupboards. In March 1953, he moved out of Rillington Place and lived rough. Within days he was arrested after the apartment's next tenant discovered the

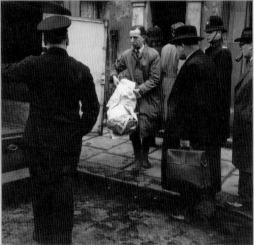

LEFT: The bones of Christie's fifth victim are removed from 10 Rillington Place by police.

grisly cause of the stench that permeated the house.

At London's Old Bailey, Christie's plea of insanity was rejected and on July 15, 1953, he was hanged for four of the murders, including that of Ethel. But who killed Beryl Evans? Christie finally confessed to her murder but two subsequent tribunals failed to overturn the verdict against Timothy Evans. In 1966, however, the lingering doubts earned Evans a long-overdue posthumous royal pardon.

Douglas Clark and Carol Bundy

Douglas Clark, the 'Sunset Strip Slayer', had a particularly gruesome fetish. He killed prostitutes, one of whom he decapitated and had sex with her head. His girlfriend Carol Bundy indulged this perversion by applying make-up to the head. Clark kept this grisly memento in his freezer for a few days, taking it out from time to time for the purpose of oral sex.

Hideous Habits Of The 'Sunset Strip Slayer'

Clark, handsome son of a former admiral in the US Navy, was 31 when, in 1980, he met Bundy, a dumpy 37-year-old mother of two, who worked as a vocational nurse in Los Angeles. He moved into her apartment in Burbank and made her his willing sex slave. He brought women and girls, as young as 11, home for sex while she watched and photographed them.

Then, in June 1980, the bodies of stepsisters aged 15 and 16 were found beside a highway. They had been snatched by Clark from Huntington Beach and forced to perform sex acts before being shot in the head. Although Bundy may not have been involved in that crime, she was an active participant in those that followed.

She and Clark would regularly drive along Sunset Boulevard to pick up a prostitute. Once parked in a quiet street, Clark would force her to perform oral sex on him while Bundy watched. As he climaxed, Clark would shoot the girl in the head.

Their murderously kinky games resulted in the bodies of prostitutes aged 17, 20, and 24 turning up during their June killing spree. Each had been disposed of in the same manner—except that in the case of the 20-year-old, her head was missing. It was found three days later in a box in the driveway of a house in Hollywood.

According to Bundy's later testimony, Clark had taken the head home with him so he could engage in oral sex with it at his leisure. She said that while her two children were out, Clark had produced the head from the freezer, ordered her to comb the hair and apply make-up to it. 'We had a lot of fun with her,' she told police. 'I was making her up like a Barbie.'

Clark's next victim was never identified. Her dismembered body turned up in Malibu in July. The final murder victim died the following month at the hands of Bundy herself. He was a former boyfriend, barman John Murray, who had foolishly confided to her that he suspected her new lover might be the 'Sunset Strip Slayer'. Bundy set up a meeting at which she shot and stabbed him, then decapitated him. His torso was discovered in his van but his head was never found.

Bundy may have been trying to prove to Clark her equal ability to kill but she could not carry it off. The overweight, mentally disturbed nurse broke down and confessed to a colleague. Police were tipped off and the killers were arrested. After initially blaming each other, Bundy confessed her involvement in the crimes, pleading guilty to the murder of Murray. Sentenced to life imprisonment, she became key witness against

ABOVE: Sunset Strip in Los Angeles, the hunting ground of Douglas Clark and Carol Bundy during the summer of 1980.

her boyfriend at his 1983 trial.

Clark was found guilty on six counts of murder and was sentenced to death. The Californian Supreme Court affirmed the sentence in 1992, leaving the 'Sunset Strip Slayer' lingering on Death Row—

surviving his partner Bundy, who died in prison of heart failure in December 2003.

Adolfo Constanzo

Adolfo de Jesus Constanzo was a practitioner of voodoo for the power it gave him over others. He was also a devotee of the strange religion because it allowed him to satiate his bloodlust with regular human sacrifices.

Human Sacrifices Of The Voodoo Cult

Born in Miami of Cuban extraction in 1962, Constanzo studied the black magic arts of Palo Mayombe, a violent sect imported from the Congo.

The cult believes the spirits of the dead exist in limbo and can be harnessed if the gods are regularly appeased with the fresh blood of human sacrifices. Constanzo would keep a cauldron constantly filled with blood and, most importantly, the skull of a human who had died a violent death.

At the age of 21, Constanzo moved to Mexico City where in 1983 he launched himself as a Palo Mayombe priest. Superstitious drugs family godfathers turned to him for magical protection at $50,000 a spell. As a consequence, his cauldron needed constant replenishment with fresh blood and skulls, and decapitated corpses were regularly fished out of rivers and lakes by police. On one occasion, the mutilated bodies of five members of the same household were discovered.

Constanzo's method of sacrifice was to have the victim beaten, then dragged to the sacred cauldron. It was essential to the success of the ceremony that there should be as much pain as possible and the victim should die screaming. So Constanzo would cut off the nose, ears, fingers, toes, and genitals of the hapless wretch and partially flay him before sodomizing

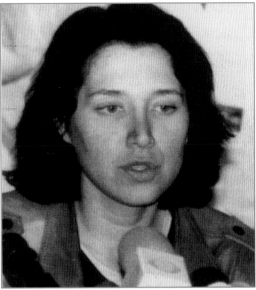

ABOVE: Sara Aldrete, a member of Constanzo's evil cult, was sentenced to 62 years without parole in 1994.

him. Only then would there be a merciful release through death.

Constanzo moved his voodoo circle to Matamoros, near the Texan border, where between May 1988 and March 1989 the gang ritually sacrificed at least 13 people. They were often rival drug dealers but also included strangers picked up at random.

Mark Kilroy was just such a victim. The 21-year-old medical student had crossed the border with friends to celebrate the end of their university term. When he became separated from them, he was bundled into the back of a truck and driven to Constanzo's remote Santa Elena ranch, where he was butchered and his brains tipped into the cauldron.

Kilroy's worried parents agitated for a properly conducted police investigation, and success was swift. Mexican police set up a road block near Matamoros, and one of Constanzo's gang drove straight through it—having been told by his leader that he was invisible! The cops simply followed him to the ranch,

ABOVE: Adolfo Constanzo's obsession with the black magic arts of Palo Mayombe drove him to make many human sacrifices.

where they unearthed human remains including those of Mark Kilroy.

Constanzo was not there. He and his favored inner circle were spotted by chance in Mexico City, where an armed siege of their apartment ensued. Out of ammunition, Constanzo huddled in a closet with a male lover and ordered another gang member to shoot them both. 'Don't worry, I'll be back,' were his last words.

The rest were taken alive. In all, 14 cultists were given lengthy jail terms on charges from multiple murder to drug running. Oddest among them was Sara Aldrete, an all-American ex-college student from Brownsville, Texas, who had thrown away a glittering future as an athlete to join the cult. Sentenced in 1994 to 62 years without parole, she was asked why she had followed Constanzo. 'I could not leave him,' she said, 'because he threatened to use witchcraft on my family.'

Eric Cooke

To say that Eric Edgar Cooke had a bad start in life would be an understatement. Born in February 1931 in Perth, Western Australia, he suffered in childhood from his father's alcohol fueled beatings. Ostracized because of his harelip and cleft palate and resulting speech defect, Cooke grew up an angry, brooding loner.

Sad Childhood Of The Random Slayer

He took a succession of semi-skilled jobs, while committing a string of crimes in his neighborhood. After the accident-prone youth suffered several traumas to his head at work, he attempted to get his life together by enlisting in the military in 1952. He was discharged three months later when it was discovered that he had failed to declare a series of convictions for theft, breaking and entering, and arson of a church.

A year later, aged 22, Cooke again attempted to settle down by marrying Sarah Lavin, a 19-year-old waitress, and fathering seven children. Family life failed to calm him, however, and he continued to roam the streets by night, being arrested for minor offenses including voyeurism.

What turned Cooke from petty crime to serial killer is unclear but, in February 1959, he repeatedly and fatally stabbed an innocent woman while she was sleeping in her Perth apartment. Ten months later, armed with a knife and hatchet, he broke into the home of a 22-year-old woman, hacking at her face after he delivered lethal stab wounds. The police discounted

sex and robbery as motives, as the girls had not been raped and nothing had been stolen.

Cooke's subsequent killing spree involved a series of seemingly unrelated hit-and-runs, stabbings, stranglings, and shootings which held Perth in a grip of terror. This was a strangely inconsistent serial killer whose methods seemed as random as his choice of victims.

Victims had been shot with a variety of different rifles, stabbed with knives, scissors, and hit with an ax. One victim was shot dead after answering a knock on his door, several were killed upon waking while Cooke was robbing their homes. Two were shot while sleeping without their homes being disturbed. After stabbing one victim, he got lemonade from the refrigerator and sat on the porch drinking it.

In August 1963, an elderly couple gathering wildflowers near the Canning River found a rifle lying in the brush and called the police. Ballistics tests confirmed it was the weapon used to kill a babysitter a week earlier. The rifle was impounded, replaced with a lookalike, and detectives staked out the scene. They waited 15 days before Cooke arrived to claim the weapon, and he was taken into custody without a struggle.

Apart from the eight or more murders of which he was suspected, Cooke admitted having committed more than 200 thefts, five hit-and-run offenses against young women, and two murders for which other men had already been wrongly imprisoned. Evidence indeed pointed to Cooke being the killer of the two women, and the convictions against Darryl Beamish and John Button were quashed—but not before they had served a total of 20 years between them.

Despite Cooke's defense citing his disturbed childhood, head injuries, and spells in an asylum, the court rejected the claim that he suffered from schizophrenia. The state permitted no other psychiatric specialist to examine him and, in November 1963, he was convicted of wilful murder after a three-day trial in the Supreme Court of Western Australia.

Cooke was sentenced to death by hanging. He ordered his lawyers not to appeal, conceding that he deserved to pay for what he had done. Aged 33, Eric Cooke became the last person to be hanged at Fremantle Prison, on October 26, 1964.

Dean Corll

Dean Corll was known as 'The Candy Man' because of the years he had spent working at home with his mother, making candies and selling them in a small store attached to their house in Houston, Texas. He had always sought the company of young men but, during a spell in the US Army, he realized he was gay—and that his sexual urges could only be satisfied by inflicting pain.

The 'Candy Man' Who Hired Kids To Kill Kids

Released from service at the age of 25 in 1964, Corll returned to his job at the confectionary factory and tried to befriend boys by giving them sweets. At roughly the same time as complaints about his sexual advances became public, his mother closed the company and retired.

Her son moved to the suburb of Pasadena and became a trainee electrician for the Houston Lighting and Power Company. He was well liked by colleagues but some of them thought it strange that he spent his free time mixing only with young teenagers. Two of them became his particular friends: Elmer Henley and David Brooks, both of whom dropped out of high school to spend more time with Corll.

In fact, what they had embarked on was not merely a homosexual relationship with the older man but a murder spree of shocking savagery.

Corll had met Brooks when the schoolboy was only 12. The older man at first paid the boy for sexual favors but then enlisted him as an accomplice. Henley, by contrast, had originally been earmarked as one of Corll's victims but avoided death by his willingness to plumb any immoral depth—and that included delivering his best friends into Corll's clutches.

The mission of these two Houston youths was to cruise the area seeking boys with whom Corll could forcibly have sex. Operating mainly in the rundown Heights area, they found they had no problem persuading young drug addicts to go to Corll's home with the promise of wild parties. There they would suffer prolonged torture at the hands of Corll before being murdered. 'He killed them because he wanted to have sex and they didn't', Brooks later told police.

All the victims were young males between 13 and 20 years old. Corll's first known victim was 18-year-old Jeffrey Konen, a student of the University of Texas who vanished in September 1970 while hitch-hiking to his parents' Houston home.

Tragically, most of those who followed were even younger. Typical was Billy Ray Lawrence, a 15-year-old friend of Henley, who was kept alive by Corll for four days before he was killed. By that August 1973, when 13-year-old James Dreymala became Corll's last confirmed victim, the tally had reached at least 27, most of them procured by Brooks and Henley, who had graduated from simply supplying the victims to helping commit the occasional murder themselves.

The official list of Corll's victims is likely to be underestimated. Forty-two boys had vanished within the Houston area since 1970 but, despite the anxiety of parents over their missing sons, police had failed to come anywhere close to solving the mystery. To the frustration of the families, many of the disappearances were written down as 'runaways'.

The breakthrough, when it came, was not due to police diligence. At 3am on August 8, 1973, Henley turned up at Corll's home with one of his friends, Tim Kerley, who had been happy to accept an invitation to a glue sniffing party but was in fact the next intended victim. Henley had also brought along his girlfriend, 15-year-old Rhonda Williams.

Corll objected to the girl's presence and, while Henley and Williams were in a drug-induced stupor, handcuffed and bound them. The 17-year-old pleaded with Corll to untie him, promising to continue helping him carry out the night's planned murder. But as soon as his hands were freed, he grabbed his captor's gun and shot him six times at point-blank range. The reign of the 33-year-old mass killer was instantly ended.

Henley called the police who found that one of the bedrooms had been turned into a 'torture room'. The centerpiece was a thick board with shackles for hands and feet. Various instruments of torture, including an assortment of dildos, were in evidence. Police also noticed that many wall and floor surfaces were covered with plastic sheeting—the better to contain the bloodstains that nevertheless spattered some of the walls.

Forced to confess his part in procuring Corll's victims, Henley led police to a boatshed where 17 decomposing bodies of boys lay in shallow graves. Corll had spread lime around them to disguise the stench of decomposition. Next stop was a local tourist spot, Lake Sam Rayburn, where more naked corpses were unearthed.

Many of the bodies recovered showed signs of mutilation and torture. It appeared that one of Corll's perverted practices was to insert a glass rod into the urethra of a victim and break it. The total body count came to 27 but police believe the higher figure of 42 was more realistic.

Henley and Brooks were tried in 1974 at San Antonio, where their pleas of insanity were rejected. Henley was found guilty of nine murders and sentenced to 594 years in prison. Brooks got life after being found guilty of one murder.

Juan Corona

Juan Vallejo Corona was at one time labeled the worst and most notorious mass murderer in United States history. Sadly, his tally of 25, killed during just a few months of 1971, did not remain a record for long. The other tragedy was that, by the nature of his crimes, many of the victims were barely missed. They were mostly Mexican migrants, largely itinerant fruit pickers, who hardly mixed with the local rural populations of California's Sutter County and of Feather River, where most of the killings took place.

Killer Dug Graves To Await Victims

Corona, born in 1933, had been an itinerant himself, having crossed the border into California as a 16-year-old in 1950. Despite his lack of schooling, he steadily worked his way up to become a successful businessman, a licensed labor contractor in charge of hiring fellow migrant workers to pick the fruit crops of the Yuba City area.

His book-keeping was meticulous—as police discovered when they followed up an anonymous tip and raided his farmhouse, near Feather River, in 1971. There they found 25 names carefully listed in a ledger. They corresponded with Mexican migrants and other itinerants all of whom had disappeared in the previous few months. Their bodies had been secreted around the farmstead after being hacked to death with knives and machetes.

The alarm had been raised on May 19, when a local rancher noticed that a hole, the size of a grave, had been dug in his peach orchard. Returning there the next day, he saw that it had been filled in with freshly dug earth. When police investigated, they unearthed the body of Kenneth Whitacre, a 40-year-old vagrant, who had been sodomized, stabbed to death, and his head almost severed with a machete.

The gruesome discovery sparked off the hunt for more buried bodies, with 25 eventually being found, although police maintained there must have been many more. The victims had all been murdered during a period of six weeks; an average of one death every 40 hours.

One grave alone yielded nine bodies. All had been subjected to homosexual rape before being stabbed and viciously slashed around the head. Corona had buried them face up, with their arms stretched above their heads and their shirts pulled up over their faces. Some had their pants pulled down.

When police searched Corona's farmhouse, they found—in addition to the notebook—a machete, a pistol, two butcher's knives, and bloodstained clothes. It became obvious that he had carefully planned the killings—digging a fresh grave in advance of each attack.

At his trial in 1973, his lawyers argued that all 25 charges of murder should be dismissed on the grounds of their client's mental instability. He had twice been treated at a psychiatric hospital where he had been diagnosed with paranoid schizophrenia, they argued. But their pleas were ignored and Corona was given 25 life sentences.

The killer lodged further failed legal appeals over the years, once telling a prison doctor: 'Yes, I did it but I'm a sick man and can't be judged by the standards of other men.'

During a parole bid in 2003, by which time he was 69, he said: 'The victims were all people who didn't have a family and they were ready to go to the next world.'

Mary Ann Cotton

Unlike most serial killers, Mary Ann Cotton was on intimate terms with all of her victims. The reason was clear, for all were members of her immediate family. It is not known exactly how many people she murdered but the candidates include her mother, three of her four husbands (one of them being bigamous), a lover, her best friend, plus 15 children, including 10 from among her own brood of 12.

Churchgoer Commits Multiple Murders With Arsenic

That was a British serial-killing record that has survived well over a century—and all the more remarkable since Mary Ann was a churchgoing girl born in 1832 far from the lure of any big city. Raised by strict Methodist parents in the County Durham mining village of Low Moorsley, Mary Ann was married in 1852 at the age of 20 to William Mowbray. They had eight children but the family appeared to

ABOVE: Mary Ann Cotton, the churchgoer who claimed around 20 victims through arsenic poisoning in the 19th century.

husband, James Robinson, asked Mary Ann to marry him. Conveniently, mother was dead within 10 days. Mary Ann herself became mother to James Robinson's five children, taking with her the surviving daughter Isabella. Within a few short months Isabella and four of the Robinson children had died from supposed natural causes. Robinson left his wife, taking with him his remaining child, and in doing so became the only husband to survive.

Mary Ann did not stay single for long, however. Even though she was still legally married, she next wed Frederick Cotton, who had two children from a previous marriage. Mary Ann soon fell pregnant and had another child but a year into the marriage, Frederick Cotton was also dead. Gastric fever was blamed.

At this juncture in her killing spree, Mary Ann met up with a former lover, Joseph Nattrass. The resumed romance was ill-fated, however, as the greedy widow found yet another way of improving her lifestyle. This time her heart was set on a customs officer by the name of Mr Quick-Manning and poor Joseph Nattrass was suddenly dispensable. Mary Ann killed him, along with her stepsons from her bigamous marriage to Cotton: 10-year-old Frederick junior and 14-month-old baby Charlie.

It was this final murder that doomed Mary Ann Cotton. Little Charlie had been fine one day and dead the next. His tiny body was subjected to an autopsy, which revealed not only the cause of his early demise—arsenic poisoning—but also the probable cause of all the other family deaths.

The suspicion was confirmed when the bodies of other family members were exhumed, and 40-year-old Mary Ann Cotton was tried for murder at Durham Assizes on March 5, 1873. Justice was swift and two weeks later she walked from her cell to the gallows.

be plagued by health problems. One by one, the brothers, sisters, and their father William himself all died of gastric fevers. In fact she had poisoned them. Only one among the family survived, a daughter named Isabella who had been sent away to live with her grandmother.

Following the death of her poor husband, Mary Ann married George Ward. Yet after only 13 months he too was dead. The widow even murdered her own mother, who became ill at the same time as her third

Thomas Cream

Dr Thomas Neill Cream stood with a hood over his head and a noose around his neck on the scaffold at London's Newgate Prison in 1892 and, so the story goes, declared: 'I am Jack the…' He was cut short when the trap door burst open beneath his feet and he was hanged.

Last Boast Of The 'Lambeth Poisoner'

Cream, tagged the 'Lambeth Poisoner', had initially been a suspect in the search for Jack the Ripper, the killer of five women in London at the close of the 19th century (see page 95). But since he could prove that he was in jail in America at the time the Ripper was operating, his cry was judged a final attempt at a dramatic exit.

Cream was born in Glasgow in May 1850 to parents who emigrated to Canada, where the studious young Thomas qualified as a doctor. In 1876 he married

ABOVE: Strychnine was the method of execution favored by the 'Lambeth Poisoner', Dr Thomas Cream.

Flora Brooks in a shotgun wedding—after her parents discovered he had carried out a bungled abortion on her that left her seriously ill. The day after the nuptials, however, Cream abandoned his wife, who later died—possibly at Cream's hands.

The callous doctor fled to Britain where he continued his medical studies in London and Edinburgh before returning to Canada and setting up a practice in London, Ontario. Soon afterward, in August 1879, the body of a woman was found in an alley near his surgery. She had earlier visited Cream to seek an abortion.

Under suspicion, Cream moved to Chicago, where he specialized in offering abortions to prostitutes. When one of his patients died in August 1880, he was taken into custody but released for lack of evidence.

Cream was again arrested a year later when the husband of one of his patients died of strychnine poisoning. There was firm evidence that Cream had supplied the wife with the poison, but when she turned state's evidence, the doctor was left to face a murder charge alone. He was sentenced to life in November 1881.

With remission, Cream was released a decade later and, with an inheritance left him by his father, returned to England and settled in Lambeth, a working-class area of Victorian London rife with crime and prostitution. In October 1891, he picked up two prostitutes, aged 19 and 27, both of whom died of strychnine poisoning.

The following April, he offered a girl some pills that he said would help clear a rash on her face. Suspicious because of her client's insistence that she swallow them all, she merely pretended to do so, thereby saving herself from the 'Lambeth Poisoner'.

But two other prostitutes hired by Cream a week later were not so fortunate. The girls, aged 18 and 21, were offered drinks the killer had brought with him and both died in agony. At last, suspicion fell on the local doctor, who was arrested at his home in June 1892. Police found seven bottles of strychnine in his rooms.

At the Old Bailey, Cream's pleas of innocence were rejected, the jury taking just 10 minutes to decide he was guilty. Seeming surprised at the verdict, he strutted from the dock, defiantly stating: 'They shall never hang me.' He was proved wrong on the morning of November 15, 1892.

Charles Cullen

Charles Cullen is the serial killer who should have kept his mouth shut. When he was brought into Lehigh County Court, Pennsylvania, for sentencing in March 2006, he became upset with Judge William Pratt and kept interrupting him. After 30 minutes of this, the judge had had enough; he ordered Cullen to be gagged with cloth and duct tape. Even then, the killer tried to mumble.

'Mercy Killing' Mania Of Suicidal Male Nurse

Cullen had already been served with 12 life sentences in various courts. Now Judge Pratt handed him another six. The multi-sentence was another record to add to the one Cullen already had— as the most prolific serial killer in New Jersey history. The former nurse had been in and out of courts since December 2003 when he told authorities that he had murdered at least 30 and possibly 45 patients during the 16 years he had worked at 10 hospitals in New Jersey and Pennsylvania.

Cullen was born in 1960 in West Orange, New Jersey, the youngest of eight children. His father, a bus driver, died when he was an infant. Two of his siblings also died. But it was the death of his mother, in a car crash while being driven by one of her daughters, that tipped young Charles over the edge.

Describing his childhood as 'miserable', he had first attempted suicide when only nine—the first of 20 attempts throughout his life. In one, he needed emergency surgery after jabbing a pair of scissors through his head. Cullen quit high school after his mother's death and enlisted in the US Navy, where he served on nuclear submarines before being given a medical discharge in 1984.

Trained as a nurse, he committed his first murder in June 1988. When a retired judge was admitted to New Jersey's St Barnabas Medical Center with circulation problems, Cullen injected him with a lethal overdose. The nurse subsequently admitted killing another 10 patients before quitting in 1992 when hospital authorities started investigating him.

Over the next five years, he took jobs at three other hospitals in the state, continuing what he dismissively described as 'mercy killings' of terminally-ill patients, until fired for poor performance in 1997. At this time, he had not only lost his job but his wife, Adrienne, she having walked out on him with their daughters. She divorced him, complaining of domestic violence.

Cullen continued to find work. A nationwide nursing shortage made it difficult for hospitals to recruit, and no reporting mechanisms or other systems existed to identify staff with mental health or employment problems.

Cullen moved to Pennsylvania, and took nursing posts at three hospitals, in Easton, Allentown, and Bethlehem, from where he was fired for poor performance. Seven nurses who worked with him at Bethlehem's St Luke's Hospital alerted the district attorney of their suspicions that Cullen had used drugs to kill patients. Investigators failed to look into Cullen's past, and the case was dropped.

Suspicion again fell on Cullen when he moved back to New Jersey and found a job at Somerset Medical Center. There, he was reported for accessing unnecessary drugs. The New Jersey Poison Information and Education System warned hospital officials in July 2003 that a number of suspicious overdoses indicated that an employee might be killing patients. The hospital put off contacting authorities until October, by which time Cullen had killed another five patients.

When he was finally arrested in December 2003, Cullen promised to cooperate with police if they did not seek the death penalty for his crimes. He was brought to court in New Jersey on a charge of just one count of murder—that of a Roman Catholic priest who died of coronary failure after being given a lethal dose of the heart drug digoxin. The single charge kept Cullen in custody on $1 million bail while investigators looked into his other crimes. He told the judge: 'I am going to plead guilty. I don't plan to fight this.'

There would have been no point in doing so. As he languished in New Jersey State Prison, Trenton, his many consecutive life sentences meant he would be ineligible for parole for at least four centuries.

Gordon Cummins

In 1942, Great Britain was in the midst of World War Two and night-time blackouts were everyday occurrences. Under the cover of darkness, the streets of London were a hive of criminal activity and residents went in fear of pickpockets and gangs as much as German bombings.

'Blackout Ripper' Stalked Blitzed City

ABOVE: Prostitute killer Gordon Cummins in his RAF uniform. It was his RAF belt and gas-mask, which he inadvertently left at one crime scene, that led to his arrest and subsequent conviction.

On the evening of February 9 Evelyn Hamilton, a 41-year-old store manageress, was walking home after a meal alone when she was strangled and robbed of her purse containing £80. Her body was discovered in an air raid shelter in Montagu Place, in the Marylebone district—her skirt hitched up and her gloves carefully placed on her chest.

A day later, Evelyn Oatley, a married, struggling singer, who had been forced to turn to prostitution to supplement her income, was found dead at her Soho apartment. Near her body was a bloodstained tin opener that had been used to slash at her naked torso.

In the coming days, the killer took two more lives, both young women who worked the streets of London's West End. Although the first victim, Evelyn Hamilton, had not been a prostitute, the quick succession of the murders drew police to the conclusion that the

'Jack the Ripper' style killings were linked. The two women, Margaret Lowe and Doris Jouannet, had been strangled with one of their stockings and knifed. Police believed their deaths were the work of a left-handed serial killer who was bound to strike again.

It was then that the killer made a fatal mistake. In the following days, two more prostitutes, Margaret Heywood and Cathleen Mulcahy, were separately attacked, but miraculously escaped by fighting back and screaming for help. The killer fled—in the first case leaving behind the damning evidence of his gas-mask and in the second attack his uniform belt, both bearing an RAF service number 525987.

The items belonged to 28-year-old Leading Aircraftman Gordon Frederick Cummins and the net around him quickly closed. Cummins was a psychopathic braggart and liked to pretend he came from an upper-class background. His background, however, was modest. He was a married serviceman whose good looks and charm made him popular with girls.

Despite the damning evidence of the gas-mask, the belt, and the discovery of his victims' personal possessions among his belongings, Cummins maintained his innocence. His trial at the Old Bailey lasted just two days and the jury took only half an hour to return a verdict of guilty. Cummins was hanged at Wandsworth Prison on June 25, 1942.

Jeffrey Dahmer

Such an ordinary, straightforward young man…that's what they all said about Jeffrey Dahmer. The sort of person who melts into a crowd, blends into any background. Yet this was the monster who held a city in the grip of terror as he kidnapped, drugged, sexually molested, and killed his victims—then, finally, ate them.

The Killer Who Was A Real-Life 'Hannibal The Cannibal'

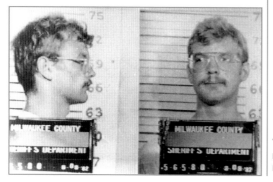

Dahmer was a homosexual, a pervert, a serial killer, a necrophiliac, and possibly the nearest thing to the fictional Hannibal Lecter in *Silence of the Lambs*. And like Hannibal the Cannibal, he had to be caged as befitting a dangerous beast, completely cut off from even his jailers inside Wisconsin's toughest prison, the Columbia Correctional Institution. There he sat isolated in an observation cell, his food passed to him through a drawer in a wall, guarded night and day from a control room. Even then, a fellow inmate managed to get to him and beat him to death.

Dahmer's insane, perverted lusts drove him to kill because only with corpses could he achieve sexual gratification. His apartment became an abattoir, a brothel, a restaurant, and a shrine—in which he could keep grotesque trophies like hands, skulls or genitals cut from his murdered and sodomized victims.

LEFT: Police mugshots of the serial murderer and cannibal, Jeffrey Dahmer, shortly after his arrest in the summer of 1991.

ABOVE: When police officers finally entered Dahmer's home on July 22, 1991, the cannibal seemed almost relieved to have been caught.

exposing himself to youngsters and was jailed for sexual abuse of a 13-year-old boy. Dahmer wrote to his trial judge seeking clemency: 'The world has enough misery in it without my adding more to it. That is why I am asking for a sentence modification, so that I can continue my life as a productive member of society.' He was jailed for eight years but was freed as a model prisoner after only 10 months.

Nine years after his first murder, Dahmer began an obsessional killing spree that would shock the world. By day he was the mild-mannered, anonymous little man who worked conscientiously in a local chocolate factory. By night he was a crazed homosexual cannibal who picked up victims from the streets or in gay bars

Choice cuts from the bodies went into his fridge for later consumption, the rest went into an acid bath he set up in the kitchen.

Even as a child, Jeffrey Dahmer had revealed an evil streak. Born in 1960 in West Allis, Wisconsin, the son of an analytical chemist, he tortured, killed, and mutilated animals for fun. He biked around his neighborhood looking for dead creatures to dissect at home, going so far as to put a dog's head on a stake.

Dahmer dropped out of high school and began drinking heavily. In 1978, at the age of just 18, he committed his first brutal murder, picking up a hitch-hiker and bludgeoning him to death after sex.

He did not kill again immediately, but he began

ABOVE: A photograph of a teenage Dahmer. He later became a self-confessed 'ghastly killer and cannibal.'

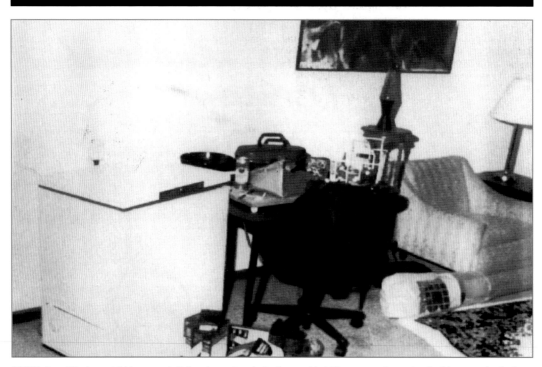

ABOVE: One of the few palatable scenes in Dahmer's apartment after it was raided. There was a strong stench of decomposing flesh.

and had sex with them before killing them. All were lured to his home, which would become infamous: Apartment 213, 924 North 25th Street, Milwaukee.

The pace of his killings increased from a single murder in 1987 to two in 1988, one in 1989, four in 1990—until the summer of 1991, by when he was slaughtering one person a week. Scandalously, it later transpired that he could so easily have been stopped...

The murder of 14-year-old Konerak Sinthasomphone on May 31, 1991, was to cause a public outcry because of a massive police blunder. The cops were called by neighbors after the teenager, a refugee from Laos, ran out of Dahmer's apartment naked, apparently drugged, bleeding from his rectum and with the marks of a power drill on his forehead.

Dahmer told them that Sinthasomphone was his 19-year-old boyfriend and that they had quarreled.

Despite the neighbors' protests, the officers believed Dahmer and returned the boy to him. Within hours, Dahmer strangled him, had oral sex with the corpse and then dismembered it, recording each stage with Polaroid photographs.

Over the next few weeks, Apartment 213 claimed four more victims: men in their 20s who were slaughtered and decapitated, their heads placed in a freezer.

His capture came about on July 22, not by diligent police work, but by Dahmer's sloppiness. Two patrolmen were sitting in their car in a seedy section of town when a young black man ran up to them, handcuffs dangling from his wrists. Tracy Edwards said someone in a nearby apartment block had threatened to cut out his heart and eat it. Edwards had taken to his heels, narrowly avoiding becoming Dahmer's 18th victim.

When the two cops hammered on the door of Apartment 213, it was opened by an innocent looking Dahmer dressed in a stylish T-shirt and blue jeans. What they instantly noticed, however, was a nauseous stench. Inside the apartment, along with pornographic pictures and kinky videos, they found hands, heads, and fingers stored in pots. In the fridge was a man's head, along with tenderized strips of meat that were later identified as human flesh.

Dahmer seemed almost relieved to have been caught. He immediately volunteered the information that he had killed 15 young men in Wisconsin and two more in Ohio. Over the next few days, scenes of white-coated forensic scientists entering the apartment and leaving with black plastic bags full of human remains became commonplace on American TV.

Victims' families turned out in force to curse the monster when his trial began on January 30, 1992. Dahmer's plea of insanity was rejected and, toward the end of the case, he made a statement to the court declaring that he would have been happy to accept the death penalty. He said:

'This was not about hate. I never hated anyone. I knew I was sick or evil, or both. I can't undo the harm I have caused, but I know I will be in prison for the rest of my life. I will turn back to God. I will cooperate with psychologists and become a human guinea pig so that they can study this bizarre mind and perhaps discover what turned a human being into a ghastly killer and cannibal'.

ABOVE: The cold-eyed stare of Jeffrey Dahmer, captured during his trial for multiple murder in 1992 in Wisconsin.

The self-serving diatribe failed to sway the jury who returned verdicts of guilty and sane. The judge sentenced him to 1,070 years in jail. He lasted only until November 1994, when he was beaten to death on a visit to the prison gym.

Albert De Salvo

Albert De Salvo has gone down in criminal history as the 'Boston Strangler'. The deaths of 13 women were attributed to him. But De Salvo was never convicted of those crimes. He was judged unfit to stand trial and was jailed in 1964 for lesser offenses.

Mystery Of The First Man Labeled 'Serial Killer'

De Salvo served only a fragment of his life sentence at Walpole State Prison, Massachusetts. On November 26, 1973, he was found dead in his cell, stabbed 16 times by a fellow inmate. Many feel the secret of the 'Boston Strangler' died with him. For although De Salvo confessed to the murders, evidence may not have committed them all.

Born in Chelsea, Massachusetts, in 1931, De Salvo was regularly battered by his drunken father who once, short of cash for booze, even sold Albert and two of his sisters to a local farmer for nine dollars. When they eventually came home, the children were taught to steal. Their father would also bring prostitutes home and make them watch as he had sex.

It is little wonder that the young De Salvo developed sexual obsessions, pursuing local girls while at the same time offering himself for homosexual favors at a price. A regular offender in minor crimes, he joined the Army and, on a posting to Germany, met and later married Irmgaard, daughter of a respectable Catholic family.

De Salvo was dishonorably discharged from the Army after being caught molesting a nine-year-old girl but the assault was covered up at the request of the abused girl's family. De Salvo, with his wife and two children, settled in Boston, where he worked as a house painter and handyman.

ABOVE: Boston Strangler Albert De Salvo photographed in Walpole State Prison, Massachusetts, in the early 1970s.

ABOVE: De Salvo shortly after his escape from a mental hospital and subsequent recapture in February 1967.

De Salvo sought sex up to six times a day, and when Irmgaard rejected his demands, her husband found a novel way of satisfying his lust. Pretending to be a model agent, he persuaded gullible girls to have their vital statistics measured, naked as well as dressed. He managed to seduce some but others put word around the district to be wary of the 'Measuring Man'.

It was then that the 'Measuring Man' became first the 'Green Man' and then the 'Boston Strangler'. He also became the first person to be given the media label 'serial killer'.

Between June 1962 and January 1964, an intruder, usually wearing green pants, gained access to the apartments of 12 single women, raped and mutilated them, then strangled them with a ligature tied in a bow. The first victim was a 55-year-old whom he strangled with the belt of her dressing gown before arranging her body in an obscene pose. The belt was then tied in a neat bow, which became the killer's trademark. The next four victims were also elderly women, aged 65 to 85.

In December 1962, the pattern changed—and the 'Measuring Man' returned. The mock 'model agent' called on a striking 20-year-old and stripped, raped, and strangled her before posing her naked body, complete with a bow under her chin. Three days later, he strangled a 25-year-old with her own stockings.

After losing one of his prey, a young girl who fought back and escaped, the killer rapist became even more violent. One victim died by having her skull crushed before being left with a fork stabbed in her breast. Another was tied to a bed, raped repeatedly, strangled and stabbed 22 times. Of one victim, De Salvo was later to confess: 'I don't know why I killed her. I wasn't even excited. Then I went home, played with the kids and watched the report of her murder on the TV.'

The final attack, on January 4, 1964, was the most horrific. Mary Sullivan, aged 19, was found propped up in a grotesque position on her bed. She had been assaulted with a broom. Between her toes, the killer had slid a card bearing the words 'Happy New Year'.

By now, some authorities believed that there might be two killers on the loose, one attacking young women and the other older women. Others suggested that the slayings were perpetrated by only one man, whose personality defect had altered over the time span of the murders.

De Salvo was eventually arrested in February 1965, although not for murder. Charged with housebreaking and sexual assault, his obviously disturbed state of mind resulted in him being committed to a hospital for the criminally insane. Only when police checked fresh witness descriptions and psychiatric profiles of the 'Boston Strangler' did they realize that he could be the man they were already holding.

Under interrogation, 33-year-old De Salvo at first denied the killings. But over seven months of questioning, he began to talk freely about them. He finally went on to admit murdering the 13 women police had linked him with, added two more to the list and confessed to raping thousands more. Much of the confession was later withdrawn, however.

Nevertheless, the gruesome details De Salvo supplied in 50 hours of tape recordings convinced police they had the right man. The clincher was when a detective observed him tying his shoelaces with the exact loops that police had come to know as the 'Strangler's Knot'. But not everyone was convinced—including the family of his last victim, Mary Sullivan, who campaigned for the hunt to be continued for her 'real killer'. The advance of forensic science may have proved them right, for in 2001 specimens of DNA obtained from De Salvo's exhumed body was compared to evidence found on Mary's. The samples did not match.

The Sullivan family's lawyer, Elaine Sawyer, said at the time: 'I think the whole theory that there ever was one Boston Strangler will be proved wrong.'

So was De Salvo the 'Boston Strangler', the 'Measuring Man', the 'Green Man' or all three? We shall never know. For his mental state allowed his lawyer, the famed F. Lee Bailey, to make a plea bargain that he admit to sexual assaults and robberies but not to murder. He never stood trial for the crimes of the 'Boston Strangler'.

'Demon Tailor'

We know the date and the place but we do not know his name. A serial killer without an identity? It happened in the unique case of the 'Werewolf of Chalons', charged in Paris in 1598 with murders so sickening that all documents were destroyed after his trial.

'Werewolf' On The Prowl

At the time, France was the scene of a spate of witch-hunts which reached their most bizarre in the pursuit of 'werewolves'. In a span of 100 years, through the superstitious 15th and 16th centuries, no fewer than 30,000 cases were reported to the authorities. Some of these could be attributed to rabies, prevalent at the time, and which turns its victims into aggressive madmen. Others might nowadays be diagnosed as cases of lycanthropy.

The term tends to be used to describe someone who is assumed to be mentally sick and believes he

ABOVE: A medieval illustration depicting a 'wolf-man' attacking his victims outside the safety of secure town walls.

has assumed wolf-like characteristics. The study of lycanthropy is the only way in which medical science can today come to terms with the long-held beliefs in werewolf delusions, which predate the birth of

ABOVE: During the 15th and 16th centuries the existence of werewolves, such as this, was accepted as unquestionable fact.

ABOVE: A depiction of a wolf-man. Lycanthropy, as it's known today, is a long-held belief which predates the birth of Christ.

Christ by 1,000 years. In France 400 years ago, for instance, church and state believed literally that such a metamorphosis could take place.

It was just as the terror of werewolves reached fever pitch that the 'Werewolf of Chalons' was dragged into the dock of a Paris court on December 14, 1598. In a case unique in the annals of serial killers, his real name has become lost in history, for he was referred to in court records only as the 'Demon Tailor'. The court was told that the tailor, who plied his trade in the ancient city of Chalons, in the Champagne region, lured into his store a string of unsuspecting victims— the younger the better. There he would subject them to gory perversions before slitting their throats and dressing the flesh, almost as if he were a professional butcher. He would then eat them at his leisure. The monster's vile habits also took him to woods around the city where he would 'assume the form of a wolf' and prey on innocent walkers.

The total number of his victims was never properly established but there is little doubt that it ran into dozens. When his house was raided, barrels of human bones immersed in bleach, along with fragments of limbs, were found in the cellar.

When he was sent to the stake the day after his trial, a huge crowd gathered to watch his final moments. And unlike many another convicted werewolves who repented of his sins as the first flames licked around his legs, the Demon Tailor betrayed no hint of remorse. He could be heard cursing and blaspheming to the very end.

Thomas Dillon

Thomas Lee Dillon, born July 9, 1950 in Canton, Ohio, was a serial sniper who shot and killed five people in the hunting forests of southeastern Ohio between 1989 and 1992. Nicknamed 'Killer' by his workmates after showing off about shooting thousands of animals, including cattle and pets, he had been aiming for live targets since childhood and was a compulsive gun collector with 500 weapons licensed to his name.

Sick Serial Sniper Smirked As He Was Sentenced

On April Fool's Day 1989, Dillon claimed his first victim, 35-year-old Donald Welling, who was jogging though the forest when he was struck down with a single shot to the back. In November 1990, Jamie Paxton, 21, was hunting wild animals through forestland in another part of Ohio. Three shots were fired and he was dead. Three weeks later, Kevin Loring, 30, was in pursuit of prey in eastern Ohio when a bullet from a high-powered rifle shattered his skull.

It was not uncommon for tragic accidents to occur during open-season hunting and police concluded that the bullets had been from the guns of hunters mistaking the victims for deer. Then, in 1991, Dillon wrote a chilling, anonymous letter to a small-town newspaper declaring that he was 'the murderer off Jamie Paxton'. In it, he boasted about killing Jamie after stalking him like an animal and described how much he loved the fun of the hunt and thrill of killing others.

He wrote tauntingly about Jamie's killing: 'The motive for the murder was this—the murder itself. With no motive and no witnesses, you could not possibly solve this crime.'

Dillon then remorsefully concluded that he only had a compulsion to kill under the influence of alcohol and hoped that curbing his excessive drinking would stop him from killing. However, in March 1992, he struck again. Claude Hawkins, 49, was shot in the back while fishing in Ohio, and two weeks later Gary Bradley, 44, was murdered the same way.

It wasn't until November 1992, when Dillon was seen firing a gun with a silencer at animals in a wildlife sanctuary, that he became a police suspect. Subsequently a friend recognized a behavioral profile compiled by the FBI and others, too, started to come forward. Wesley Tucke, 45, also a hunter, read a newspaper report of Dillon's arrest and concluded that this was the same man who had shot him 13 years earlier through the window of his home.

A psychological report on Dillon after his arrest revealed that he had been having fantasies about murdering for several years. He was an alcoholic with an aggressive personality and obsessive compulsive traits. Dillon told the psychologist: 'Five minutes after I shot Paxton I was drinking beer and had blacked out all thoughts of what I had just done from my mind. I thought no more about shooting Paxton than if I'd been shooting bottles at the garbage dump.'

It was also discovered that the murders were not the only crimes he'd committed. A map of Ohio was found in his office with 40 circles marked on. They matched the sites of 160 fires, mostly started in barns of vacant houses. He admitted to starting them, causing over a million dollars' worth of damage.

Having disposed of his guns, the evidence against Dillon was still circumstantial and he stood a chance of beating a murder charge. But the threat that if he did end up being charged with murder he would automatically be given the death sentence prompted him to plead guilty to the killings in exchange for a lesser sentence. At his 2002 trial, Dillon smirked through his sentencing. 'I'm very sorry for breaking the law', he said. He was incarcerated at the Southern Ohio Correctional Facility for 165 years for aggravated murder.

Nannie Doss

Nannie Hazel Doss was also known as 'Arsenic Annie', the 'Jolly Black Widow', and 'the Giggling Grandma'. A cuddly creature with twinkling eyes and a wide smile, she was a born romantic, a compulsive reader of pulp fiction who was just looking for the perfect love match. She married five times in a bid to find it. She failed principally because she poisoned four of those five husbands…along with two children, her two sisters, her mother, a grandson, and a nephew.

Cuddly Nannie Doss Left A Trail Of Dead Husbands

Doss was named Nancy when she was born in Blue Mountain, Alabama, one of five children of James Hazle. A cruel father hated both by the children and their mother, Hazle forced Nancy to work on the family farm rather than pursue her schooling. At the age of seven, she suffered a severe knock on the head and subsequently blamed that for her erratic behavior in later life. There is also the suggestion that she experienced sexual abuse during her childhood before escaping from her home and family by marrying, in 1920, at the age of just 15.

She had met her husband, Charlie Braggs, only four months before. He was the only child of his unmarried mother, who insisted on living with them at their new home in Tulsa, Oklahoma. Nancy, by now known as 'Nannie', came to hate the arrangement.

Nannie gave birth to four daughters in just four years, but the marriage was falling apart and her husband began seeing other women and staying away from the marital home. Nannie, having failed to find the love for which she had always yearned, turned to drink and lost herself in true-romance magazines.

When Charlie Braggs returned home one day in the spring of 1927 to find two of their four children dying on the floor, allegedly poisoned, he walked out, taking the surviving oldest child and leaving his wife with the youngest. He later claimed that he had left 'because I was frightened of what she would do'. They divorced the next year but Nannie had already lined up a prospective new spouse.

Husband Number Two was not around for long; Frank Harelson died of stomach trouble within a year of the marriage. Husband Number Three, Arlie Lanning, survived until 1952 before succumbing to the same affliction. Number Four, Richard Morton, left a healthy insurance policy. Nannie's mother, her two sisters and the nephew of one of her deceased husbands were added to the list of mysterious deaths.

It was only upon the death in 1954 of Nannie's fifth husband, Samuel Doss, that an autopsy was ordered. It was discovered that there was enough arsenic in him to kill 20 men. Arrested, she chuckled and giggled through police interrogation, not appearing to realize the gravity of her crimes. She was still smiling when, at her trial, police estimated the total tally of her victims to be 11.

Mrs Doss showed neither regret nor remorse and calmly explained that she had poisoned the last four of her five husbands because they were 'dullards'. Basically, she found that they did not live up to the glamorous images of the fictional men in her paperbacks and magazines. She was sentenced to life imprisonment and died in prison of leukemia in 1965.

John Duffy and David Mulcahy

'We would have balaclavas and knives,' boasted rapist John Duffy. 'We used to call it hunting. We did it as a bit of a joke, a bit of a game.'

Sick Crimes Of The Railroad Killers

Duffy was a brutal rapist, attacking as many as 50 women during the 1980s, as he stalked lonely paths and isolated spots beside railroad lines throughout the London area. During that time, he also turned killer, murdering three women.

The search for the 'Railroad Rapist' was one of the

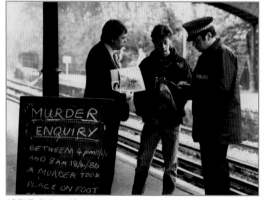

ABOVE: Police officers interview a witness following the murder of Dutch schoolgirl Maartje Tamboezer in April 1986.

biggest manhunts in British criminal history. After the first murder, by which time police realized the rapist was working with an accomplice, the pair became known as the 'Railroad Killers'.

Duffy first raped in October 1982, repeating his violent attacks until his first murder in December 1985, when he seized 19-year-old secretary Alison Day as she got off a train in Hackney, east London. Alison was garrotted with a strip of her own shirt and her body thrown into a river. The fact that Duffy had an accomplice in this attack was unknown at the time, and police did not identify David Mulcahy for another 14 years.

Four months after the first murder, 15-year-old Dutch schoolgirl Maartje Tamboezer was seized, raped, and strangled as she cycled through fields in East Horsley, Surrey. In May 1986, Duffy killed 29-year-old Anne Lock, a local TV host, who was snatched after getting off a train at Brookmans Park.

Despite this being one of the biggest manhunts they had ever conducted, police twice let Duffy slip through their net. He was questioned over the murder of Alison Day but was freed because he provided an alibi. Later, police found him loitering outside a station with a knife but let him go after he told them it was for a martial arts class.

A psychological profile of the killer indicated that he was a martial arts fanatic, did semi-skilled work and was likely to have a failed marriage behind him. Duffy was a carpenter with a police record for raping his wife. All this information supported police suspicions that Duffy was the killer and he became the first offender in

English legal history to be identified by 'Psychological Offender Profiling'.

Duffy was arrested after the rape of a 14-year-old girl in Watford in October 1986. Police later spotted him as he stalked a woman in a park. At his North London apartment, detectives found a collection of knives, assorted house keys belonging to his victims, fibers from Alison Day's coat, and string identical to that used to bind the hands of Maartje Tamboezer.

Police also arrested Duffy's closest associate, David Mulcahy. Both born in 1959, they had been friends since childhood and both worked on building sites in North London. However, at the time, Duffy was refusing to admit that he had acted with an accomplice and Mulcahy was released due to lack of evidence.

In February 1988, Duffy went on trial charged with seven rapes and the three murders, although it was ruled there was insufficient evidence to convict him of Anne Lock's killing. He received seven life sentences.

It was another 11 years before police were able to nail David Mulcahy. Arrested in February 1999, he faced his former accomplice across a courtroom at the Old Bailey, where Duffy gave detailed evidence against him over 14 days. The prosecution alleged that Mulcahy was the chief perpetrator of many of the attacks and was the first to decide that rapes were an insufficient thrill and that the pair should try murder. Mulcahy was convicted of three murders and seven rapes and handed three life sentences.

Peter Dupas

On the evening of April 19, 1999, Rena Hoffman called on her friend Nicole Patterson for dinner at her home in the Melbourne suburb of Northcote. Upon entering the unlocked apartment, where 28-year-old Nicole worked as a psychotherapist, Rena found her friend dead on the floor.

Pervert Freed To Kill Again And Again

Nicole had suffered 27 stab wounds to her chest and back and numerous defense wounds to her hands. She was naked from the waist down, with her underwear around her ankles. Small pieces of tape were attached to her body. Both of her breasts had been removed using a sharp knife and were nowhere to be found at the murder scene.

The killer had meticulously cleaned up the crime scene but had overlooked Nicole's diary, containing an appointment at 9am that morning for a meeting with 'Malcolm' and a telephone number next to the name. 'Malcolm' turned out to be a student who had an alibi at that time. But he said he had passed his number on to Peter Dupas, a 46-year-old furniture maker, who had been known to Australian police for more than three decades.

A search of Dupas's home uncovered a black balaclava, a newspaper cutting about the murder, PVC tape, and a picture of Nicole Patterson slashed with a knife. In a bin was a torn-up note with the words 'Nine O'clock Nicci' and 'Malcolm'.

Peter Norris Dupas, born in 1953, had previously served numerous prison sentences for rape. And upon each and every release, he had gone on to commit further crimes against women, with increasing levels of violence.

His first attack had been against a Melbourne neighbor in 1968 when he was just 15. He was put on probation while being treated as an outpatient in a psychiatric hospital. After applying to join the police service—and being rejected for being an inch too short—Dupas was arrested again in 1972, this time for rape.

Serving five years in jail, Dupas was released, only to be rearrested two months later for molesting women in four separate attacks over a 10-day period. In each case, he used what would become his trademarks: a knife and a balaclava.

After another five-year stretch, he was released—and only four days into his freedom raped a 21-year-old woman as she lay sunbathing at Blairgowrie Beach. Under arrest, Dupas was also questioned about a previous attack on a nearby beach, in which a mother-of-four had been beaten to death while sunbathing 16 days earlier—at a time when Dupas had been on temporary leave from prison.

Jailed for the Blairgowrie rape, Dupas served seven years of a 12-year sentence before being released in 1992. Two years later he was back inside for attacking a woman at a picnic spot. He was freed in September 1996—sealing the fate of poor Nicole Patterson.

By the time of his conviction for Nicole's murder, handed down in August 2000, Dupas already had 16 prior convictions involving acts of sexual violence. As he began a life sentence, police began investigating other, previous killings. These resulted in two further life sentences for Dupas. In August 2004, he was found guilty of the 1997 murder of prostitute Margaret Maher, 40. And in August 2007, he got a further life sentence for the slaughter, also in 1997, of Mersina Halvagis, 25, who suffered 87 stab wounds when attacked from behind while placing flowers on her grandmother's grave.

Dupas attempted suicide several times while serving out his sentences, knowing that in addition to his three convictions, he was a prime suspect in at least three other murders committed in the Melbourne area during the 1980s and 1990s.

Marc Dutroux

Serial killer and child rapist Marc Dutroux was an unemployed electrician and father of three whose 25-year criminal past included male prostitution, violent mugging, drug-dealing, and auto theft. Such activities helped him amass a property portfolio of seven houses—one of which concealed a self-built dungeon where he tortured, raped, filmed, and murdered several young girls.

Terrible Ordeal Of Girls Caged In Killer's Dungeon

Dutroux, born in Brussels in November 1956, received the first of a series of convictions for minor offenses in 1979. In 1986, he and his wife Michelle Martin, whom he met and married in jail, were incarcerated for the kidnapping and rape of five young girls. Deeming Dutroux to be safe for release, he was freed after three years of his 13-year sentence.

Despite his early release, his mother feared her eldest son's intentions and she wrote to the prison director warning: 'What I do not know, and what all the people who know him fear, is what he has in mind for the future.' The letters apparently went unanswered. His mother was right to be fearful…

On May 28, 1996, 12-year-old Sabine Dardenne was cycling to school in the Belgian city of Charleroi when she was grabbed by Dutroux and stuffed into a trunk inside a van. Once back to his house, she was chained by the neck to a bed and ordered to undress. She was raped and photographed and, in the days that followed, he began a malicious assault on her mind as well as her body. He said he was working as part of a team and his 'boss' wanted Sabine dead because her parents were not prepared to pay the 3 million-franc ransom to save her. Dutroux asked her if she wanted to live or die. If she chose to live, he would keep her in the house, but she

ABOVE: The dungeon of torture at the home of Marc Dutroux, where several young girls met their death.

would have to relocate to the dungeon hidden behind a false wall in the basement. If the 'boss' found out about her, he would kill her and her parents.

Sabine asked to live, and there she continued her life of terror in the 3ft x 9ft (0.9m x 2.7m) cell. Her prison contained only a dirty mattress and some crayons in which to write letters to her parents. Dutroux took the letters and told Sabine that he had posted them. He then made up replies from her mother, such as: 'She said to make sure you eat properly, that you never were much good at washing yourself, and that you should enjoy the sex…'

On August 9, 1996, 14-year-old Laetitia Delhez was brought into the dungeon. She had been on her way home from a public swimming pool when Dutroux bundled her into his van, but this time the police had an eyewitness who remembered enough of the license plate for it to be traced to Dutroux.

ABOVE: Dutroux's home at Sars-la-Buissiere, where the bodies of Julie, Melissa, and Bernard Weinstein were found.

ABOVE: Belgian pedophile and murderer Marc Dutroux in police custody on March 27, 1998.

found in the grounds of one of Dutroux's houses.

The rescued teenagers, Sabine and Laetitia, had survived their ordeal. Others imprisoned by the monster had not…

In June 1995, Dutroux had kidnapped two eight-year-old girls, Julie Lejeune and Melissa Russon, and kept them in his cellar where they were subjected to repeated sexual abuse and used to produce pornographic videos.

During the children's imprisonment, Dutroux was arrested for auto theft and jailed for three months. While he served his sentence, his wife Michelle was too afraid to enter the basement to feed the chained girls and they starved to death. Their bodies were later found at one of Dutroux's properties.

In August 1995, 17-year-old An Marchal and 19-year-old Eefje Lambrechts were kidnapped while

ABOVE: Pictures of Melissa Russon and Julie Lejeune, who Dutroux's wife Michelle allowed to starve to death.

Dutroux was arrested on August 13, 1996, but investigators initially found no sign of the girls at the house. It was two days later, when he confessed to the crimes, that he led investigators to Sabine Dardenne and Laetitia Delhez, who were found alive in the basement.

The police made further arrests—for Dutroux was working, not with a 'boss', but with accomplices. Dutroux's wife, Michelle Martin, knew about the girls. And two drug addicts, Michel Lelievre and Bernard Weinstein, had helped in the kidnappings, for which they were paid in narcotics. Weinstein's body was later

ABOVE: Dutroux's defense counsel listen to evidence during the trial in March 2004.

on a camping trip to Ostend and kept chained in the upstairs bedroom of Dutroux's home. Both teens were killed several weeks later, although the specific manner of their deaths was never discovered.

Dutroux's trial began in March 2004 in the southern Ardennes town of Arlon, Luxembourg, nearly eight years after his initial arrest. On June 22, he received the maximum sentence of life imprisonment with no possibility of parole, bringing an end to a case that had haunted Belgium for nearly a decade.

Michelle Martin was sentenced to 30 years in prison for the deaths of the two eight-year-olds who had starved to death. For his complicity in the kidnappings, Michel Lelievre was sentenced to 25 years behind bars.

The case led to judicial and police reforms, and crackdowns on child sex crimes within Belgium. It also proved so shameful to Belgians that more than a third of those with the last name 'Dutroux' applied to have their name changed during the two years following the monster's arrest.

Amelia Dyer

Single parenthood and illegitimacy were stigmatized in Victorian Britain. Facing scandal and poverty, unmarried mothers struggled to survive, often being forced to give up their offspring to the lucrative and exploitative practice of 'baby farming'. For an upfront fee, unwanted newborns were secretly adopted or fostered out to individuals.

Brutal 'Baby Farmer' Disposed Of Her Tiny Charges

Unfortunately, many unwanted offspring were starved to death as baby farmers cut costs and failed to care for them properly. They were often quietened with tonics laced with opium derivatives—and mothers who tried to reclaim or simply check on the welfare of their children would be too frightened or ashamed to tell the police if they were missing.

When pretty 25-year-old barmaid Evelina Marmon gave birth in January 1896, she found it impossible to earn a living and care for illegitimate baby Doris. She dearly loved her, but in desperation she placed an advertisement in the *Bristol Times* for someone to adopt her daughter until she could earn enough money to look after her again.

Quite by chance, next to her own advert was one placed by a 'Mrs Harding'. It stated: 'Married couple with no family would adopt healthy child, nice country home. Terms, £10.' Evelina felt her prayers were answered. She responded to the advert, and in April a meeting was arranged.

Despite Evelina's concerns about the woman's age, at 57, Mrs Harding seemed respectable and caring. Harding insisted upon adopting the baby instead of fostering, but Evelina could visit when she wished. With nowhere else to turn, she tearfully handed Doris over, together with £10 and a box of baby clothes. The next time she was to see her was on a mortuary slab. 'Mrs Harding' was an alias of ex-nurse Amelia Dyer, a callous brute who had already been convicted of neglect of the babies in her care.

Seventeen years earlier, in 1879, Dyer's doctor had raised concerns over the number of child deaths he had been called to certify and Dyer was sentenced to six months hard labor. Upon her release, she attempted to resume her nursing career but reverted to the easy money of the unwanted baby market—only this time, she would dispose of the bodies herself, relocate frequently and use a succession of aliases to evade suspicion.

It was to be the body of a six-month-old baby girl, Helena Fry, found floating in the River Thames in March 1896 that would put an end to the span of evil

ABOVE: The weathered features of Amelia Dyer, the murderous former nurse and 'baby farmer'.

killings. Helena had died from strangulation; around her neck was white dressmaker's edging tape. Dyer had neglected to weight the baby girl down, and among the brown parcel paper containing her body was the name 'Mrs Thomas' and an address in Reading, Berkshire.

When police raided the address, they were immediately struck by the stench of human decomposition. No bodies were found, yet bundles of telegrams arranging adoptions, receipts for advertisements, pawned children's clothes, letters from mothers inquiring about their babies, and white tape exactly like that found around Helena's neck.

Police concluded that in the past few months alone, at least 20 children had been placed in the care of 'Mrs Thomas', now revealed as Amelia Dyer. They had most likely all met the same fate.

The river was dragged and five further children emerged—among them, tiny Doris, whose body was found inside a weighted carpet bag she shared with 13-week-old Harry Simmons, taken 'into care' only a day after Doris. Both babies had been asphyxiated using the same tell-tale white tape around their necks—which, as Dyer would later tell police, 'was how you could tell it was one of mine'.

Dyer was arrested and appeared at the Old Bailey where, despite the untold numbers of her tiny victims, she pleaded guilty to just one murder, that of Doris Marmon. It took the jury only minutes to find her guilty and she was hanged at Newgate Prison on June 10, 1896.

Dyer's conviction caused the introduction of greater protection for foster children. A shocking report on the baby farming trade was published by *The British Medical Journal*, which prompted Parliament to pass the Infant Life Protection Act.

Donald Leroy Evans

Seemingly full of remorse for killing a defenseless child in 1991, the drifter picked up for the crime made a full confession—to more than 60 other murders. And that is what made the case of Donald Leroy Evans so strange. For although he wished to be punished for so many slayings, he was only ever prosecuted for two.

'I Slew 60' Claimed Texan-born Weirdo

Evans, born in 1958 in Galveston, Texas, had embarked on a life of violent crime after being kicked out of the Marine Corps in 1977. In the years immediately following, according to his confession, he raped and killed six women in Florida, Illinois, and Texas.

As Mississippi police drew out further admissions from their dim-witted prisoner, the body count mounted—to more than 50 men and women in 22 states across America. Most of the murders and rapes took place at rest stops and public parks.

Authorities were originally skeptical of Evans's claims, but many of his descriptions were perfect matches to those unsolved cases to which he confessed in Florida and Illinois. His own legal adviser certainly believed him. Said Fred Lusk: 'There is a strong possibility that he is telling the truth. The count could go higher.'

Through Lusk, Evans then offered a strange pact with police—he would try to locate the bodies of all his victims as long as was given the death sentence. According to Lusk: 'He said he lived by the sword and wanted to die by the sword.'

Others, however, were less ready to give Evans's wilder claims credence. The Mississippi authorities believed that he was a serial killer, probably with a tally of up to 16 murders. But they suspected he was jumping on the bandwagon of the notoriety of cannibal killer Jeffrey Dahmer (see page 54), whose sick slayings were making headlines shortly before Evans decided to 'come clean' about his own multiple murders.

In the event, Evans was initially charged only with one murder. It was the final crime that had caused him to give himself up in 1991: the murder of 10-year-old Beatrice Rough, abducted from her home in Gulfport, Mississippi, then raped and strangled. The district attorney who prosecuted him described Evans as 'as close to evil as I've ever seen'.

After being tried, convicted, and sentenced to death in 1993 for the Rough killing, Florida authorities in 1995 successfully prosecuted him for an earlier murder. He was given a second life sentence after admitting to the killing of Ira Smith, a black woman, in Fort The professed white supremacist caused outcry in the court by asking if he could wear a Ku Klux Klan robe. He also petitioned the court to refer to him

ABOVE: Donald Evans's older brother, Larry, speaks about his evil sibling to a TV reporter.

not as Donald Leroy Evans during proceedings but as 'Hi Hitler'. In both of his trials, and during his entire incarceration, Evans made similar ludicrous requests and launched risible appeals.

Leroy Evans's execution was eventually carried out, but not by the authorities. In January 1999, while on Death Row in Mississippi State Penitentiary, 41-year-old Evans was stabbed 17 times with a makeshift knife. The white supremacist met his fate at the hands of a black fellow inmate, Jimmie Mack.

Raymond Fernandez and Martha Beck

The terms of endearment expressed by the two lovers would, in other circumstances, have been touching. 'I wanna shout it out: I love Martha!' said Raymond Fernandez. The object of his desire, Martha Beck, responded: 'My story is a love story. But only those tortured by love can know what I mean. Imprisonment in the Death House has only strengthened my feeling for Raymond.'

'Lonely Hearts Killers' Preyed On The Lovelorn

Those were the official last words of the lovebirds who, despite tumultuous arguments, often professed their affection for each other in the most florid terms. The pair knew quite a lot about romance. They were known as the 'Lonely Hearts Killers' because of the manner in which they lured their many victims.

Raymond Fernandez and Martha Beck met in 1947 and formed a unique but deadly coupling. Fernandez, then aged 33, was a Hawaiian-born Spanish-American who, having deserted his wife and four children, made his living as a confidence trickster. Beck, a 27-year-old divorced mother of two, was lonely, overweight, and looking for love.

Beck was to have been just another of Fernandez's victims when he spotted her advertisement in a newspaper's lonely-hearts column. When he discovered that she had no hidden wealth, he initially tried to ditch her, but when she persisted, he began to regard

ABOVE: Fernandez and Beck sit either side of their attorney Herbert E. Rosenberg at Bronx Supreme Court on July 13, 1949.

ABOVE: Fernandez and Beck stand between Nassau County police on arriving at New York's Laguardia Airport on March 15, 1949.

her with admiration, then with real affection, and the two of them joined in an evil union.

The con-artist and his 200lb (90kg) lady love traveled the United States targeting vulnerable women, stealing from them and murdering as many as 20 in little over two years. Fernandez, wearing a wig to cover his balding head, would join a lonely-hearts club and win over a fading female with his glib patter. Eventually, he would suggest marriage. Beck would be introduced as his sister and, in many cases, would move in to the target's home along with Fernandez as marriage plans were made.

This was the web they weaved in 1949 when widow Delphine Dowling, 28, allowed the conspirators to stay with her and her two-year-old daughter at their house in Grand Rapids, Michigan. Her fatal mistake, however, was not being in sufficient hurry to hand over her financial affairs to the couple. Anxious to get their hands on her money, Fernandez shot her in the head and Beck drowned her daughter in a washtub.

Tipped off by the widow's family, police found the bodies under a concrete slab in the cellar. They arrested the killers and linked them with the deaths of

18 other lonely hearts throughout the country.

Fernandez confessed to most of the murders—but suddenly recanted when told that he was being moved from Michigan, which had no death penalty, to New York State, which did. There, the couple were tried for two further murders.

It was too late, however, and the duo were convicted. After writing their final professions of love, they were both executed in the electric chair at Sing Sing prison on March 8, 1951.

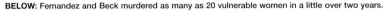

BELOW: Fernandez and Beck murdered as many as 20 vulnerable women in a little over two years.

Albert Fish

Albert Fish is one of the most reviled killers in American criminal history. He molested, tortured, castrated, and occasionally ate his victims—all children. He is also one of the oldest serial killers ever arrested, for it was not until he was in his 60s that the vile pervert was caged. By then, he had subjected at least 100 children to torture and depraved acts, had murdered at least 15 more and had devoured at least four of them.

Reviled Cannibal Killer Cooked Kids In A Stew

Born in Washington DC in 1870 to a family with a history of mental illness, Albert Howard Fish attributed the root cause of his terrible crimes to the experience of watching boys ruthlessly whipped at the orphanage where he grew up.

His sadomasochistic urges manifested themselves in extraordinary ways. He would dance naked in the moonlight and harm himself with hot pokers and nail-studded paddles. Apart from consuming human flesh, he ate excrement and drank human urine and blood. He stuffed cotton wool balls soaked with lighter fuel into his rectum and set fire to them. He drove 29 needles into his body, mostly around his genitals.

The monster's life might well have been different. In 1898, at the age of 27, he married and had six children before his wife ran off with a younger man. After that, Fish's behavior changed. He heard voices, had hallucinations and became fascinated with evil, pain, and sacrifice.

He moved to New York in 1928 and in June of that year claimed his first known murder victim: 10-year-old Grace Budd, whom he lured from her Manhattan home with the promise that he was taking her to a children's party. Instead, he led her to a derelict cottage at White Plains. Armed with what he called his 'instruments of hell', including a butcher's knife and a cleaver, he strangled her, dismembered her body and carried parcels of her flesh home to cook them in a stew.

Fish went on to abuse children in several states. Constantly on the move, his trade as a house painter meant he had access to basements and attics, where he could take child victims. Most of them came from poor, black families. Fish said this was because they 'didn't make such a fuss' if their children disappeared or returned home in distress.

At the height of his killings, Fish became known as the 'Moon Maniac' because of his habit of striking when there was a full moon. The press also labeled him the 'Thrill Vulture' and 'Vampire Man'.

He was finally arrested after sending the parents of Grace Budd a cruelly sick letter in November 1934. In it, he recounted: 'I came to your house on June, 3, 1928,

ABOVE: Albert Fish mutilated and murdered more than 100 defenceless young children, even eating the flesh of some victims.

and under the pretence of taking your daughter Grace to a party at my sister's, I took her up to Westchester County, Worthington, to an empty house up there and I choked her to death. I didn't fuck with her. She died a virgin.'

Fish had failed adequately to erase an address on the back of the envelope, and police swooped on his room in a squalid New York boarding house. He was brought to trial at White Plains, New York, in March 1935, charged with Grace's murder. Convicted, he confessed to dozens of other assaults and murders, claiming to have violated as many as 30 children a year.

Even hardened detectives were sickened by Fish's description of the manner in which he had cooked the buttocks of one little boy: 'I put strips of bacon over each cheek and put them in the oven. When the meat was roasted for about a quarter of an hour, I poured a pint of water over for gravy and put in the onions. At frequent intervals I basted with a wooden spoon so the meat would be nice and juicy. In two hours it was nice and brown. I never ate any turkey that tasted half as good as his sweet, fat little behind did. I ate every bit of the meat in about four days.'

Fish went to the electric chair at Sing Sing prison on January 16, 1936. He spoke of the prospect of electrocution as 'the supreme thrill' and even helped his executioners fasten the straps that held him in place. Because of the needles in his body, which caused short-circuits, the first charge failed to kill him. Witnesses told how wisps of blue smoke floated over his head before the second, fatal charge coursed through him.

Catherine Flanagan and Margaret Higgins

Known as the 'Black Widows of Liverpool', Catherine Flanagan and Margaret Higgins led a gang of women who poisoned between 17 and 23 people, including their own families, to claim insurance payouts. Arsenic was fed to husbands, children, grandchildren, boarders, and friends.

The 'Black Widows' Of Liverpool

Flanagan, born in 1843 and Higgins in 1829, were sisters of Scottish descent who were ringleaders of a small group operating in the northern part of Liverpool in the 1870s and early 1880s. The likelihood of their targeted victims surviving was in inverse ratio to the amount of insurance on their lives.

Their crime wave came to light after Margaret's husband Thomas died in October 1883, poisoned by arsenic extracted from flypapers. It was a slow death, long premeditated. By the time the women had got rid of him, his life was insured by five different societies for a total of £108. It was a considerable sum at a time when the wage of a working man was less than £1 a week.

Thomas's brother became suspicious, however, and a coroner was asked to perform a post-mortem, which revealed traces of arsenic in the body. Other mysterious deaths in the sisters' household were recalled, and three more bodies were exhumed, each containing arsenic. As in Thomas's case, all three had been heavily insured.

Under arrest, Flanagan accused her sister and two other women of poisoning six victims. Students of the case, however, point to collaboration between as many as a dozen women and a death toll as high as 23. Among the many victims were Thomas Higgins's 10-year-old daughter from a previous marriage, Catherine Higgins's 22-year-old son, and an 18-year-old female who had boarded with the killers.

The trial of the sisters in February 1884 was a sensation, the reporting of their crimes in the local press fueling the anger of the large crowds that swelled the Liverpool courtroom. *The Liverpool Daily Post* described them as 'squalid, ignorant' and displaying 'brute-like sullenness', while lamenting the fact that 'society does not investigate too curiously into the deaths of its worthless members'. The medical journal *The Lancet* alleged that the practice of disposing of relatives in this way had been widespread in poorer city areas of Britain for many years.

Catherine Flanagan and Margaret Higgins were hanged side by side in the city's Kirkdale Prison on March 3, 1884. The reviled sisters' effigies were placed in the Chamber of Horrors of the London waxworks Madame Tussaud's, where they remained for the better part of a century.

Wayne Ford

He was arrested after he walked into the Humboldt County Sheriff's office in Eureka, northern California, in 1998 with a woman's severed breast in his pocket and confessed to horrified cops that he was the serial killer they had been hunting. His name was Wayne Adam Ford.

Tearful Confessor Bore A Grisly Memento

The previous night, November 2, 1998, Ford, a 37-year-old truck driver, had been slumped over a motel bar, unsure whether to drink himself into a stupor or unburden his conscience. When the barman asked him if he was all right, Ford told him all he wanted to do was get drunk and blow his brains out.

His brother Rod joined him at midnight and the pair sat up most of the night talking. At daybreak, they drove to Eureka and Wayne Ford made his startling confession. Shedding tears and clutching a Bible, he said he had killed and mutilated four women and strewn their body parts in rivers and ditches across California.

To support his claim, he produced a plastic bag containing the severed breast of a 29-year-old prostitute he had picked up two weeks earlier. She had been found the next day dumped in an aqueduct after being bound, raped, battered around the head, strangled, and mutilated.

A search of Ford's trailer-park home revealed body parts of other girls in his freezer and buried nearby. He told detectives that he was in the habit of picking up prostitutes or hitch-hikers and taking them back to his trailer for bondage games. When that went too far, he would strangle them and mutilate the bodies.

Despite his detailed description, police failed to identify his first victim, killed in 1997. He said he had chopped up her body, storing her legs in his freezer and burying other parts by the banks of northern California's chillingly named Mad River. A second victim had also had a breast hacked off, which psychiatrists said was a clear signal of the killer's hatred of women.

Police had sufficient evidence for the four slayings but were still puzzled as to what had driven the quiet family man to become a serial killer.

The all-Californian boy, born in 1961 to a military family, had served in the US Marines but was discharged in 1984 following a mental breakdown. He took a job driving a bus for disabled children before becoming a long-haul trucker. He attended a Bible study group and frequented a Christian bookstore. The only clue as to what may have tipped him over the edge was a feud

ABOVE: A Death Row cell at San Quentin prison, similar to that inhabited by serial killer Wayne Ford.

with his estranged second wife who would not allow him to see his toddler son.

It was not until June 2006 that Ford was tried and found guilty of four counts of first-degree murder. He was sentenced to be executed—joining California's 600-plus inmates on Death Row. The case did not close then, however.

Despite his supposedly frank confession back in 1998, Ford was suspected of as many as eight other murders. Which put into question the notion that he was that rare breed, a truly remorseful serial killer.

'It's a rarity, almost without precedent,' said Mike Rustigan, a criminologist at San Francisco State University. 'Serial killers usually delight in trying to outwit the police—and they have absolutely no sympathy for their victims. To see genuine remorse in a guy capable of such savagery is extremely surprising.'

Michel Fourniret

In what was to be one of France's worst serial killer cases of all time, 66-year-old Michel Fourniret was convicted in 2008 of the murder, rape, and attempted rape of nine people between 1987 and 2001. The victims, mostly French girls between the ages of 12 and 21, were either strangled, shot or stabbed with a screwdriver and were, according to prosecutors, targeted in an effort to feed Fourniret's obsession with virgins.

Evil Abductor Who Had Obsession With Virgins

Fourniret, a former carpenter, forestry worker, and school supervisor, was sentenced to life imprisonment and his wife, Monique Olivier, a 59-year-old nurse, was sentenced to 28 years with no possibility of parole for helping him lure his victims to their deaths.

Fourniret confessed to his crimes after his wife gave information to the police, apparently fearing a conviction similar to the 30-year sentence handed down to Michelle Martin, wife of Belgium's notorious pedophile and murderer Marc Dutroux (see page 64).

Even though Olivier claimed to have not been involved in the abductions and murders, prosecutors believed she played a vital role. Olivier, latterly accompanied by her baby son, Selim, was used as a lure to put potential victims at ease. And once Fourniret had abducted his victims, he would order Olivier to watch him rape and kill them.

ABOVE: Michel Fourniret's evil lust for virgins knew no bounds and saw him rape and murder at least nine victims over a 14-year period.

Fourniret, dubbed the 'Ogre of the Ardennes' after the forested border region between France and Belgium where many of his crimes occurred, was a known pedophile and had already served three years of a seven-year sentence for trying to abduct a 13-year-old Congolese girl. Some of Fourniret's victims were buried within the grounds of his château on the Franco-Belgian border, a property he and his wife had purchased after stealing the spoils of a bank robber with whom he had shared a prison cell.

Fourniret's youngest victim was a 12-year old Belgian girl, Elisabeth Brichet, who disappeared after playing with a friend in Namur in 1989. Olivier helped to trap Elisabeth so that Fourniret could strangle her. Elisabeth's disappearance was long thought to be at the hands of Marc Dutroux—until Fourniret led police to her burial site on his estate.

Olivier was also the accomplice in the killing of Natacha Danais. At just 13, Natacha was kidnapped, sexually assaulted, and stabbed to death near Nantes, western France, in November 1990. Her body was

ABOVE: Police teams excavate the grounds of Fourniret's house in July 2004 looking for the remains of one of his victims.

ABOVE: A Belgian investigator outside Fourniret's house in Sart-Custinne, shortly after his arrest in July 2003.

found three days later on a beach on the French Atlantic coast. The couple had lured Natacha into their van in the car park of a supermarket and Fourniret stabbed her during an attempted rape. The coroner suggested Fourniret sexually assaulted the girl after killing her.

During the trial, at Charleville-Mézières, northeast France, in March 2008, state prosecutor Francis Nachbar described the couple as 'inhuman and cruel criminals, the likes of which our country could have never imagined'. He called the serial killer a 'necrophiliac monster' and said that, together with Olivier, they formed a 'devil with two faces'.

The jury heard Fourniret admit that he had a sexual obsession with virgins. He told the court: 'I remain an extremely dangerous individual.' Although he was convicted of the murder, rape, and attempted rape of nine people between 1987 and 2001, it is believed the tally of his victims is higher. Fourniret faced charges in three other cases, including the 1990 killing of British student Joanna Parish, 20, who was working as a teaching assistant when she was raped and murdered.

In court, Fourniret's wife Monique proved herself a more enigmatic character. She had no prior criminal record before meeting the killer, to whom she wrote in reply to his advert for a pen pal while he was serving a prison sentence in the 1980s. Her lawyers sought to portray the short, gray-haired woman as the weak and fearful wife of an overpowering and violent husband, who would have killed her and their son if she had lifted a finger to intervene.

However, state prosecutor Xavier Lenoir described her as a willing accomplice, a 'bloody muse' and a 'deceitful witch' who displayed 'a deafening silence' to the screams of girls being raped by her husband. Found guilty of complicity to murder, Monique Olivier expressed some remorse at the end of the trial, saying: 'I regret everything that I have done. That is all.'

ABOVE: Fourniret leaves Dinant court house in handcuffs after an appearance in July 2003.

Wayne Gacy

It was a late hour to attend a job interview but 15-year-old Robert Piest was eager. As he prepared to leave the family home in Des Plaines, Illinois, on the evening of December 11, 1978, his only thought was the prospect of earning some extra cash for the school vacation. His appointment was for 9pm at the local pharmacy where his prospective employer, a building contractor, was carrying out renovation work.

Foul Smelling Morgue Of The 'Killer Clown'

As he stepped out of the front door, his mother urged him to return speedily. It was her birthday and a family party was getting into full swing. When there was still no sign of Robert by midnight, his worried mother phoned the police to report that he had not returned. He never did.

As soon as police established the identity of the builder Robert had been due to meet, they realized that this was not simply a 'missing persons' case. John Wayne Gacy, aged 36, had a long criminal record as a sexual deviant.

After Piest's disappearance, the local force decided to keep a watch on Gacy. He boldly invited the officers sitting outside his home to pop in for a cup of coffee. The cops immediately smelled a strong odor, which Gacy put down to a drainage problem. A warrant was obtained and Gacy was arrested as police began a search of the house.

What they discovered was one of the most gruesome scenes in the history of American crime. No fewer than 29 bodies were found covered with lime and dirt in

ABOVE: Several thousand protestors stage a Gacy Day Parade in May 1994, to celebrate the murderer's imminent execution.

the 'crawl space' beneath his home and in the plot surrounding it. The victims ranged in age between nine and their mid-20s. Some were homosexuals and some were men who had worked for, or sought work from Gacy. All had endured savage sexual torture.

Gacy, born in Chicago in 1942, was the son of a Danish mother and Polish father who was abusive toward him. The young Gacy suffered from dizzy spells in his youth, the result of being hit in the head by a swing at the age of 11. Nevertheless, he completed a good education at business school, moving to Iowa and becoming a successful shoe salesman.

When he married Marlynn Myers in 1964, he took a management position in his father-in-law's fast-food business. At this point, Gacy seemed the most normal of family men. He was a pillar of the community in the city of Waterloo, Iowa, being a leading light in the Junior Chamber of Commerce. But disturbing forces were coming to the surface.

In 1968 he sexually assaulted a young male employee at the Waterloo fried chicken restaurant business which he managed. The terrified boy was handcuffed while 280lb (127kg) Gacy subjected him to a vicious attack. The boy fought back against attempts to sodomize him and force him to perform oral sex and afterward went to the police.

Gacy was convicted of sexual molestation and given a sentence of 10 years' imprisonment. He served only 18 months, his reputation as a model prisoner convincing his parole board that he was no longer a risk to the public, but it was long enough to send his life into a tailspin. His wife divorced him, taking their two children, so he moved back to his hometown of Chicago.

In 1971, he was questioned by police for trying to force a teenage boy into having sex, but the case was dropped after the boy failed to turn up for the preliminary hearings.

A second marriage, to Carole Hoff in 1972, also ended in failure. Police were later to learn how Hoff was puzzled by his lackluster sexual performance and terrified of his violent temper. Also, she complained to him constantly about the fetid smell that hung around the house.

Gacy worked to regain his social standing and began his own construction business. He became involved in the local political scene. He was also much in demand as a children's entertainer, his character being 'Pogo the Clown'. But there was nothing funny about the pornography-addicted Gacy; all the while, he was a predatory serial killer on the loose.

Shamefully for the police, one incident that could have stopped him in his tracks went largely unpunished. In March 1978, 27-year-old Jeffrey Rignall told police how he had been approached by a fat man driving a distinctively colored Oldsmobile car. Invited to sit in the passenger seat for a smoke of cannabis, he had been rendered unconscious when a chloroformed

ABOVE: Chicago Police use a ground penetrating radar device to seach for the bodies of those murdered by Gacy.

handkerchief was held to his face.

Rignall remembered regaining consciousness in his abductor's house where he was beaten with whips and repeatedly raped. He promised that he would leave Chicago forever if Gacy would free him, and the following morning he was dropped off in Chicago's Lincoln Park.

When police failed to launch a full investigation, Rignall launched his own search for Gacy's car and turned him in. Gacy denied all knowledge of any homosexual rape and, as there were no witnesses to challenge his statements and alibi, the incident resulted in only a misdemeanor charge.

When police raided the builder's home at 8213 West Summerdale Avenue nine months later, the stench of rotting flesh was unmistakable.

Stored in the cramped 'crawl space' were seven corpses in different stages of decomposition. Eight more were dug out of crude lime pits in the backyard. In total, the remains of 29 teenage boys and young men were accounted for in the house and grounds. Having run out of space, another five victims, including Robert Piest, had been thrown into the Des Plaines River.

Gacy's explanation for his crimes was a hatred of homosexuals. He denied that he was one himself, and pleaded not guilty by reason of insanity at his trial in Chicago in February 1980. The plea was rejected and he was sentenced to death. After a failed string of appeals, he was executed by lethal injection at Stateville prison, near Chicago, on May 10, 1994. His last reported words to a warder were: 'Kiss my ass.'

Gerald Gallego

Sociologists and forensic psychiatrists might argue that Gerald Armand Gallego never really stood a chance, given his difficult background. Born in 1946, he never met his father, who was locked up in San Quentin at the time. Gallego Sr. was a triple-killer who was executed in a Mississippi gas chamber at the age of 28.

Sick Coupling Of The Genius And The Sadist

Gallego Jr. seemed destined to go much the same way. A burglar at the age of six and a sexual offender at 12, he wed at 17 and by the age of 32 had married seven times. At 22, he was jailed for armed robbery. He went on the run in 1978 after his daughter complained to police that he had been abusing her from the age of six.

Thereafter, Gallego embarked on a killing spree with a strange accomplice: 22-year-old Charlene Williams, a bisexual, drug-taking violinist with a genius-level IQ. The pair would tour central California, southern Oregon, and Nevada by van, procuring victims to fulfill Gallego's sex-slave fantasies. The girls would be lured into the van with the promise of drugs, whence Gallego would pounce on them, rape them, and murder them while Charlene sat coolly in the front seat.

Their first known murders were in September 1978 when two girls, aged 16 and 17, were enticed into the van in Sacramento. Gallego repeatedly raped them throughout the night before bludgeoning them, shooting them, and leaving their bodies in a ditch.

Possibly their most horrific crime was the June 1979 murder of 21-year-old Linda Aguilar who was four months pregnant when Charlene offered her a ride at Gold Beach, Oregon. Her body was found in a shallow grave with her legs and hands tied and her skull shattered

A post-mortem revealed that the injuries had not killed her—but that she had been buried alive.

Later that month, girls aged 13 and 14 were lured into the van at the Washoe County Fair, Nevada. Driving through the desert, Charlene watched through the rear-view mirror as Gallego repeatedly raped the girls. Parked up, he then watched Charlene force them to perform sexual acts on each other before beating them to death with a shovel.

Gallego and Charlene, now bigamously married, killed 10 people before finally being identified. In November 1980, Craig Miller and Beth Sowers were leaving a dance in Sacramento when a woman brandishing a gun forced them into the back of a van. A friend tried to follow them and took down the license plate.

The kidnapped couple were later found dead in separate locations but police at last caught up with the killers. Charlene Gallego turned state's evidence when she realized she faced a death sentence. She was sentenced to 16 years in jail and was freed in 1997.

Gallego was tried in both California, where he was sentenced to death in June 1983, and in Nevada, where a year later he was again condemned to death. He remained on Death Row through a series of appeals until his death through rectal cancer in July 2002.

ABOVE: Gerald Gallego calmly lights a cigarette as he hears the jury's verdict in his murder trial on April 11, 1983 in Martinez, California.

Luis Garavito

Colombians are accustomed to violence, but not on this scale. Described in South America as 'the world's worst serial killer', Luis Alfredo Garavito confessed to the murder and rape of 140 boys over a period of five years. The number of his victims, based on the locations of skeletons listed on maps that Garavito has drawn in prison, could eventually exceed 300—possibly even beating the 'score' of his compatriot Pedro López (see page 134).

Is This The World's Worst Serial Killer?

The mutilated corpses of the mostly male victims, aged between eight and 16, have been discovered near more than 60 towns in at least 11 of Colombia's 32 provinces. The hunt for more corpses has now moved to neighboring Ecuador, where Garavito once lived.

Most of the bodies so far unearthed since his capture in 1999 had been beheaded and bore signs of having been tied up and mutilated. The killer's 'signature' method of execution meant that police forces across the country, who once thought they were seeking a number of serial killers, now know the murders are the work of only one man: Luis Alfredo Garavito, aka 'Goofy' (because of his prominent front teeth), 'The Madman', 'The Priest' or simply 'La Bestia' (The Beast).

Born in December 1956 or January 1957 in Colombia's western coffee-making region, Garavito was the oldest of seven children. He was regularly beaten by his father and claimed to have been raped by two male neighbors. Ill educated, he was considered a simpleton and managed only menial jobs. He was also an alcoholic.

He probably committed his first murder in 1992 but his killing spree started in earnest in 1994. His prey were poor or homeless children lured by the promise of money, food, drink or drugs. Many of them were the children of street vendors who had been left unattended in parks and at city traffic lights to beg money from motorists.

To win their confidence, Garavito would pretend to be a street vendor or beggar himself. He also posed as a cripple and even a monk, hence his nickname 'The Priest'. Led to a quiet location, he would tie the children, torture, rape, and kill them by cutting their throats. Finally, wherever possible, he would decapitate them.

Since Columbia has one of the highest murder rates in the world, little was done about the discovery of a single child's body. And since Garavito frequently moved around the country, the killings appeared to be spasmodic and unrelated.

Authorities were unaware that such a monster was on the loose until a mass grave was discovered in 1997. The bodies of 25 boys were in a ravine beside an overgrown car park in the western city of Pereira. The victims had their throats slit. Some showed signs of torture and rape.

Police initially believed the children were massacred in some sort of black magic ritual. Authorities also considered social cleansing, organ trafficking and a pedophile gang. But when another 16 bodies were found a few miles away and a further 27 in a bordering county, they finally realized they were looking for one of history's worst serial killers.

After an 18-month investigation, Garavito was arrested in the eastern city of Villavicencio in April 1999 on suspicion of attempting to rape a child. That's when the 42-year-old monster confessed to killing 140 children. He was eventually charged with murdering 189. Because the death penalty had been abolished in Colombia, Garavito was sentenced to 835 years in prison.

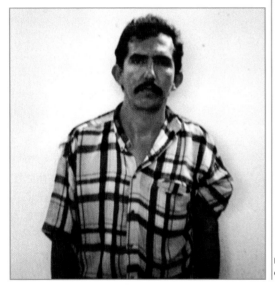

LEFT: Luis Garavito was charged with murdering 189 young boys during the 1990s, but the final death toll may prove to be far higher.

Donald Gaskins

Born Donald Henry Parrott Jr. in March 1933, he became 'Pee Wee' Gaskins following the marriage of his mother, the nickname being acquired because of his diminutive 5ft 4ins (1.62m) stature. With a violent stepfather, Gaskins's home life was, he later said, 'unbearable'. He grew up unruly and, as a youth, was sentenced to reform school for planting a hatchet in the head of a woman who upset him. She surprisingly survived.

Pervert 'Pee Wee' Claimed Over 100 Murder Victims

'Pee Wee' might have been small but he had a ferocious temper and was feared in the town of Prospect, South Carolina, where he drove around in a hearse and boasted about his 'personal graveyard'. Many believed him—and were right to do so.

Gaskin carried out a string of arson attacks, burglaries and an attempted murder, for which he received a prison sentence. While incarcerated, he killed a fellow prisoner whom he claimed had sexually abused him, and this earned him a further nine-year sentence for manslaughter.

Following parole in 1962, Gaskins committed more offences, including the rape of a 12-year-old girl, and served further prison terms. Surprisingly, he was granted parole once more in November 1968, but it was not until 1975 that the real extent of his evil came to light. Police were investigating several disappearances around Florence County, including that of a 13-year-

ABOVE: Donald Gaskins directs officers to an area in Florence County, South Carolina, where human bones were found.

old local girl, when, because of his record and due to a tip-off by a former burglary accomplice, Walter Neeley, suspicion fell on the obvious suspect.

Gaskins was captured trying to escape over the state line and was initially charged with eight murders, most of the victims being neighbors who, in some small way, had offended him. Eventually, he confessed to 13 slayings over the previous five years. They included the murders of his own 15-year-old niece, her 17-year-old friend and, most horrifically, a pregnant woman and her baby daughter.

Gaskins led police to remote woodland east of Prospect where they uncovered the bodies of three men and three women, killed by having their throats cut or by gunshot, execution style. One mile away, the gruesome discovery was made of the bodies of the pregnant woman and her baby girl—who, at just 20 months old, had been raped.

Questioned about the abhorrent act, Gaskins described it as 'the best sexual experience of my life'. He later told police: 'I am one of the few that truly understands what death and pain are all about. I have a special kind of mind that allows me to give myself permission to kill.'

In May 1976, Gaskins was found guilty of the murders, along with his burglary accomplice Neeley, who had been charged with complicity in three of the

ABOVE: The 13 murders committed by Gaskins included those of a pregnant woman and her baby daughter.

killings. Both were sentenced to death, later commuted to life imprisonment.

But Gaskins had not yet finished killing. While serving his nine life sentences, he accepted a contract to murder a Death Row inmate, Randolph Tyner, a task he carried out with explosives, removing half his head and laughing during the process. For this, Gaskins finally received the death penalty, being convicted in 1982 and eventually going to the chair in September 1991.

Before his death, Gaskins wrote his autobiography outlining what he termed his 31 'serious murders' and introducing a further 80 or 90 recreational 'coastal kills'. Describing the first of these, carried out in September 1969, he recalled picking up a girl hitch-hiker, torturing, then disemboweling her before burying her body on the Carolina coastline. This was his first of many 'pleasure kills'.

Although the authorities have been unable to substantiate the full numbers of his claimed victims, 'Pee Wee' Gaskins still goes down in history as one of America's most prolific killers.

Edward Gein

Edward Gein has a unique claim to infamy. His heinous deeds were so macabre that they were used as the basis of not one but three Hollywood movies. He was the inspiration for the character of schizophrenic transvestite Norman Bates in Hitchcock's Psycho, as Leatherface in The Texas Chainsaw Massacre and, through his liking for wearing human skin, as Jame 'Buffalo Bill' Gumb in The Silence of the Lambs. No morbid fiction, however, could hope to match the horrors perpetrated by Gein, who exhumed corpses from graveyards and fashioned trophies and keepsakes from their bones and skin.

Psycho Who Inspired Three Movies

Edward **Theodore Gein** was born in 1906 to an alcoholic carpenter and a strict Lutheran mother. He and his elder brother Henry were not allowed to mix with other boys but made to work long hours on the family's poor farmstead near Plainfield, Wisconsin.

After Edward's father died of drink in 1940, his widow Augusta became even more possessive of her sons. Four years later, Henry went missing while fighting a brush fire—Edward being suspected of fabricating an 'accident'—and shortly afterward Augusta suffered a stroke. Edward nursed her for 12 months until she died in December 1945.

The large, ramshackle farmhouse now became a time capsule, the boarded-up rooms unchanged from the moment of his mother's death—with her corpse remaining behind the locked door of her bedroom.

Gein, then aged 39, grew fascinated with corpses and began making night-time visits to three local graveyards to exhume recently buried bodies and investigate their sexual organs. They were all female and, generally, they were of the age of his mother.

His sickness progressed from adorning himself with bits of their flesh to draping himself in the skin and parading around the house wearing a woman's scalp on his head, a woman's chest over his own, and women's genitalia strapped to his groin. He would arrange a dead woman's skin over a tailor's dummy as though he were somehow trying to resurrect his mother.

Finally, Gein graduated to murder. And although the tally of his two known victims would not normally qualify him as a 'serial killer', the nature of his crimes and the suspicion that more corpses may have been 'created' rather

than exhumed have made him notorious.

In December 1954, he shot bar owner Mary Hogan, dragged her body home on a sled, skinned it and dissected it. Over the next three years, he put an end to an unknown number of victims, probably including two abducted teenage girls, before striking for the last time. In November 1957, he shot dead store owner Bernice Worden, decapitated and disembowelled her corpse, then hung it like a deer's carcass.

When police visited the farmhouse, they found a stomach-churning array of artifacts, including lampshades, belts, and socks made of human skin, skulls mounted as ornaments and skullcaps used as bowls. In this weird, stinking charnel house were the remains of the two known victims, as well as body parts including those of two teenagers.

After being judged 'incompetent to stand trial', Gein was locked in a mental institution for 10 years before doctors finally gave the go-ahead for a trial in November 1968. Found guilty of murder but legally insane, he was returned to a mental institution in Madison, Wisconsin, where he died of cancer in July 1984.

ABOVE: Edward Gein (right) in custody. Gein was the inspiration for the character of Norman Bates in Hitchcock's Psycho.

Harvey Glatman

Harvey Glatman was an ugly, jug-eared career criminal who pretended to be a professional photographer to lure the beautiful women he would not otherwise have a chance of attracting. He murdered three times during the 1950s and earned himself brief notoriety as the 'Lonely-hearts Killer'.

Death At The Hands Of A Jug-Eared Monster

Born in 1927 and raised in Colorado and New York, Glatman exhibited sadomasochistic tendencies from his teens, when he would break into women's apartments, tie them up, molest them, and take pictures as souvenirs. He was caught in 1945 after pulling a toy gun and ordering a woman to strip. Charged with attempted burglary but set free on bail, he kidnapped another woman and molested her before letting her go. Glatman went to prison for eight months.

On his release, he moved to New York where he was rewarded for a spate of street muggings and burglaries with a five-year stretch in Sing Sing. Upon his further release in 1951, he made his home in Los Angeles, where he set himself up as a TV repairman. But the sight of California's sun-kissed beauties turned him back to crime and, using false names and credentials, he began posing as a professional photographer to entrap them.

In August 1957, he arranged to meet blonde model Judy Ann Van Horn Dull for a picture shoot 'for a detective magazine'. He picked her up at her apartment and drove her to his makeshift Hollywood studio

LEFT: Posing as a photographer, Harvey Glatman murdered three young women in the Californian desert in 1957 and 1958.

Shirley Bridgeford, a 24-year-old divorcee, was the next to die, in March 1958. After meeting her through a dating agency, he drove her into the desert where he bound and gagged her before strangling her. He photographed her suffering right up to the moment of her death.

Four months later, Glatman talked his way into the apartment of model Ruth Mercado, 23, bound her, bundled her into his car and again drove her into the desert to meet the same fate.

The killer's last target, 27-year-old model Lorraine Vigil, managed to turn the tables on her attacker as he tried to tie her up in his car in a dark Los Angeles side-street. She bravely wrested his gun away from him despite suffering a flesh wound to the leg in the struggle. As they rolled out of the car and onto the sidewalk, they were spotted by a passing motorcycle cop who pounced on Glatman.

A search of his home revealed photographs of the three dead girls that finally sealed his fate. He confessed to the three known murders and led detectives to the bodies in the desert. Glatman was also suspected of the 1954 killing of an unidentified girl in Boulder, Colorado. Found guilty of first-degree murder, he was executed in the gas chamber at San Quentin on September 18, 1959.

where he tied her up for some bondage shots. But instead of freeing her, he assaulted her before driving her into the desert where, at gunpoint, he made her pose for obscene photographs. Finally he tied a noose around her neck and slowly throttled her.

John Glover

John Glover's series of murders earned him unchallenged notoriety as Australia's worst serial killer. He was the 'Granny Killer'. His known crimes, the battering to death of six elderly women for which he was jailed for life, were horrific enough. But police who investigated those killings believe there were many more.

'Granny Killer' Was Australia's Worst

In 2005 Glover committed suicide at the age of 72 in Lithgow Prison, New South Wales. He was found hanging from a crude noose attached to a shower fitting in his cell.

John Wayne Glover, born in 1932, came from a broken family, left school at 14 and emigrated to Australia from Britain in 1957 with 30 shillings in his pocket and no qualifications other than his driver's license. In 1962, he was convicted of assaulting two women in Melbourne and put on probation for five years. Three years later, he was convicted of 'being unlawfully on premises' and was jailed, a police officer marking his file with the notation that he would probably become a 'serious sex offender'.

Glover married in 1968 and the couple moved to Sydney to live with the bride's parents in the North Shore suburb of Mosman. There is no evidence of Glover killing over the ensuing 20 years, by which time he was 57 and had two children.

Early in 1989, and soon after his mother's death, he attacked an 84-year-old, but she survived and provided police with an accurate description of her assailant. On March 1 of that year, he claimed his first murder victim, Gwendolin Mitchelhill, 82. On May 9, he murdered Winifred Ashton, 82. He struck three times in June of that year, assaulting women residents of retirement homes. In August he battered an old lady in the street, and in October, pretending to be a doctor, he molested a blind nursing home inmate. Later that month, he violently attacked another retirement home resident, smashing her face into a brick wall. The victim gave a clear description, which provided police with an Identikit picture—of a young man, possibly a teenager.

In November, he murdered Margaret Pahud, 85, in Lane Cove and the very next day attacked and killed Olive Cleveland, 81, at a retirement community in Belrose. Later that month, he followed Muriel Falconer, 93, to her home in Mosman and battered her to death, but left a clear footprint at the scene.

In January 1990, he entered Sydney's Greenwich Hospital and molested an elderly woman, who pressed an alarm button. Glover fled, downed a bottle of Scotch, wrote a suicide note saying there would be 'no more grannies', then got into a hot bath. He survived but by now was a prime suspect and under police surveillance.

Nevertheless, he managed to strike one last time, on March 19, 1990. The victim was Joan Sinclair, with whom he had a longstanding but apparently platonic relationship. He went to her Beauty Point home, smashed her head with a hammer, removed her pantyhose and strangled her with it. He then ran a bath, swallowed sleeping pills and a bottle of Scotch, slashed a wrist and waited to die. At that point, police burst in and found him in a coma.

At his trial, Glover pleaded not guilty on the grounds of diminished responsibility. A psychiatrist said pent-up hostility toward his mother and then his mother-in-law was the trigger for the crimes. Judge James Wood had no sympathy for the plea and gave Glover consecutive life sentences, ordering: 'He is never to be released.'

His wife agreed. She never went to see her husband in jail, instead leaving Sydney for New Zealand with their daughters. Her husband, she said, would be 'better off dead'. That was not the view of New South Wales Police, however. They wanted him to confess to further crimes, so easing the pain for families of at least five other murder victims.

The unsolved killings included that of a woman he knew, Sydney socialite Florence Broadhurst, found bludgeoned to death in her apartment in 1977. Seven other elderly women were murdered in similar style in the Sydney area, and two close to where Glover once lived in Melbourne.

But prison visits by murder squad detectives could elicit no more than vague hints from Glover right up until his suicide in September 2005.

Belle Gunness

It is quite likely that Belle Gunness got away with murder—at least 18 and possibly more than 40 of them. For, although police closed their files after finding what they thought was the lady's corpse, it is highly likely that she faked her own death and continued her murderous career 'from beyond the grave'.

Wily Widow Wooed Victims With Words Of Love

ABOVE: Belle Gunness invited many rich male suitors to stay at her home…then murdered them with a meat cleaver.

Belle was not her real name. She was born Brynhilde Paulstadder, a stonemason's daughter, in Trondheim, Norway in November 1859. At the age of 24, she arrived as an immigrant to the United States and married a Swede, Mads Sorenson, who died in suspicious circumstances. Although his body was later exhumed, no evidence of foul play was detected.

Sorenson was insured—and so was the couple's house, which burned down shortly afterward. Belle invested in a bakery, which also burned down, although this time the insurance company refused to pay up.

Belle moved to Indiana, where she married widower Peter Gunness, and they settled on a lonely farm near the town of La Porte. He was persuaded to take out heavy life insurance and was dead shortly afterward, his head crushed by a blunt object. According to his widow, a sausage grinder had fallen from a shelf under which he had been sitting and split his skull.

That was not the version of events that was reported by their 14-year-old adopted daughter, Jennie, who went to the police to report Mr Gunness's slaying. They did not believe her and she returned home, only to be murdered too.

Now a widow in her 50s, Gunness found difficulty making the mortgage payments on her farm, so she advertised for suitors through the matrimonial columns of newspapers. One of her adverts read: 'Rich, good-looking woman, owner of a big farm, desires to correspond with a gentleman of wealth and refinement, object matrimony. No replies by letter will be considered unless the sender is willing to follow an answer with a personal visit. Triflers need not apply.'

Gunness would invite prospective suitors to stay at the farm but insisted they bring along a sum of money to prove their willingness to invest in the property. Belle would feed them, sleep with them, then drug them. Once comatose, she would hack them to death with a meat cleaver, dispose of the body and make off with their savings.

To one deluded suitor, Andrew Helgelein, she wrote: 'My Andrew, I love you. PS, Be sure and bring the $3,000 you are going to invest in the farm and for safety's sake sew them up in your clothes, dearest.' Andrew traveled from his home in South Dakota and was never heard of again.

Belle's one-woman crime wave ended in 1908, although the circumstances surrounding her demise are still shrouded in mystery. It appears that

Belle had an accomplice in many of her crimes, a hired handyman and lover, Ray Lamphere. They had recently fallen out, however, and Lamphere had gone to police with a seemingly far-fetched tale of 42 murders having been committed at the farm over the past four years. They had disbelieved him and Lamphere had been fired by his employer.

On the night of April 28, the farmhouse was burned to the ground. Lamphere was seen running from the scene and police assumed he had torched the farm in revenge for his firing. He was subsequently jailed for a year for arson. Yet it is far more likely that the arsonist had been Gunness herself. Inquiries were being made by relatives of the missing Andrew Helgelein and it is probable that she wanted to cover her tracks and simply vanish.

This she seemed to have successfully achieved. When police searched through the burned-out farm buildings, they found several bodies. Fourteen male corpses were discovered in a pigsty, and among the ashes in the basement of the house were the burned bodies of Gunness's four children. Alongside them lay the headless body of a woman—presumed to be that of Belle herself because her false teeth were recovered nearby. However, the corpse was considerably shorter and lighter than the strapping widow and there were traces of poison in it. Had Belle Gunness lured yet another victim to the farm, this time a woman, and callously murdered her alongside her own children in order to conceal her escape?

RIGHT: Gunness with three of her four children. Their bodies were later found, almost certainly murdered, in the basement of her farm.

Fritz Haarmann

Werewolf scares were common in the Middle Ages, as evidenced by the case of Peter Stump (see page 195). But this was the 20th century—and the notion of a half-man half-beast prowling the streets of a German city, even in the dark days following World War One, was an obvious nonsense.

The 'Werewolf' Who Bit Boys To Death

Yet this was the period when the defeated country found itself sucked into the kind of monster-hunting hysteria that belonged to an earlier age, as people by the dozen mysteriously vanished from the streets. At the same time, housewives became suspicious about cuts of meat they had bought—and it was suggested to police that the odd-tasting joints might be human flesh.

Soon it would be proved that a monster was indeed on the loose. His name was Friedrich 'Fritz' Haarmann, and he would soon become known by the epithets 'Werewolf of Hanover', 'Vampire of Hanover' and 'Butcher of Hanover'. His prey was young boys, over the years, his victims numbered at least 27 and possibly as many as 50.

Haarmann found his prey by prowling around Hanover's central railroad station, luring young male prostitutes and vagrants back to his apartment and killing them by biting through their throats while sodomizing them. He would then chop up his victims and sell the flesh as black market pork.

Born in 1879, young Friedrich adored his invalid mother but hated his father, a railroadman who rejected him as feeble minded. He turned to petty crime, his center of operations being the railroad station. There, even the charity workers manning the soup kitchens for the poor and homeless came to regard Haarmann as one of their team. And the police saw him as a useful source of criminal information.

They were forced to question their informer in September 1918, however, when it was reported to them that a missing 17-year-old youth had last been seen in his company, but the killer was cleared. At his trial six years later, he was to boast: 'When the police examined my room, the head of the boy was lying wrapped in newspaper behind the oven.' Haarmann now believed he was invincible. The following year he teamed up with a homosexual lover, 20-year-old Hans Grans, who picked out victims for Haarmann to abduct. Grans made a living by selling the clothes of the murdered young men—even instructing his elder partner to murder a boy 'because I like what he's wearing'.

As newspapers wrote hysterically about the 'Werewolf of Hanover', one claiming that 600 people had disappeared in the city within a year, the finger of suspicion increasingly pointed to Haarmann. In June 1924, police raided his apartment and discovered blood-splattered walls and heaps of clothes of varying sizes. Haarmann broke down and confessed everything.

At their trial in December 1924, Haarmann and Grans were jointly charged with the murders of 27 boys aged 12 to 18. Grans was sentenced to life imprisonment, served 12 years and died in Hanover in the early 1980s. Haarmann was sentenced to be executed and was beheaded by guillotine.

ABOVE: The 'Werewolf of Hanover', Fritz Haarmann, who murdered at least 27, and possibly as many as 50, young boys.

John Haigh

John Haigh relished the title bestowed on him by the press: 'The Acid Bath Murderer'. He used industrial acid to dissolve away evidence of his crimes and, but for one careless oversight, would almost certainly have gone on to claim the lives of many more victims. It was his mistaken belief that a corpse could be completely disposed of by chemicals that led him to the gallows in 1949.

Deadly Charm Of The 'Acid Bath Murderer'

John George Haigh was a charmer. Born in 1909 and raised in a Yorkshire village by parents who were strict followers of the Plymouth Brethren sect, he grew up a bright scholarship pupil and choirboy. But when, at the age of 21, he was fired from an early job for stealing cash, he turned his hand to forgery and

ABOVE: Dr Archibald Henderson and his wife Rose on holiday in 1944. They were both killed by the Acid Bath Murderer.

ABOVE: Haigh arrives at Horsham Magistrates Court handcuffed to a policeman, on April 1, 1949.

ABOVE: Haigh's vile crimes make the front page of the Daily Express newspaper on March 3, 1949.

in September 1944, Haigh smashing his skull with a pin-table leg and dissolving his body in a 40-gallon (180 liters) water butt filled with sulphuric acid. The little that was left of McSwann was then poured down a drain.

Haigh contacted the young man's parents, wealthy businessman William and wife Amy, with a message

ABOVE: Rose Henderson in 1945. After murdering Rose and her husband, Haigh used forged papers to embezzle £7,000.

fraud, specializing in selling cars he didn't own. As the cash rolled in, Haigh acquired a gleaming sports car and a pretty wife. He lost both when he was jailed for fraud in 1934 and again in 1938.

Incarcerated in bleak Dartmoor prison, Haigh studied chemistry and worked in the tinsmith's store where he had access to sulphuric acid. The idea of dissolving bodies in acid began to take shape. He experimented on small animals brought in as pets by prisoners on outside work parties. He made careful notes about the time taken for acid to dissolve flesh and bone.

Freed in 1944, Haigh moved to the capital and set up his own business repairing pin-tables in basement rooms in London's Gloucester Road. His first murder victim, a draft dodger named Donald McSwann, was killed here that their son had gone into hiding to avoid his call-up papers. When they turned up to learn more, they too were murdered and their remains swilled down the drain. Using forged papers, Haigh seized control of £4,000 of their assets and moved into the nearby Onslow Court Hotel. With money came a passion for gambling, however, and Haigh's debts mounted. He decided that new victims were needed.

The killer had moved his repair workshop to Crawley, Sussex, where, in February 1948, he lured London doctor Archibald Henderson and his wife Rose, murdered them and consigned their bodies to the acid vat. After forging letters giving him authority over their assets, he embezzled £7,000.

Haigh's final victim was a fellow resident of the Onslow Court Hotel, 69-year-old colonel's widow Olive Durand-Deacon. Lured to Crawley in February 1949, she was shot in the back and heaved into the acid vat. The resultant gunge was then poured onto the earth at the back of the workshop. Haigh had been too hasty, however. When police arrived, at the behest of a friend of the victim who knew of her appointment with Haigh, they found bone and false teeth which the acid had failed to dissolve.

Although police suspected Haigh of up to 15 murders, he confessed to just six. A jury at Lewes Assizes took just 17 minutes to declare him guilty. The deadly charming con-man was hanged at London's Wandsworth prison on August 10, 1949.

ABOVE: A crowd gathers outside Wandsworth prison in anticipation of news of Haigh's hanging.

Archibald Hall

Archibald Thompson Hall, the son of a Glasgow postman, experienced a taste of the good life at 16 when he was seduced by an older woman. They attended the best hotels and enjoyed the finest restaurants, and this made Hall determined that the elegant lifestyle would be his from then on.

The Butler Did It— In Savage Style

His youthful misdeeds began modestly: collecting for the Red Cross, but keeping much of the charitable proceeds in his own pocket. From this, it was a small step to more serious theft, and in 1943, at the

ABOVE: Hall committed his first murder after being released from prison in 1977.

ABOVE: Archibald Hall, aka Roy Fontaine, a fake butler whose yearning for the high life led him to murder.

aged of 19, he embarked on a crime spree that earned him several brief terms in prison and two spells in mental institutions.

Then, in 1951, Hall reinvented himself as 'Roy Fontaine' and became a 'gentleman's gentleman'. Using forged references, he gained positions as a butler, which allowed him to live the high life he so yearned for. Among his stunts over the next five years were intercepting an invitation to a royal garden party where he met the Queen, posing as a rich Arab to fool jewelers, and playing the part of a wealthy American to gain access to exclusive functions.

A string of thefts from his employers caught up with him in 1956 when he was given a 30 year jail term. Paroled in 1963, he was back inside the following year, only to escape and go on the run for two years before his recapture.

Free again in 1977, Hall played his usual trick of creating fake references to obtain a post as butler to Scottish heiress Lady Peggy Hudson. On his recommendation, David Wright, a homosexual lover from prison, was taken on as gardener on her Dumfriesshire estate. It was a short-term position for Wright—because when the pair fell out, Hall shot him and buried him in a shallow grave.

Hall's next post was in London with wealthy ex-MP Walter Scott-Elliott and his wife Dorothy. In ailing health, Scott-Elliott was an easy mark for Hall, who called in two accomplices, Mary Coggle and Michael Kitto, to help relieve him of his valuables. When Mrs Scott-Elliott caught the two men in her bedroom, Hall suffocated her. Then, with her body stuffed into a car boot and her drugged husband in the back seat, the three conspirators drove to Scotland, where the old man was also killed and both bodies buried in the countryside.

Hall's next victim was his accomplice Coggle who, when she refused to return Mrs Scott-Elliot's stolen jewelry, was also killed and her body dumped in a stream. The remaining two villains then returned to England, breaking their journey at the Cumbria home of Hall's hated half-brother Donald, a pedophile just out of prison. Hall placed a chloroform-soaked cloth over the man's face and drowned him in his bath.

With yet another body in the car boot, Hall and Kitto returned to Scotland where, during a meal stop, a suspicious hotel manager phoned police and the pair were arrested. Tried for different murders in both London and Edinburgh, both received life sentences, Hall's being without hope of parole.

From his cell, Archibald Hall wrote his autobiography, published in 1999 under the title *A Perfect Gentleman*. He died in prison in October 2002 at the age of 78.

Donald Harvey

How Donald Harvey ever got a job working in hospitals is a mystery to many of the families of those he murdered. In 1987, he confessed to killing between 85 and 100 patients. His mental state made it difficult to sift fact from fiction, however, and, in three separate trials, he was convicted of 40 murders.

Scourge Of The 'Angel Of Death'

Born in 1952 and raised in Booneville, in the Appalachian Mountains, Harvey was a homosexual obsessed with the occult. He also had a fascination for all things medical. At the age of 18, he took a part-time post as a junior orderly at Marymount Hospital in London, Kentucky. There, he was later to confess, he killed 12 patients in 10 months by suffocation or removing their oxygen supply 'to ease their suffering'.

In 1972 he joined the US Air Force but was discharged less than a year later and was subsequently committed to the Veterans' Administration Medical Center in Lexington, where attempts were made to cure his mental disorders by the application of electroshock therapy. Undeterred by this dramatic treatment, Harvey disguised his recent medical history and secured part-time jobs as a nursing assistant at two Lexington hospitals and as a clerk at a hospital in Fort Thomas. There are no records of any deaths at his hands in those hospitals but the killings started anew when he moved to Ohio in 1975 to work at the Cincinnati Veterans' Association Medical Center in jobs ranging from nursing aide to laboratory technician to mortuary assistant.

Harvey literally got away with murder for 10 years.

ABOVE: Donald Harvey during a court appearance. The Cincinnati prosecutor called him 'a compulsive killer'.

In 1985, he was searched by security guards and was found to be carrying hypodermic needles, cocaine-snorting equipment, and a .38 caliber pistol. He was fined $50 and fired but that was no impediment to his getting another hospital job. Within a few months he picked up a new post as a nurse's aide at the city's Drake Memorial Hospital.

Patients were now regularly dying at Harvey's hands, his methods including injecting air into their veins, sprinkling rat poison on their food, disconnecting life support machines, and suffocation with plastic bags and wet towels. He sometimes inserted a coat hanger into a catheter, causing an abdominal puncture and subsequent peritonitis. His favorite methods, however, were poisoning by arsenic, cyanide, insulin, morphine or fluid tainted with hepatitis B or HIV.

Harvey's colleagues were now calling him 'Angel of Death' because so many patients died on his shifts. Yet it took an autopsy on one of his victims to reveal that a poisoner was on the loose. Harvey was arrested in April 1987 and was found to have kept a diary of his crimes. It revealed that during his 10 years at the Cincinnati Veterans' Association Medical Center, he had murdered 15 patients. In his 13 months at Drake Memorial, he murdered another 23. He had also attempted to murder his gay lover, Carl Hoeweler, after they had fallen out. Hoeweler ended up in hospital but survived. So did Hoeweler's mother, to whom he had also administered poison. His father was similarly admitted to hospital but died in May 1983 after Harvey had visited him and sprinkled more poison on his food.

As Harvey's trial date loomed, the killer began a

spate of plea bargaining to avoid Ohio's death penalty. In an apparent bid to demonstrate insanity, he first confessed to 33 murders, then 50, then 80-plus. The view of the Cincinnati prosecutor's office was clear, however: 'This man is sane and competent but is a compulsive killer.'

In court in Cincinnati on August 18, 1987, Harvey was given four consecutive 20-years-to-life sentences after pleading guilty to 25 counts of murder. A further trial opened in Kentucky in November, when he pleaded guilty to 12 murders at the Marymount Hospital and was sentenced to eight life terms. Back in Cincinnati in February 1988, he pleaded guilty to three further murders and three attempted murders, drawing three further life sentences. That made a total of 40 murders—far short of his last confessed total of 87. Since Harvey is notable for keeping his crimes undetected over 17 years, their true extent may never be known.

Javed Iqbal

Javed Iqbal never completed his 700-year jail sentence, of course. The serial killer with the most victims in the history of Pakistan was found dead in his cell in Kot Lakhpat prison on the morning of October 8, 2001. Iqbal and one of his accomplices Shahzad Sajid had apparently committed suicide by hanging themselves with bedsheets, though their deaths looked suspiciously like murder. Autopsies revealed that they had recently been beaten.

Letter To Newspaper: 'I Killed 100 Kids'

Iqbal (full name Javed Iqbal Mughal), born in Lahore in 1956, had a relatively privileged upbringing, his father being a well-off businessman in the city. His son followed in his footsteps. Yet in December 1999, at the age of 42, he wrote the most astonishing letter to a Lahore newspaper. He confessed to killing 100 children and mocked police for failing to catch him. Then he went on the run.

The fugitive became the target of Pakistan's biggest ever manhunt. It was a month before he turned himself in at the offices of a newspaper, telling journalists that he feared that the police would kill him. He allegedly confessed: 'I have no regrets. I killed 100 children. I could

RIGHT: Javed Iqbal was Pakistan's most prolific serial killer. 'I killed 100 children', he boasted. 'I could have killed 500.'

have killed 500. This was not a problem, nor was the money. But I pledged to kill 100 and I never wanted to violate this.'

Although he later reneged on his confession, the evidence against him was overwhelming. In a sickening rampage, he had plucked children from the streets of Lahore, sexually abused them, throttled them, then hacked their bodies to bits. The 100 he had killed had all been aged between six and 16. In his letter, he had claimed to have strangled and dismembered the victims, mostly runaways and orphans, and disposed of their bodies using vats of hydrochloric acid. He had then dumped the remains in a river.

Police who swooped on his three-bedroom apartment found bloodstains on walls and floors and on the chain with which he had strangled many of his victims. There was a huge vat of acid but the remains of only two children. However, there were photographs of some of the missing youngsters. Tearful parents were able to identify only 25 out of the 100 ill-fated children, mainly by their belongings which the murderer had kept in five sacks.

Four accomplices, teenaged boys who had shared Iqbal's home, were arrested. One of them died in police custody, apparently by jumping from a window. When the remaining three appeared in court with Iqbal in March 2000, they pleaded not guilty to charges of murder, abduction, and sodomy. Astonishingly, so did Iqbal himself.

At their trial, the court heard evidence that one of Iqbal's young helpers, 19-year-old Shahzad Sajid, had purchased sulphuric and hydrochloric acid to fill his master's vats. On March 16, 2000, Iqbal was found guilty of 100 murders and Sajid of 98. The third accused, aged 15 at the time of his arrest, was found guilty of complicity in 13 killings and the youngest boy, then just 13, of aiding in three killings. The two minors were given extended jail sentences of 162 and 42 years respectively.

The judge then sentenced Iqbal and Sajid to life sentences, in the ringleader's case specifically 700 years, being seven years for each of the bodies he had dissolved in acid. He added that he wished he could have made the punishment fit the crime under Islamic 'Qisas' law—by having the pair strangled in a public park in front of their victims' families, cut into 100 and 98 pieces respectively, and thrown into an acid bath.

Colin Ireland

Colin Ireland made the leap from morbid daydreamer to serial killer as a conscious lifestyle choice. Labeled London's 'Gay Slayer' in the tabloid press, he reveled in his notoriety. As his crimes were reported in the newspapers, he would telephone detectives to taunt them. 'I've got the book,' he once said. 'I know how many you have to do.' The 'book' was the FBI handbook which stated that only someone who had murdered 'one over four' could count as a serial killer. Colin Ireland was desperate to achieve that level of infamy—which is why, after his fifth victim, he jubilantly boasted: 'I've done another one.'

Sick Revenge Of The Gay Slayer

Ireland was a burglar and robber who decided to become a serial killer as a New Year resolution at the beginning of 1993. With two failed marriages behind him, he claimed to be 'a normal guy'—but his obsessive hatred of homosexuals proved him otherwise. The survival enthusiast launched his vendetta against them after being fired at Christmas 1992 from the night hostel for the homeless where he worked in Southend, Essex, following a row with a gay man.

Intent on revenge, he began frequenting the

Coleherne pub, in London's Earl's Court where, on March 9, 1993 he met 45-year-old theater director Peter Walker and was invited back to his apartment for a sadomasochistic sex session. There, Ireland bound him, whipped him, placed a plastic bag over his head and suffocated him. Two days later, he rang the Samaritans charity to request someone go round to the address to feed Walker's two pet dogs.

ABOVE: Police mugshot of 'gay slayer' Colin Ireland, who decided to become a serial killer as a New Year's resolution in 1993.

Ireland struck again on May 29 after being invited to the apartment of 37-year-old librarian Chris Dunn. Ireland handcuffed him to his bed, beat him with a belt and held a cigarette lighter to his testicles before strangling him.

Ireland's next fatal Coleherne assignation was with Perry Bradley III, 35-year-old son of a US Congressman, who invited the killer back to his stylish apartment in Kensington on June 4. Bradley agreed to be tied up and handcuffed to the bed but was then strangled. Ireland's pick-up four days later followed a similar pattern. Andrew Collier, a 33-year-old warden at an old people's home, ended up being spread-eagled on his own bed, beaten, and strangled.

Encouraged by the way his crimes were being reported but frustrated that police had not taken his 'crusade' sufficiently seriously, Ireland phoned Scotland Yard and again taunted them: 'Doesn't the death of a homosexual man mean anything? I will do another. I have always dreamed of doing the perfect murder.'

Ireland's final murder was far from perfect, however. On June 13, he tortured and strangled Emmanuel Spiteri, a 42-year-old chef. But within days, police knew the face of his killer, because the pair had been caught on a security camera. When they apprehended Ireland, they recognized his voice from the anonymous phone calls. A single fingerprint he had left at Collier's apartment was further evidence.

At the Old Bailey in December 1993, Ireland was handed five life sentences after Lord Justice Sachs told him: 'The fear, brutality, and indignity to which you subjected your victims are almost unspeakable. You expressed a desire to be regarded as a serial killer. That must be matched by your detention for life.'

Jack The Ripper

One of the most infamous serial killers, yet with only five murders to his credit over a relatively brief period of less than three months, Jack the Ripper or the 'Whitechapel Murderer' still fascinates and mystifies experts and amateur sleuths alike. More than a century later, researchers pour over the gory evidence and clues he left behind, trying to put a name to this savage slayer of the East End of London.

The Unanswered Question: Who Was 'Jack The Ripper'?

What is certain, from the surgical precision the Ripper used to mutilate and disembowel his victims, is that he (or even she) was no stranger to anatomy or handling a scalpel. Each victim had her throat slashed, was disemboweled, and her entrails removed.

Jack first struck on August 31, 1888, the victim being a 42-year-old prostitute, Mary Ann Nichols, known as 'Pretty Polly'. The police surgeon reported that 'only a madman could have done this' and commented on the skill with which he had used his knife. Local residents were so upset by the murder that they petitioned to have their street renamed. It was duly retitled Durward Street but no longer exists.

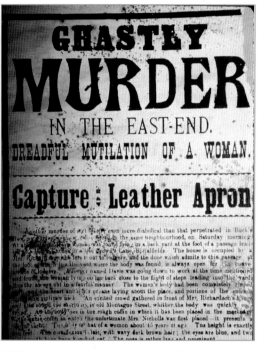

ABOVE: A newspaper report on the death of Annie Chapman, on September 8, 1888.

ABOVE: Bucks Row, renamed Durward Street, where the body of the Ripper's first victim, Mary Ann Nichols, was discovered.

Just a week later, Jack struck again, butchering 47-year-old 'Dark Annie' Chapman. Her disemboweled corpse lay alongside her few paltry possessions and her still-steaming entrails. Following this murder, a Fleet Street newspaper received a letter purporting to be from Jack. He told how he was targeting prostitutes and wouldn't stop until he was caught. He also described how he would cut the ears off his next victim, 'just for jolly'.

Victim Number Three was 44-year-old Elizabeth 'Long Liz' Stride, found in Whitechapel on September 30. Although her throat was cut, her body remained intact, leading the police to believe Jack had been disturbed. However, the very same day, he struck again. Catherine Eddowes, 46, a drunkard recently released from police cells after causing an affray, was

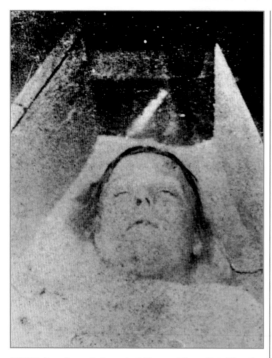

ABOVE: A mortuary photograph of 42-year-old prostitute Mary Ann Nichols, known as 'Pretty Polly'.

victim, met her grisly end on the night of November 9 in her own apartment, giving Jack plenty of time to mutilate her body in private. Her horrifying remains were discovered the next day by her landlord when he called to demand his rent. After this final murder, London waited with baited breath, but the killings had ended.

Fascination with the case for modern-day criminologists has never faded. There have been endless publications and television investigations on the grisly subject, all speculating on Jack's identity.

Several authors favor Montagu John Druitt, an impoverished barrister with some medical training. His body was found floating in the Thames a few weeks after Mary's murder. Another theory is that Jack was really Jill, a twisted midwife and abortionist. Other

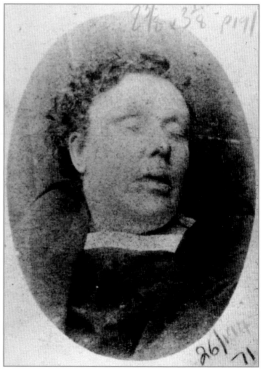

ABOVE: The body of Annie Chapman was discovered alongside her steaming entrails, meaning she was very newly killed.

discovered disemboweled, with her intestines draped over her shoulder. As promised, her ears were missing and her face had been hacked off. A chalk message was scrawled on a nearby wall: 'The Jewes (sic) are not men to be blamed for nothing.'

This fueled a theory that the murders were being committed by a Jewish ritual slaughterman. Others believed the killer must be an insane surgeon, or possibly a butcher. Indeed, Inspector Robert Sagar, a leading officer in the investigation, later revealed that a chief suspect lived in Butcher's Row, Aldgate. He was kept under close surveillance, but his friends committed him to a private asylum. After his incarceration, the killings stopped.

Mary Kelly, at age 25 the Ripper's final and youngest

A diary discovered in 1993 in Liverpool was said to prove that James Maybrick, a wealthy cotton broker, had committed the atrocities. Crime writer Patricia Cornwell suspected Walter Sickert, an artist whose works reflected the murder scenes. In 1996 an American doctor named Tumblety was implicated by a television documentary, which suggested he killed after discovering his wife was a prostitute. His effects upon his death contained a collection of preserved female reproductive organs.

The mystery intrigues thousands each year who come to visit the capital and join one of the guided tours of the area where Jack dispatched his victims. But after so long a gap and so much speculation, the question remains unanswered: Who was Jack the Ripper?

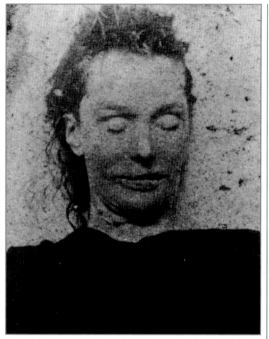

ABOVE: The corpse of Elizabeth Stride. She had her throat slit but was not mutilated, leading police to believe the killer was disturbed.

names include William Bury, who was hanged for murdering his prostitute wife five months after the last Ripper murder, and Aaron Kosminski, a Polish Jewish hairdresser known to be a prostitute hater. Even Prince Albert, a grandson of Queen Victoria, fell under suspicion. It was believed that he had contracted venereal disease which sent him insane.

Author Melvin Harris named Robert D'Onston Stephenson as his prime suspect in his respected book *The True Face of Jack the Ripper.* Stephenson was obsessed with black magic, had some medical experience, and had boasted of killing a black woman in West Africa. Harris believes Stephenson killed his wife, who disappeared in 1887, perhaps giving him the taste for murder. Stephenson became a self-professed expert on the Ripper murders, even having detailed articles published on the subject.

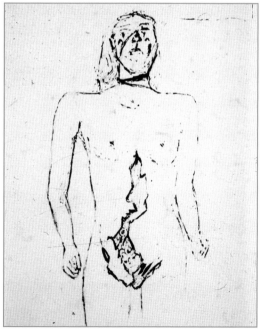

ABOVE: A mortuary sketch of the violated body of the Ripper's penultimate victim, Catherine Eddowes.

Jack The Stripper

Beneath the glitz and glamor of the swinging Sixties, London was a city in fear. Seventy years after Jack the Ripper conducted his reign of terror, killing prostitutes in the East End, the body count had begun again. And, like his mysterious predecessor, this new butcher, nicknamed 'Jack the Stripper', was never caught.

Did 'Jack The Stripper' Die Of Shame?

The first possible 'Stripper' victim was prostitute Elizabeth Figg, dragged out of the River Thames in June 1959. She had been strangled. Another probable victim was 22-year-old Gwyneth Rees, found in a shallow grave on the banks of the Thames in November 1963. She had been sexually assaulted and was naked apart from one stocking.

In February 1964, the body of Hannah Tailford, aged 30, was recovered from the river. She was naked apart from her stockings, her panties having been stuffed down her throat. In April, when the nude body of yet another street girl, 26-year-old Irene Lockwood, was found floating in the river, alarm bells began to sound at Scotland Yard. At this stage, although the incidents were concentrated within a few miles of each other

ABOVE: Detective Superintendent William Marchant of Scotland Yard holds up an Identikit picture of his prime suspects.

ABOVE: A policeman and young volunteers near the spot on the Thames towpath where the body of Gwyneth Rees was discovered.

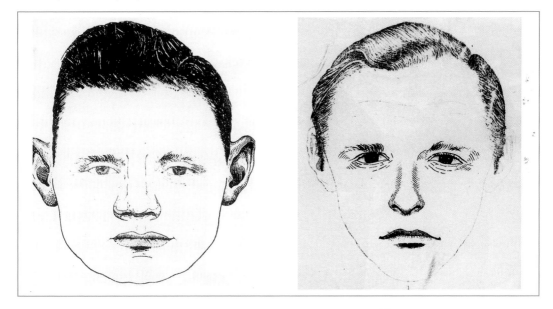

ABOVE: As the Stripper was never caught, it is not known if these Identikit images were a good likeness.

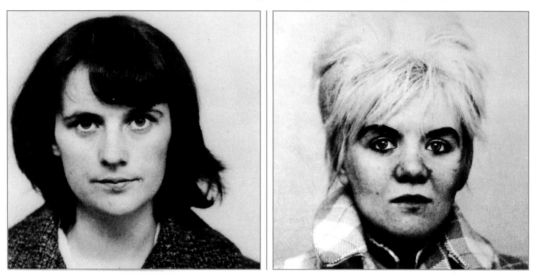

CLOCKWISE FROM TOP LEFT: Gwyneth Rees, discovered on a towpath in November 1963; Irene Lockwood, whose naked body was found floating in the Thames in April 1964; 21-year-old prostitute Margaret McGowan; and Bridget O'Hara, the Stripper's final victim.

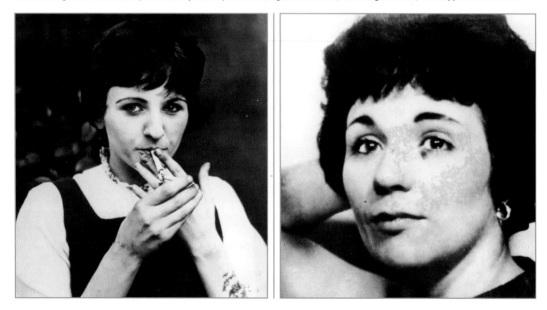

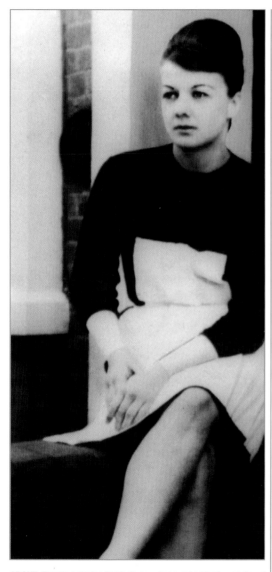

ABOVE: Prostitute Helen Barthelemy, whose naked body was found in a London sports field on April 24, 1964.

ABOVE: Policemen guard a spot on the edge of a North Acton playing field where the corpse of Bridget O'Hara was found.

in West London, there was no firm link between the victims.

That same month, Helene Barthelemy, age 20, became the first victim found away from the river. Her naked body had traces of multi-colored spray paint, suggesting it had been kept in a paint store before being dumped beside a sports field. In July, 21-year-old Mary Fleming was discarded, nude and lifeless, on a garage forecourt, her body bizarrely arranged with legs crossed and chest slumped forward. The body of Margaret McGowan, 21, was found in November with the familiar traces of paint on her skin. Last to die was 27-year-old Bridget O'Hara, found in February 1965 in shrubbery on an industrial estate. Her corpse was partially mummified, as if it had been stored in a warm, dry place.

Police now had their first lead. The Heron Trading Estate, where Bridget's body had been dumped, contained a car body-shop from which flecks of paint were emitted through an air extractor. They questioned all 7,000 workers on the estate without success.

Like the 'Jack the Ripper' killings, the 'Stripper' reign of terror seemed to cease on its own, and there were few solid clues for police to follow. But the policeman in charge, Chief Superintendent John Du Rose, subsequently professed his certainty that the killer was a security guard on the Heron Trading Estate, his rounds including the paint store where at least some of the bodies may have been stored after death. In March 1965, a month after Bridget's murder, just such a guard gassed himself, leaving a note saying: 'I cannot stand the strain any longer.'

Pointing to the man's guilt, Du Rose wrote in his memoirs, *Murder Was My Business*: 'The man I wanted to arrest took his own life… (but) because he was never arrested or stood trial, he must be considered innocent—and will therefore never be named.'

However, the cessation of the crimes is not proof, and it is still unclear whether the murders listed above are the work of one man or more. Police put the killer's tally at a certain five, a probable six, and a possible eight. But there remains doubt over the numbers because the first possible victims did not entirely fit the killer's modus operandi: asphyxiation during sex. For this reason, the Scotland Yard file on 'Jack the Stripper' remains open to this day—just as it does on his more famous namesake 'Jack the Ripper'.

Hélène Jégado

An illiterate French peasant girl, Hélène Jégado once complained: 'Wherever I go, people died.' They certainly did—because she poisoned them, her victims including her masters, mistresses, their relatives, her fellow servants, and her own sister. As many as 36 people are known to have succumbed to her habit of lacing their food and drink with arsenic.

'Wherever I Go, People Die'

Born in Lorient, Brittany, in 1803 and orphaned in childhood, Hélène entered a convent as a novice when she was in her early 20s. She was expelled from her first convent for stealing and from a second convent when the nuns suspected they were being poisoned. They did not inform the authorities, thus failing to save many innocent lives.

Apart from her spells in holy orders, Jégado worked throughout the region as a domestic servant, usually for members of the clergy. The seemingly pious servant could not resist stealing from her venerable masters, however, and she covered up her petty thieving by poisoning potential witnesses. Jégado would mix arsenic with their food and, upon their agonizing deaths, would go into convincing mourning.

Her first suspected poisoning was in 1833 when she was working for a family in Guern, Brittany. In the space of three months, seven members of the household and their house guests died suddenly, including the parish priest and her own visiting sister. Her apparent sorrow and pious behavior was so convincing she was not suspected. Coming shortly after a cholera epidemic the previous year, the deaths were attributed to natural causes.

After an initial spate of killings between 1833 and 1841, Jégado seems to have stopped for eight years before a final spree starting in 1849. That year, while working as cook for a family in Rennes, Jégado was fired for theft but, before leaving, poisoned the entire household. All recovered, but in her next job in the city,

working for a university professor, two of his servants died mysteriously. An autopsy revealed arsenic in the second victim's body and Jégado was suspected.

Her mistake was protesting her innocence too volubly, revealing details of the murders that had yet to be put to her. Initially accused of 17 killings, the poisoner was eventually brought to court in December 1851 on three charges of murder and three of attempted murder. Her behavior in court was bizarre, from pronouncements of innocence to loud and violent outbursts against her accusers.

She was led to the guillotine on February 26, 1852, and executed in front of a large crowd in the town center of Rennes.

LEFT: An engraving of the execution, by guillotine, of serial poisoner Hélène Jégado.

Genene Jones

Genene Jones was a pediatric nurse who is feared to have lethally injected up to 47 infants and children in her care over a four-year span in clinics around San Antonio, Texas, in the early 1980s. Jones, it appeared, thrilled in putting children in mortal peril and thrusting herself into the role of heroine when they pulled through. Sadly, many did not.

Tiny Innocents Fell Victim On The 'Death Shift'

Jones had always been viewed by many of her colleagues as a strange character. Born in 1950, her nursing career started shakily, with her having to leave a number of nursing positions because of her difficult and sometimes aggressive behavior. Despite this, she landed a job in the intensive care section of the pediatric unit of Bexar County Medical Center Hospital. There, it was apparent to colleagues from the onset that she was odd. She was described variously as an unlikeable character, one who wouldn't take orders and a 'bragging attention seeker'.

It was noted by hospital staff that when a baby died, Jones would be grief-stricken as if it were her own child. She would sit by the body for hours and insist on taking it to the morgue herself. Despite her peculiar behavior, she had the support of her Head Nurse, who liked and protected her. This, it appears, gave Jones a feeling of invincibility.

In 1981, Jones was granted authority to oversee the hospital's sickest children, giving her access to an unlocked cabinet of freely available medications on the ward. It was not long before babies started dying on her shifts—at one point as many as seven in two weeks. The babies had been admitted because of common childhood symptoms such as fevers, vomiting or diarrhea but, while in Jones's care, they developed unexplained seizures and went into cardiac arrest.

One of those babies was month-old Rolando Santos, who was being treated for pneumonia. His unexplained

ABOVE: Many of the babies in the care of Genene Jones suffered cardiac arrest. During one two-week spell in 1981 she killed seven.

cardiac arrest, extensive bleeding, hemorrhaging, and finally coma all occurred or intensified on Jones's shifts. The baby recovered only when he was placed under 24-hour surveillance.

Jones's on-duty hours became known as the 'Death Shift', because of the many occurring resuscitations and deaths. Her boss, Dr. James Robotham, head of the pediatric unit, made a formal complaint about her after an autopsy on one of the babies in her care revealed traces of Herapin, a drug that causes the heart to stop. Tragically, hospital administrators decided not to follow up on an investigation that could draw negative attention to their hospital, but they asked for the drug to be carefully monitored within the ward.

Further infant deaths continued but, with Herapin restricted, toxic amounts of another drug, Dilantin, began to come up in laboratory tests. When investigators failed to pin the deaths on just one nurse, a staff restructure was ordered and Jones was moved away from pediatrics.

She immediately resigned and, in 1982, she joined a newly opened pediatric clinic in Kerrville, Texas. After she started work there, seven children succumbed to seizures in a two-month period, culminating in the death of 15-month-old Chelsea Ann McClellan, who was treated by Jones in a routine check-up.

As with all the other six babies who had unexpected seizures, Chelsea had immediately been transferred to Kerr County's Sid Peterson Hospital. From the sheer volume of children admitted, staff there became suspicious, especially since the babies normally recovered quickly once in their care.

A doctor at Sid Peterson Hospital investigated the deaths and discovered a similar spate of emergencies at Bexar County Medical Center Hospital where Genene Jones had previously worked. At last the finger of suspicion was pointed at the 'Death Shift' nurse.

Chelsea's body was exhumed in October 1982 and it was found that a powerful muscle relaxant, Succinylcholine, had been injected. In February 1983, a grand jury was convened in San Antonio to look into a shocking total of 47 suspicious deaths of children at Bexar County Medical Center Hospital. All had occurred over a four-year period coinciding with Jones's tenure at that facility.

Jones was finally indicted on charges of poisoning Chelsea McClellan and went on trial for that single murder in January 1984. She was sentenced to 99 years in prison and earned another 60 years in a second trial the same year when she was found guilty of injuring Rolando Santos by injection.

Jones's final death count may never be known because hospital officials at Bexar County Medical Center Hospital shredded records of her employment and activities, thus destroying crucial evidence that was under the grand jury's subpoena. But it has been speculated that Jones may have murdered almost 50 helpless infants dating back to the beginning of her nursing career in 1977.

Jones will serve only one-third of her sentence because of a law in place at the time to deal with prison overcrowding, meaning she will receive automatic parole in 2017. She is currently eligible for early parole every two to three years, but has been constantly denied it.

Patrick Kearney

Patrick Kearney became known as the 'Trash Bag Killer' and the 'Freeway Killer' because his victims were found scattered along Californian roadsides. The first epithet is the one that has stuck—mainly because, in the sick 1970s, there were so many murderers roaming the United States West Coast highways. 'Freeway Killer' is a nickname Kearney had to share with two other separate serial killers, William Bonin (see page 23) and Randy Kraft (see page 122).

Dismembered Bodies Were Mark Of The 'Trash Bag Killer'

Born in Texas in 1940, Patrick Wayne Kearney was a sickly child who was bullied at school. He was to admit years later that he fantasized about killing people from his teen years. After a brief marriage ended in divorce, he moved to California and took a job in Los Angeles as an electronics engineer for Hughes Aircraft Co. He was withdrawn and avoided small talk with colleagues.

He killed his first victim, a hitch-hiker, around 1965 and claimed several more victims over the next two years before he teamed up with a younger, homosexual lover, David Hill, and the pair moved to a rundown house at Redondo Beach.

The California 'trash bag' case officially opened on April 13, 1975, when the mutilated remains of

21-year-old Albert Rivera were discovered near San Juan Capistrano. Over the next seven months, five more bodies were found dumped between Los Angeles and San Diego. All the victims were drifters or young men who frequented gay bars. All came to a similar end, stripped naked, shot in the head with a small-caliber gun, dismembered, and their body parts packaged in plastic garbage bags which were left by the roadside.

As the number of corpses continued to mount, detectives realized that the abduction of gay men seemed to be linked to the company of two particular, mysterious prowlers, but they had no idea of their identities. The last known victim of Kearney and Hill was 17-year-old John LaMay, who left his home in March 1977 to meet an acquaintance he had named to his parents only as 'Dave'. Five days later, the teenager's dismembered body was found beside a highway near Corona. Police questioned LaMay's gay friends, one of whom was able to identify 'Dave' as David Hill. The net was closing in on the evil duo, who fled to Mexico and laid low.

The pair were eventually caught, not by fleet-footed

detective work, but by their dramatic appearance at Riverside County Sheriff's office on July 13, 1977. Kearney, then aged 37, and Hill, 34, walked up to the desk, pointed to a wanted poster and announced: 'We're them!' They had decided to turn themselves in under pressure from family members.

The evidence against Kearney and Hill included fibers, binding tape, and a bloodstained hacksaw found at their Redondo Beach home. But when the older man assumed full responsibility for the murders, the Riverside County Grand Jury refused to indict Hill, and the charges against him had to be dropped through lack of evidence—to the great frustration of investigating officers. Hill fled California and returned to his home town of Lubbock, Texas.

Kearney, who explained that killing 'excited me and gave me a feeling of dominance', signed confessions to 28 murders but was initially charged with the deaths of only three of them, including John LaMay, whose blood it was on the hacksaw. At his trial in December, he was sentenced to life imprisonment, having been spared the death penalty because of his cooperation in clearing up other cases. The judge said: 'This defendant has perpetrated a series of ghastly and grisly crimes. I can only hope he will never be released. He appears to be an insult to humanity.'

Kearney was back in court in 1978 to plead guilty to the murders of 18 boys and young men and to provide information relating to a further 11 gay victims, bringing the probable total of his victims to 32, including two children, aged five and eight. Given a fresh string of life sentences, he spent his years in Californian state prisons as an avid writer of essays and of letters to his many, sick-minded pen-pals.

Edmund Kemper

Edmund Emil Kemper, otherwise known as 'The Co-ed Killer' because of the female college students he targeted, could hardly be described as a normal child. Born in December 1949, his parents separated when he was nine and young Edmund lived mostly with his grandparents on a ranch in North Fork, California. He had a terrible relationship with his mother, who would constantly belittle and humiliate him. Finding it difficult to make friends, Kemper lived in a fantasy world involving the torture and slaughter of helpless animals. The decapitation of his pet cat was an indication of his future trademark.

He Practiced Killing By Decapitating The Family Cat

At the age of 15, Kemper shot his grandmother three times with her own gun, then dispatched his grandfather with a shot to the back of his head. He was diagnosed as paranoid and psychotic and committed to Atascadero State Hospital, where he used his time expanding his fantasies. On release in 1969, he was ready to start his trail of sickening killings and mutilations.

Disappointed at being turned down for the police force—he was too tall at 6ft 8ins (2.03m)—Kemper frequented bars used by off-duty cops, gradually becoming a regular participant in their conversations about guns. He even customized his car to resemble an unmarked police vehicle. During this time, he often picked up young female hitch-hikers, indulging in bizarre sexual fantasises involving murder and necrophilia.

It was in May 1972 that he started to put his preparations into practice. Kemper embarked on a spree of murders, picking up hitch-hikers, killing them, having sex with them, and then dissecting them. Two hitch-hiking students, Mary Ann Pesce and Anita Luchese, never reached their destination. His next young victim was a 15-year-old Korean girl, Aiko Koo, on her way to a dance class. He suffocated her, raped her and, after a few beers in a local bar, cut off her hands and head.

In 1973, now living back home with his mother in Santa Cruz, Kemper struck again. The first of his next three victims, Cindy Schall, was shot before he had sex with the body. Her head was buried in his backyard and other body parts thrown off a cliff. Cindy was followed by Rosalind Thorpe and Alice Lui. He abused Alice's headless body in the apartment of his mother, who throughout had no idea of her son's depravity.

Just one month later, on Easter Sunday, Kemper battered his mother to death with a hammer while she slept. He decapitated her—some reports detailing that

ABOVE: Kemper's evil fantasies prompted him to cut off the hands

he performed oral sex on her head before using it as a dartboard. He stuffed her voice box into the waste disposal unit 'to put an end to her constant nagging'. He ended his killing spree by strangling Sally Hallet, his mother's friend, having invited her for dinner while his mother's mutilated body lay in a cupboard.

Kemper fled the murder scene and, with the two women's heads in a bag in his car, he drove aimlessly for 18 hours until, reaching Pueblo, Colorado, he used a payphone to call Santa Cruz police and make a full confession. He had to make several calls before they would believe him.

At his trial in October 1973, he pleaded insanity but was found guilty of eight counts of murder. He asked for the death penalty but received life imprisonment at Folsom maximum-security jail.

ABOVE: Aged 15 Edmund Kemper was imprisoned for murdering his own grandparents, but he was released...to kill again and again.

Bela Kiss

Perhaps it was the infidelity of his wife that made Bela Kiss resort to murder. Certainly, he gained sympathy from neighbors in the Hungarian town of Czinkota when, in 1912, he told them that Marie Kiss, some years his junior, had found herself a lover and the couple had run off together.

Kiss Of Death For Lonely Widows

Kiss, however, took immediate advantage of his new bachelor status. He replaced his wife with an elderly housekeeper, and invited a regular flow of women to his home, 10 miles (16km) from the capital Budapest.

This seemingly romantic period in his life ended in November 1914 when, at the age of 34, he was drafted into the Hungarian army and sent to fight in Serbia. In the spring of 1916, word got back to his home town of Czinkota that Kiss had been killed in action and had been buried at the battlefront.

That, it seemed, would be the last anyone would hear of Bela Kiss. But in June of that year, a squad of soldiers visited Czinkota looking for illegally stockpiled gasoline, in severely short supply during the First World War. In the course of their search, they visited Kiss's home and discovered a number of suspicious oil drums in a workshop where he had carried out his trade as a plumber and tinsmith.

Prizing open the lid of one, they found the perfectly preserved naked body of a woman. The contents of a further six drums was the same. Each woman had been garrotted and then pickled in alcohol.

A search of the surrounding countryside revealed another 17 drums, each with a pickled corpse inside. One contained Marie Kiss, another her lover Paul Bikari, who was the only man among the 24 victims.

Kiss's motives had been both sex and robbery. From papers and letters found in his house, it became clear that Kiss had been advertising himself under the name Hoffman as a 'lonely widower seeking female companionship'. He had, it appeared from the bodies, been successful at attracting lovelorn females.

He had also been successful at avoiding the consequences of his murderous ways. For Kiss had not died on the battlefield, as reported. He had simply switched name tags with a dead comrade and was now on the loose.

Bela Kiss was later spotted back in Hungary in the spring of 1919. Someone who had known him as 'Hoffman' spotted him on Budapest's Margaret Bridge across the Danube—the place where at least two lonely widows had last been seen with him. There were three further reports of Kiss. In 1924, a fleeing French Foreign Legionnaire told police about a fellow deserter who had boasted at his proficiency with the garrotte. His name was Hoffman.

In 1932, New York homicide detective Henry Oswald, who earned the nickname 'Camera Eye' because of his memory for mugshots, chased a man he was convinced was Kiss through Times Square before losing him in a subway. He again proved elusive in 1936, fleeing before police could check out a 'Mr Hoffman', the aged janitor in a Sixth Avenue apartment block. Bela Kiss was never caught.

Randy Kraft

The epithets applied to Randy Steven Kraft when arrested in 1983 included the 'Scorecard Killer' and the 'Freeway Killer'. Another was 'California's worst-ever serial killer', because Kraft's case stands out among the spate of slayings at that time—in that he probably accounted for as many as 67 murders.

Sick 'Scorecard' Of A Sadistic Mutilator

Kraft, born in 1945, was a star pupil at high school in Westminster, California, and at his college, at Claremont, where he joined the Reserve Officer Training Corps and, unlike many of his peers, demonstrated in support of the Vietnam War. In 1964,

ABOVE: A face of pure evil. Randy Kraft was dubbed 'California's worst-ever serial killer.' His murder count probably totaled 67.

he campaigned for right-wing presidential candidate Barry Goldwater. The following year, he began working as a bartender at a local gay club.

Kraft joined the US Air Force in 1968 but was discharged only a year later on undisclosed 'medical grounds'. He went back to bartending for a while, but his especially high IQ of 129 was finally put to use and he went on to forge for himself a successful business career. A computer expert, he became a sought-after trouble-shooter for companies' technology problems, earning himself a large salary. But it was while on these business journeys up and down the Pacific Coast that Kraft picked up homosexual partners and murdered them.

His first suspected victim was Wayne Dukette, a 30-year-old gay barman missing since September 1971 and whose decomposing body was found beside a highway near San Juan Capistrano. Kraft's first

confirmed victim was Edward Moore, a 20-year-old Marine whose body was found near Seal Beach in December 1972. He had been strangled and sexually assaulted.

For the next two decades, dozens of what were believed to be Kraft's victims turned up along the freeways of California and Oregon. The victims were young men and teenage boys. Many were in the military, hitch-hiking their way between homes and bases. Some were teenage runaways. Others were picked up by the killer in gay bars.

Kraft's method of dispatching his victims varied; they had been strangled, shot in the head or had died as a result of torture. Most of the bodies showed signs of sexual mutilation by a sadistic killer. It was established that some of his victims had been alive and conscious while Kraft hacked at their genitals.

In May 1983, highway police stopped Kraft near San Diego for drink-driving and were surprised to discover that his passenger was dead. Terry Gambrel, a 25-year-old Marine, had died either of strangulation or an overdose of drugs. Also in the car was a briefcase containing a notebook with the killer's own detailed account of his murders—his 'scorecard'. It gave names, places, how the victims were murdered, and the mutilations carried out.

The briefcase also held 47 photographs of young men, some naked, some dead. Among those pictured were victims whose deaths were on the police 'unsolved' list. One of them was shown lying dead on the couch at Kraft's house in Huntington Beach, where police found property and fibers that helped identify further victims: three from Oregon and one from Michigan, both in locations where Kraft visited in his work. It was suspected that he had also killed on business trips to New York, Washington, and Ohio.

Kraft confessed to none of the murders and, by manipulating the legal system, managed to delay his trial for five years. He stretched the hearings out over 13 months, running up a bill for his Orange County trial of $10 million. But time ran out for him in May 1989 when he was finally convicted of 16 counts of murder and sentenced to death.

He remained on San Quentin's Death Row, raising a string of appeals to delay justice. Meanwhile, of Kraft's suspected 67 victims, 22 bodies remain unrecovered and unidentified.

ABOVE: Kraft (right) during his much delayed trial costing $10 million. He was eventually convicted of 16 murders in May 1989.

There was one more mystery that remained unsolved: had Randy Kraft always acted alone? Forensic evidence in two cases point to an accomplice: an extra set of footprints and semen that did not match Kraft's DNA. His trial prosecutors believed that Kraft's roommate, Jeff Graves, occasionally helped him carry out or cover up the killings. Graves died of AIDS before police could question him, so the matter was never raised in court.

Joachim Kroll

When police finally caught up with German 'Cannibal Killer' Joachim Kroll, they found themselves interrogating a pathetic, mentally retarded 43-year-old lavatory attendant, small and balding with tinted glasses, who embarrassedly told them he had killed so many people that he could not remember the details.

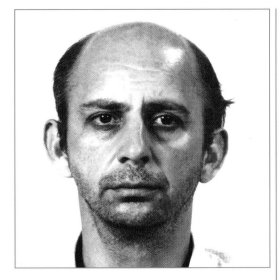

LEFT: When police raided the home of Joachim Kroll they found him cooking a meat stew…containing a child's hand.

he considered to be young and tender. When they checked through the files, they found that the skinnier of the victims had been left with their bodies unbutchered.

Kroll would surprise his victims and strangle them quickly. Afterward he would strip the body and have intercourse with it. Among Kroll's younger victims were two 13-year-old girls whose buttocks, thighs, and forearms he carved steaks for his dinner table. But it was two murders of mere youngsters that caused the German press to howl for the apprehension of the 'Ruhr Hunter', as he was then known—while freshly labeling him the 'Cannibal Killer'.

In 1966 he strangled five-year-old Ilona Harke in a park, raping her and carving chunks of flesh from her buttocks and shoulders, and in 1976, he snatched four-year-old Marion Ketter from a street, took her to his apartment and cut up her body.

Kroll was caught only because, while performing his duties as a lavatory attendant in the apartment complex where he lived, he had warned a neighbor not to use

Cannibal Who Killed For The Cookpot

As they searched his rooms in Duisberg, an industrial city of the Ruhr, they found plastic bags filled with the flesh of his victims. Cuts of meat were laid out on plates in the refrigerator. And on the stove was a stew of carrots, potatoes…and a tiny human hand.

Kroll admitted killing at least 14 women and children between 1955 and 1976, their ages ranging from four to 19. Most had been raped and slices of flesh taken from their bodies. He said he had begun raping women in 1955, when he was aged 22, but had discovered that he was unable to have sex with a conscious woman.

He committed his first murder shortly afterward, his victim being a 19-year-old girl whom he lured into a barn and strangled. Four years and four victims later, he began cannibalizing the bodies. After raping and strangling a 16-year-old girl, he carved slices from her buttocks 'because meat in the shops is so expensive'.

Kroll was later to tell detectives that he only ate those

ABOVE: The bespectacled rapist, murderer, and cannibal admitted he could only have sex with his victims after they were dead.

a particular toilet because it was 'stuffed up with guts'. It was in fact blocked with the remains of Marion Ketter.

Now relabeled in the press as the 'Duisburg Man-Eater', Kroll tried to explain his vile habits by complaining to police about the price of meat in the stores. In custody, the simpleton believed that he would be freed again after undergoing an operation to cure him of his homicidal urges. Instead he was charged with eight murders and one attempted murder.

In April 1982, Kroll was convicted on all counts, given nine life sentences and sent to a secure hospital for the criminally insane. He died of a heart attack in 1991.

Peter Kurten

One of 13 children, home life for Peter Kurten was brutal and harsh. His father was an alcoholic and beatings were commonplace, as was the sight of his father raping his mother and sisters. At the age of nine, the local dog catcher initiated him into the act of bestiality. It was then that Kurten developed an insatiable fascination for spurting blood—and for murder. In 1893, when he was just 10 years old, he drowned two young friends while out on the Rhine on a raft together.

Evil Bloodlust Of The Vampire Of Dussledorf

As a teenager on the streets of Dusseldorf, Kurten embarked on a career of petty crime, including arson and housebreaking, receiving a two-year prison sentence. On his release, he progressed from torturing animals to attacking women. He savagely beat and raped a girl in woods at Grafenburg and left her for dead. The traumatized victim never reported his vicious attack. This was followed in May 1913 by the murder of eight-year-old Christine Klein. Kurten discovered her during a burglary. He cut her throat and raped her, relishing the sound of her blood gushing to the floor.

His killings were curtailed by the arrival of World War One, which Kurten spent entirely in prison for desertion and petty crimes. On his release in 1921, he took a job in a local factory and got married. His wife was an ex-prostitute but she did not satisfy Kurten for, over the next few years, he had several mistresses, all of whom seem to have enjoyed his penchant for sadistic torture. He achieved his orgasms by wounding them and watching their blood drip. It was not long before he transferred his sick practices to strangers, now drinking blood from horrific wounds he inflicted, thus earning the nickname 'The Dusseldorf Vampire'.

The citizens of the city were now living in terror, believing there was a vampire prowling their streets. Kurten struck next in 1929, when he stabbed to death two sisters, aged five and 14, followed by an attack on a 26-year-old housemaid who, despite her appalling injuries, survived. On another day, he killed again, cutting down three victims within 30 minutes.

For his next attacks, Kurten chose to hammer his victims to death before stabbing them. The more wounds, the longer he had taken to reach orgasm. Poor little Gertrude Albermann, aged just five, had 36 separate stab wounds. She was the last of Kurten's murder victims, although his vicious attacks continued.

In May 1930, he befriended Maria Budlick, a 21-year-old maid. He took her first to his apartment and then, on a walk through Grafenburg woods, he raped and half-strangled her. But she survived and, although inexplicably she did not immediately go to the police, she was later able to provide as evidence the address to which Kurten had taken her: 71 Mettmannerstrasse.

Meanwhile, realizing that the police were closing in on him, Kurten told his wife his grisly secret, and it was she who tipped off the police. Kurten remained calm throughout his arrest and subsequent trial. His counsel failed to convince the jury of his client's insanity and

Kurten was sent to the guillotine on July 1, 1932. He asked if he would hear the sound of his own blood gushing from his neck—forecasting that it would be 'the pleasure to end all pleasures'.

ABOVE: Two photographs of Peter Kurten after he was taken into police custody in May 1929.

Ilshat Kuzikov

For some reason, the Soviet Union has bred a high proportion of serial killers with a penchant for cannibalism. One of the most enthusiastic of recent times was Ilshat Kuzikov, a St Petersburg street sweeper. Neighbors in Ordzhonikidze Street recalled him as a cheery, likeable man who was always ready to help his elderly neighbors with jobs around the house. He was devoted to his cat, Dasha, but appeared to have few human friends. He was also on the register at his local psychiatric hospital.

Special Ingredients Of A Killer's Kebabs

In November 1992, a piece of human torso turned up in the basement of a house close to Kuzikov's home. Police failed to link him to the crime, just as they failed to make the connection two years later when the severed head of a vagrant was found in a communal trash dump on Ordzhonikidze Street. But in August 1995, another severed head was found, this time belonging to one of Kuzikov's fellow psychiatric patients, Edik Vassilevski. Police realized the two men were friends and made 35-year-old Kuzikov their main suspect.

When they raided the dingy apartment block in which he lived, detectives found a plastic bag hanging outside a window in the cold, which contained human flesh marinating with onions, probably destined to be for Kuzikov's evening meal. In the hallway leading to his front door were two arms and two legs. And when they broke into his single-room Apartment 22, they found a human abattoir. Near the oven was a casserole dish containing human bones. Nearby was a small sack of human ears and other parts. Pickle jars sat around the room filled with vinegar and what turned out to be pickled human meat. On a shelf was a fizzy drink bottle full of blood. Next to it was an old gherkin jar used to store dried skin and ears. And, last but not least, there was an aluminum cooking pot containing the last remains of Edik Vassilevski. He had been cut up for Russian-style kebabs.

As he was sent to an institution for life, psychologists said Kuzikov was a sexual sadist for whom cannibalism was the ultimate way of controlling his victims. As he put it himself in interviews with police: 'You know, I always wanted to be a surgeon, but it's better to be a cannibal. If you're a surgeon you have to put the body back together and you stop having any control over it. But a cannibal kills and then he can do what he wants with the body. After he kills, he owns it forever.'

Leonard Lake and Charles Ng

To outsiders and even close members of his family, Leonard Lake was a model citizen. He was a volunteer firefighter and a charity worker with the elderly. But behind this façade, he was a sadistic murderer who kidnapped his victims before subjecting them to terrifying torture and mutilation, capturing the images on film which he then sold from his perverted mail-order business.

Deadly Partnership Of The Sickest Of Killers

His interest in photography and film started in his childhood in San Francisco when his mother encouraged Leonard to take pictures of young naked girls and to take pride in the human body. She could never have guessed that these early movies and photographs were just practice for his later 'snuff movies'.

Lake had a variety of jobs, from teacher to circus performer, but in 1966 joined the Marine Corps. During his service, he spent two years undergoing psychiatric treatment for unspecified mental problems before his discharge in 1971. He then moved to San Jose, California, and had a short-lived first marriage. Lake was known to be making porn movies featuring his wife and several other women at that time.

In 1981 he moved again, to rural Ukiah, California, joining a commune whose residents dressed in 'Renaissance' style clothing and led bizarre lives. While living at the commune, he married Cricket Balazs, who became another star of his sadomasochistic movies.

At this time, he met Charles Chitat Ng, the son of a wealthy Hong-Kong based businessman, who had been sent to boarding school in England after being arrested at the age of 15 for shoplifting. He was expelled from that school for theft and continued his education in San Francisco, joining the Marines in 1981. However, unable to stop his thieving ways, he was caught stealing weapons worth $11,000 and sentenced to 27 months in a military jail. He managed to escape and made his way back to San Francisco, where he applied to an advertisement in a survivalist magazine for a 'mercenary'.

The advert had been placed by Lake, who was himself a 'survivalist' and believed the 'holocaust' was coming. He had constructed a sick fantasy in his mind that he labeled 'Operation Miranda', where he saw himself in total world domination surrounded by his 'sex-slaves'. When he and Ng met up, a barbarous partnership was forged. The year was 1982; Lake was aged 37, Ng aged 21, and a three-year killing spree was about to begin.

It was Ng's clumsy shoplifting habit that was to bring to light the horrific murders he and Lake were committing in the wooded hills in Wisleyville, Calaveras County, about 150 miles (240km) east of San Francisco. In June 1985, police officer David Wright responded to a call about an oriental man attempting to shoplift a $75 vice from a South San Francisco store. By the time Wright arrived, the young thief had fled but his older friend was vainly trying to pay for the item.

The officer became suspicious and ran a vehicle check, which revealed that the car belonged to a local businessman, Paul Cosner, who had been reported missing. Lake gave his name as Robin Scott Stapley, a

ABOVE: A grinning Leonard Lake on one of his wedding days. It's not known if his two brides were aware of his grisly activities.

further police check revealed Stapley to be 26 years old and also missing.

Lake was arrested and taken to the police station where he was momentarily left with a pencil and paper to write out his statement. He calmly wrote a note begging forgiveness from his wife and family—and took a cyanide capsule he always carried on his person. He collapsed and died four days later, never having regained consciousness.

Finding an electricity bill on Lake, the police contacted the local Calaveras County sheriff, who confirmed that a young oriental man and a 'Charles Gunnar' lived at a ranch in Wisleyville. He had been keeping an eye on the pair as they were always advertising second-hand furniture and effects for sale and he thought these were possibly stolen goods.

When officers arrived at the small woodland cabin, they were horrified and sickened. Charred human bones were found in shallow graves, along with decomposing human remains. Inside the house they found bloodied women's clothing, a box containing shackles, and a collection of chains, hooks, and manacles hanging from the bedroom walls and ceiling. In an outhouse they found a blood-stained chainsaw.

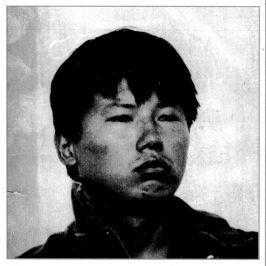

ABOVE: Charles Ng's compulsive shoplifting habit led to the arrest of the deadly duo, and signaled the end of their murderous spree.

But worse was to come. The discovery of a subterranean bunker a few days later provided more gruesome evidence of the activities of Lake and Ng. Lake had filmed and photographed their terrified victims, chained and shackled to beds or a chair, as they were tortured, raped, and sexually abused. Some movies showed the final terrifying moments of the victim's life. Ng and Lake found this 'snuff movie' trade a most lucrative addition to their already established drug-trafficking business.

In the course of fingerprint checks, it was discovered that Lake was wanted under another name for burglary in Humboldt County, where police discovered he had started another bunker. It was here they found the remains of Lake's own brother, Donald, murdered when he had come asking for a loan. The grave of Charles Gunnar was also discovered, a colleague of Lake's from the Marines, whose identity he had later taken.

Among the known victims of Lake and Ng were two babies, taken from their mothers and used to get the women to perform sickening sex acts with empty promises of their return. And all recorded by Lake for his own video library. For variety, Lake and Ng had set some victims free in the woods, only to be hunted down like animals with rifles or doused with gasoline and burned alive.

With one murderer dead, the investigation focused on tracing Ng. Again it was his bungled attempts at shoplifting that were to give him away. In July 1985, he was caught stealing in Calgary, Canada, and wounded an officer during capture. Initially, he denied any involvement in the murders, although he admitted knowledge of them. He was sentenced to four-and-a-half years for armed robbery in Canada, during which time he fought extradition to California to face the murder charges.

After a long extradition battle, Ng was finally handed over to the United States authorities and convicted of 11 murders, the victims being six men, three women, and two babies. The trial was one of the longest and most expensive in Californian history. He was sentenced to death on June 30, 1999, and is languishing on Death Row in San Quentin State Prison, where he has submitted a string of appeals in his attempt to beat the might of the American legal system.

Henri Landru

Henri Landru was born in 1869 to a poor but honest hardworking couple. They gave him the middle name Desiré, meaning much desired. And indeed, despite his small stature, Landru would in time prove to be a magnet for the opposite sex. Given the nickname 'Bluebeard', he preyed on the women of Paris during World War One while their menfolk were away fighting— and it cost at least 11 of the ladies their lives.

French 'Bluebeard' Was A Ladykiller

ABOVE: Henri Landru pleads his innocence from the witness box during his trial in November 1921.

Landru married in 1893 and had three children but he gave up his job as an architect's clerk to lead a life of petty crime. On the run from the law, he started advertising for a new wife, even though he was still married. A widow aged 39, Jeanne Cuchet answered him and was greatly impressed by 'the widower Monsieur Diard', as Landru was calling himself. In December 1914, she gave up her apartment and, with her son, moved in with 'Diard' at his rented villa outside Paris.

Mme Cuchet and her son then vanished without trace, leaving Landru in possession of 15,000 francs worth of jewels, furniture, and securities. Over the next five years, Landru entertained scores of other women, at least 10 of whom never returned home. They ranged from a 19-year-old serving girl to a 44-year-old widow pretending to be aged 29.

Alarmed relatives began contacting the local mayor seeking help in tracing their loved ones. When he put

ABOVE: Two guards stand next to the oven in which Landru burned the bodies of his many victims.

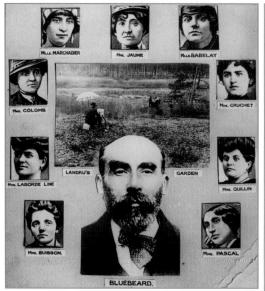

ABOVE: 'Bluebeard', the murderous womanizer and nine of the victims he killed for money.

An arrest warrant was issued and, in April 1919, Landru was spotted strolling down a Paris street arm in arm with his proposed next victim. Police searched his city lodgings and recovered a handwritten book meticulously recording the women he had met through his advertisements, together with an account of their riches. A search of his country villa revealed the cause of thick, black, oily smoke that neighbors had noticed emitting from the chimney. Almost 300 fragments of bones and teeth were recovered from the stove where Landru had burned the dismembered bodies.

Landru vehemently denied all charges, so there was

them in touch with one another, the families realized that the common factor in the disappearances was the bearded charmer, now confusingly going under the various names 'Fremyet', 'Cuchet', 'Guillet', 'Dupont', and 'Diard'.

ABOVE: The courtroom at Seine-et-Oise during Landru's trial. He was found guilty and sentenced to death in November 1921.

ABOVE: Landru burned the bodies of his victims in a stove in this house, pictured here in 1921.

never an answer to the question of how many victims he had claimed—many more than the 11 known about, it was suspected. At his trial at Seine-et-Oise court in November 1921, he was found guilty and, to hysterical scenes inside and outside the courtroom, was sentenced to die.

He faced his death, at Versailles prison in February 1922, like the gentleman he pretended to be. He refused the priest's offer of a confession, and instead wrote a note to the chief prosecutor at his trial: 'Farewell Monsieur. Our common history will doubtless die tomorrow. I will die with an innocent and quiet mind. I hope, respectfully, that you may do the same.' The next morning, after persuading the warders not to shave off his beard, Landru's shirt was ripped open and his neck laid on the guillotine. His last words were: 'I shall be brave'.

ABOVE: An artist sketches the scene of one of Landru's murders, in 1921.

Bobby Joe Long

Who knows what goes on in a brain as severely traumatized as that of Bobby Joe Long? He could not understand the forces that drove him to rape more than 50 women; neither could he control them. He was utterly disgusted with what he was doing but could not stop. And when his sexual obsession turned to murder, he knew that he just had to get himself caught.

The Serial Rapist Who Wanted To Get Caught

Robert Joe Long, born 1953 in Kenova, West Virginia, was the product of a broken home and was completely dominated by his mother, who was constantly on the move seeking new jobs and new partners. At the age of 11, he was struck by a congenital disorder which caused his glands to produce extra oestrogen, making him grow breasts. Surgeons had to remove tissue from his chest but, although the physical abnormality was largely fixed, he was mentally scarred by the experience.

At 19, Long enlisted in the Army and six months later married his childhood sweetheart, who by all accounts was as dominant as his mother. At 20, he suffered a fractured skull in a motorcycle crash that left him in a coma for weeks. When he came round, he found that the least annoyance would make him erupt in violence. It was also, he said, when his uncontrollable sexual fixations began.

He demanded sex from his wife at least twice a day and masturbated obsessively. As a result, she divorced him and left with their two children. Sex also dominated his working day. He was a hospital X-ray technician but was fired from several posts for propositioning female patients, for showing a young girl pornographic pictures, and for ordering women to undress unnecessarily.

In 1976, he began raping regularly. Operating in and around Miami, Fort Lauderdale, and Ocala, Florida, he earned the nickname 'The Classified Ad Rapist' by ringing numbers from newspaper adverts and making appointments with housewives alone during daytime. Having gained entry to their homes, he would pull a knife, tie the victim up, and rape her.

From 1983, Long began murdering the women he abducted. At first in Jacksonville and then in the Tampa Bay area, he would cruise around looking for prostitutes or pick them up in seedy bars. He would take them to his apartment, bind them with rope and neck ligatures, then strangle them, bludgeon them or cut their throats. The bodies would be dumped, displayed in crude postures. During an eight-month period, he murdered at least nine women in the Tampa Bay area alone.

Long finally allowed himself to be caught by freeing one of his last victims, a 17-year-old girl whom he pounced on in November 1984 as she cycled home from her night-shift job at a bakery. He drove around with her blindfolded in his car for 26 hours and, although he raped her, he did not kill her. 'I knew when I let her go that it would only be a matter of time,' he said later. 'I just didn't care any more. I wanted to stop. I was sick inside.'

Nevertheless, two days later he struck again, strangling his final victim and driving around with her naked body but, on this one occasion, failing to rape her. Four days later, police identified him from the evidence of the freed 17-year-old. The following year, Long was found guilty of nine murders and given 32 life sentences and one death sentence.

He stalled all of the state's efforts to send him to Florida's electric chair, however, successfully gaining two new trials in one of the killings, though he was found guilty and re-sentenced to death both times. He was still sitting on Death Row two decades after his arrest.

A clue as to what made Bobby Joe Long tick came in a prison interview he gave. Talking of a stripper who accosted him up in a bar, he said he killed her because he was revolted by her. 'She picked me up,' he said. 'I didn't go after her. She was a whore. She manipulated men and she wanted to manipulate me. Once I had her in the car, I tied her up and raped her. Then I dumped her body along the highway. Next morning I couldn't believe what I had done. I was sick. Then I met another girl…and it happened all over again.'

Pedro López

Pedro López explained his murderous ways to police thus: 'I lost my innocence at the age of eight—so I decided to do the same to as many young girls as I could.' Born to a penniless prostitute in Tolmia, Colombia, in 1949, Pedro was one of 13 children. When the eight-year-old was caught sexually molesting one of his sisters, his mother threw him out of the house.

Did 'Monster Of The Andes' Kill 300?

Left to beg and steal on the streets, López was himself molested by a man who pretended to befriend him. At 18, he was jailed for auto theft and, on his second day in jail was gang-raped by fellow inmates. He got his revenge by murdering three of them with a knife he had fashioned—a revenge that cost him another two years behind bars after he pleaded that he had acted in self defense.

By the time he was finally freed, López was a hardened criminal and a killer beyond compare in South American criminal history. He earned himself the title 'Monster of the Andes', eventually confessing almost 10,000ft (3,000m) up in the Andes, unearthed the remains of some of his victims. Days later, López was caught by townspeople while trying to abduct a 12-year-old girl from a marketplace. Under arrest, he refused to answer questions, so police used an old ploy to trick him. They placed a priest in the same cell posing as a prisoner. The ruse worked almost too well. López confessed to such revolting acts of sadistic violence that the priest asked to be removed.

Confronted with the evidence, López finally cracked. He told of his five years as the 'Monster of the Andes', relating countless abductions of young girls, whom he would rape and then strangle while staring eagerly into their eyes. He said watching their death throes gave him heightened sexual pleasure.

López confessed to killing as many as 110 girls in Ecuador, 100 in Colombia, and 'many more than 100' in Peru. His story was only fully believed when he led police to his 'killing fields'. Near Ambato, mass graves held 53 girls aged between eight and 12. Police unearthed 28 other graveyards, although in many cases they had already been disturbed by wild animals.

Lopez was given a life sentence, segregated from other prisoners at Ambato prison following threats to castrate him and burn him alive. Prison director Major Victor Lascano said: 'We may never know how many young girls Lopez killed. His estimate of 300 may even be too low.'

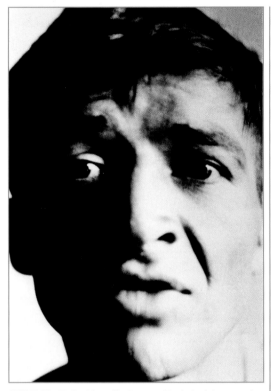

ABOVE: Vile Pedro López liked to see his victims' faces as they were murdered, so he always operated during daylight hours.

to the murder of 300 girls and, for a while, winning notoriety as the world's worst serial killer.

Roaming the impoverished countryside, his early victims were members of the native Indian tribes living on either side of the borders with neighboring Peru and Ecuador. López would stalk his young victims, sometimes for days, before approaching them with a supposed message from their mothers. López would then lead the girls to the outskirts of town where he would rape and kill them. He never worked at night because, as he later explained, he wanted to see his victim's face as she was murdered.

The hunt for a mass murderer began in earnest in April 1980 when a flash flood near Ambato, Ecuador,

ABOVE: López during police interrogation in April 1980. He eventually confessed all to a priest, who was posing as a prisoner.

Henry Lee Lucas

Was Henry Lee Lucas the worst serial killer in American history? Given the glaring inconsistencies in his various confessions, it is impossible to know. He admitted to being, among other things, a cannibal, Satanist, contract killer, and born-again Christian. He claimed more than 500 murders. He might be responsible for over 100. He was convicted of just 11. Perhaps not even Lucas himself could filter fact from fiction in his warped and addled brain.

America's Worst Serial Killer?

Lucas was born in 1936, the youngest of nine children whose home was a one-room log cabin in Blacksburg, Virginia, where his alcoholic father ran an illegal whiskey still. Lucas Sr., who had lost both legs when a freight train ran over his drunken body, was later frozen to death when his wife locked him out of the cabin in mid-winter. She also starved, abused, and brutally beat her youngest son, probably causing him brain damage. He was once in a coma for three days after she hit him with a plank. She earned her living as a prostitute and allowed young Henry to watch her satisfying her clients.

Henry later said of his mother: 'I was brought up like a dog. No human being should have been put through what I was.' In 1960, at the age of 23, he took revenge on her by stabbing her to death. It was also suggested that he may have raped her.

Lucas was committed to a mental institution but, against his own better judgment, was chosen for release on parole in 1970. 'I told them not to let me loose', he said. 'I told them I would do it again. They wouldn't listen.' He was soon back inside with a four-year sentence for kidnapping and attempted rape, his victim being a woman who had rejected his advances.

Released again in 1975, by which time he was aged 39, Lucas became a drifter, roaming the American South and taking short-term jobs. In Florida in 1976, he teamed up with Ottis Toole, a transvestite. They became friends and, according to Toole, lovers. The pair continued on the road together taking with them Toole's 12-year-old niece, Becky Powell, who was on the run from a juvenile detention center.

ABOVE: Henry Lee Lucas was a self confessed cannibal, Satanist, and contract killer—but how many did he murder?

ABOVE: A local sheriff at Stoneburg, Texas, points to the site where an 80-year-old victim of Lucas had been buried.

The unprepossessing Lucas—tattily dressed, unshaven, with straggly hair, and a glass eye—and Becky, who was slightly retarded, seem to have had a genuinely deep affection for each other. It was possibly the only such relationship he had ever enjoyed, and it ended in 1982 when Becky disappeared while the couple were drifting through Texas. By then, Toole and Lucas had split up, the former returning home to Florida and later being jailed for arson.

In October 1982, Texas Rangers were investigating the disappearance of an 80-year-old widow at Stoneburg when inquiries led to a squalid hut, dubbed by locals 'the Chicken Shack'. There, they found the dagger that had killed the old lady.

Under interrogation, Lucas confessed not only to her murder and posthumous rape but a catalog of sex-murders across the Deep South and Southwest states. He told of rapes and torture, kidnapping and mutilation, death by gunshot, knife, rope, and even crucifixion. Some were carried out by him alone, some with Ottis Toole. Among his solo victims, he said, was the feeble-minded Becky.

Detectives at first believed the confessions were a fantasy, possibly dreamed up to justify a plea of insanity. But Lucas was often able to produce irrefutable evidence. He recalled how he had scattered over the body of a 76-year-old lady he had bludgeoned to death—information that had never been released to the media. Police also obtained verification of many of the crimes from Toole, who consequently had a death sentence added to the 20 years he was serving for arson.

ABOVE: Lucas is led by Texas Rangers to the site of one of the many unsolved murders they hoped he would confess to.

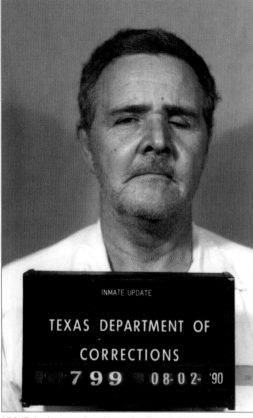

ABOVE: A prison mugshot of Lucas in a Texas jail. While incarcerated his own estimate of his murder tally rose to 600.

Some of these confessions he later retracted. But in many cases, his claims enabled the bodies of missing persons to be recovered, most having been raped, sometimes after death.

Lucas needed to be locked up for life. His 1983 trial for the murder of the Texas widow—during which he shocked the judge by telling him he should take into account 'another 100' murders—resulted in a 75-year sentence. Then came his trial for murdering Becky, during which he sobbed in court and told the jury that he loved her and didn't want her dead.

His case wasn't helped by a videotaped confession in which he said: 'I had sex with her. It's one of those things that I guess got to be part of my life, having sexual intercourse with the dead.' A sentence of life imprisonment resulted, after which a smiling Lucas shook hands with the prosecutor and said: 'You did a good job.'

In prison, Lucas continued recalling murders he had supposedly committed all over the country. A list of female victims from 19 different states produced a spate of requests from other forces for samples of hair and saliva. But over the months, the information he gave became increasingly bizarre. Lucas's own estimate of his victims eventually grew to about 600. In 1983, frustrated representatives of law enforcement agencies from 19 states gathered in Louisiana to exchange information on Lucas and Toole. They concluded that there were links between the pair and 81 murders, and many of those cases were thereby closed.

Convicted of only 11 of his indeterminate number of murders, with a further 20 murder charges pending, Lucas languished on Death Row in Texas. In June 1999, as a fresh execution date neared, doubts arose about his guilt in the case of one his unidentified victims, and Texas governor George Bush Jr. stepped in to commute his death sentence to one of life imprisonment. Lucas died of natural causes in March 2001.

Toole, who died in prison of cirrhosis of the liver in 1996, told Florida investigators: 'We picked up lots of hitch-hikers. Lucas killed most of the women himself. Some of them would be shot in the head and the chest, and some of them would be choked to death, and some of them would be beaten in the head.'

Meanwhile, in Texas, Lucas's official murder confessions rose to 360, although he hinted that he had committed 500 or more—which would have made him the worst serial killer in American history.

Michael Lupo

Michael Lupo was an outrageous homosexual who claimed to have had 4,000 lovers. He indulged in sadomasochistic activities of the weirdest kind, including slitting the scrotum of his partners so that he could massage their testicles. And when he began killing some of those gay partners, he gained the nickname 'Wolf Man of London'.

Crazed 'Wolf Man Of London'

Before arriving in Britain in 1975 at the age of 22, the ex-choirboy had served in an elite Italian commando unit. He got a job as a hairdresser in London, and worked his way up to owning a fashion and make-up store, which he grandly called a 'styling boutique'. His clients were said to include some of London's High Society names, with gay lifestyles they were eager to keep secret.

Lupo bought himself a house, one room of which he kitted out as a torture chamber. But his kinky promiscuity was to cost him his life, and that of four others. For after he was diagnosed with AIDS, he began a bloody rampage, slaughtering four men whom he picked up in bars—his weird 'calling card' being to slash their naked bodies and smear them with excrement.

Police inquiries began in March 1986 when the body of a 37-year-old man was found in a derelict apartment in Kensington, London. The investigation made no progress because there was no connection between victim and perpetrator. But Lupo was already a killer. He was responsible for the murder of a young hospital worker, found strangled in West London, and an unidentified man who was killed beside the River Thames, near Hungerford Bridge. And Scotland Yard subsequently passed their case file to forces in Germany and the United States because of similar mutilation murders in Berlin, Hamburg, Los Angeles, and New York at times coinciding with Lupo's travels.

In April 1986, a 24-year-old man was found strangled to death with his own scarf on a railroad embankment in Brixton. It was the discovery of this final victim that convinced police a serial killer was at large.

His existence sent terror through the capital's gay glitterati.

Lupo was arrested on May 20 after two terrified men who had managed to escape his orgiastic clutches went to police with their stories. In July, under his full name Michele de Marco Lupo, he was found guilty at the Old Bailey of four murders and two attempted murders and was sentenced to life in prison, where he died from an AIDS related illness in February 1995.

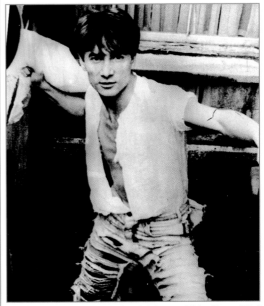

ABOVE: Ex-choirboy and full-time hairdresser, Michael Lupo, killed four gay lovers in London in the 1980s.

Charles Manson

By the age of 32, Charles Manson was so institutionalized, having spent most of his life in prison, that he pleaded to stay in jail. If only the authorities had granted his wish. Two years later he had gathered a cult of impressionable devotees who were willing to kill to stay in his evil sect, which they referred to as 'The Family'.

Bloody Massacre By Manson And His 'Angels Of Death'

Manson was born in Cincinnati in 1934 to Kathleen Maddox, a 16-year-old prostitute. The name on his birth certificate was No Name Maddox. He never knew who his father was and grew up in an environment of violence and drugs, spending long periods of his adolescence in juvenile institutions. At one detention center, Manson held a blade to a fellow inmate's throat as he violently raped him.

Although mainly homosexual during his teens, Manson married Rosalie Jean Willis, a 17-year-old waitress, in 1954. She was pregnant when he was next sentenced to three years in prison for auto theft. She visited him regularly at the start, bringing Charles Manson Jr. with her, but eventually met someone else and the visits stopped. Manson was never to see his son again. He remarried between jail sentences and had another son, also named Charles Manson Jr., but that marriage also failed.

In 1967 Manson found himself in San Francisco in the heyday of 'flower power' and drug-taking. He had a magnetism that seemed to attract drop-outs and middle-class young women alike. He formed a sect and settled in California's Santa Susana mountains, at Spahn Ranch, a one-time movie set.

Manson was convinced that an uprising between American blacks and whites was coming. He heard messages in the lyrics of Beatles tracks. He prophesied that only his disciples and the 'Chosen Blacks' would survive the mass slaughter and go on to take over the world. His followers, he believed, must rise up and strike out at the white establishment.

BELOW: In his warped mind, Manson foresaw a mass uprising of American blacks and whites which his 'Family' would survive.

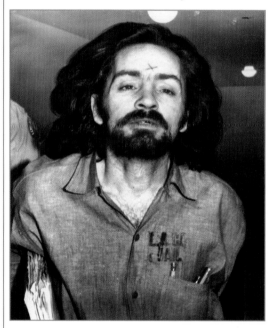

He called his devastating plan 'Helter Skelter' and on the night of August 9, 1969, sent four of his disciples— Susan Atkins, Patricia Krenwinkel, Linda Kasabian, and Charles Watson—to 10050 Cielo Drive, Benedict Canyon, Los Angeles, to begin the horrific slaughter. Movie producer, Roman Polanski and his pregnant wife, Sharon Tate, were renting the property. Polanski was away filming but Sharon and friends were partying at the house when the self-styled 'Angels of Death' broke in.

ABOVE: Polish film director Roman Polanski and American actress Sharon Tate at their wedding in 1968.

Displeased with the previous night's messy events at the Tate residence, Manson led the next 'Helter Skelter' mission on August 10. The four Tate murderers were again summoned, along with Steve Grogan and Leslie Van Houten, a former college queen and youngest member of the cult. They cruised the better neighborhoods of Los Angeles in search of potential victims before settling on the home of Leno and Rosemary LaBianca, who owned a small chain of supermarkets. Manson burst into their Waverly Drive mansion, tied them up and left them to the mercy of three of his cult slaves, Watson, Krenwinkel, and Van Houten.

The LaBiancas were subjected to horrific injuries, inflicted with a sword, knives, and forks. 'War' was carved on Leno's stomach and a fork was protruding from his body. He had been stabbed 26 times and, with a blood-soaked pillowcase acting as a hood, symbolically hung. Rosemary also had multiple stab wounds in her back and buttocks, was inscribed with 'War', hooded, and hung. The walls were covered with slogans written in their blood. They had misspelled 'Healter Skelter' on the fridge.

They showed no mercy in their frenzied attack. Watson is said to have chanted 'I am the devil come to do the devil's work' as he battered Voytek Frykowski, a Polish movie director, who was then stabbed by Atkins. Jay Sebring a hairdresser, was stabbed and shot.

The most shocking murder was that of heavily pregnant Sharon Tate and her unborn son, who was stabbed 16 times. They tied a nylon rope around her neck, looped it over a ceiling beam and tied the other end around the hooded head of Sebring. Eighteen-year-old Steven Parent, a friend of the Polanskis' caretaker, was shot as he drove from the house. Abigail Folger, a coffee heiress, was slashed to pieces trying to escape the massacre. 'Pigs' was written in blood on the door of the mansion.

There is a theory that Manson's gang had killed the wrong people. The house in Cielo Drive had once been rented by record company boss Terry Melcher, Doris Day's son. He had apparently shunned Manson's attempts at breaking into the recording business. However, it is also believed that Frykowski and Sebring were drug dealers, whose business Manson coveted.

ABOVE: Manson shadowed by police officers in 1970. The spell he managed to cast over his followers was incredible.

LA5)LOS ANGELES, Dec.2--CULT
LEADER?--Charles Manson, above,
34, was described today by the
Los Angeles Times and attorney
Richard Caballero as the leader of a quasireligious cult of
hippies, three of whom have
been arrested on murder warrants
issued in the slayings of actress Sharon Tate and four others

ABOVE: A police mugshot of a crazed-looking Manson after his arrest in 1969.

Los Angeles police did not initially connect the two raids, and it was only the arrest of Susan Atkins in another investigation that brought the evil cult to justice. She was picked up in connection with the slaying of drug dealer Gary Hinman at his Topanga Canyon home 10 days before the mass murders. Atkins could not help boasting about her role in the Tate raid, describing her feelings of sexual satisfaction when stabbing the actress and hearing her scream for mercy. She even claimed she drank Tate's blood.

The police arrested the Manson 'Family' and, after a sensational trial that lasted 38 weeks, on March 29, 1971, they were all found guilty and sentenced to be executed—commuted to life imprisonment the following year when California quashed the death penalty.

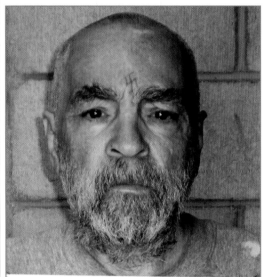

CALIFORNIA STATE PRISON
MANSON, C
B-33920
3/18/09

ABOVE: Manson, as he appears today, the swastika tattoo on his forehead a reminder of his sickening past.

Leslie Van Houten succeeded in gaining two retrials in the late 1960s because her lawyer had disappeared during her initial trial. His remains were found later in the mountains, and members of the Manson cult were suspected of his murder. Van Houten failed to win her freedom and was again sentenced to life imprisonment.

America relived the horrific deaths in 1994, when a 'Free Susan Atkins Campaign' was launched. Her supporters felt she was now rehabilitated. However, after hearing evidence from Sharon Tate's sister, Patti, who was only 11 at the time of the murders, her appeal was refused. Patti told of her mother's distress each time a member of the murdering gang applied for parole and of the indifference of the gang as they left behind the sickening murder scene at Cielo Drive and moved on to the massacre at the LaBianca home. Atkins remained in custody, as does Manson, who admits he will kill again if he ever gets his freedom.

ABOVE: Manson during his trial in 1970. He was vowed to kill again if he is ever released from prison.

Peter Manuel

Peter Manuel turned to crime at an early age. When only 11, he was caught breaking into stores. At 15, he attacked a woman with a hammer. As a consequence, he spent a large part of his teen years in an approved school and in Borstal—all of which helped make him a hardened villain ready to turn to violence to obtain either money or sexual satisfaction.

Families Shot Dead By Gun-Toting Burglar

On his release from Borstal in 1946, the 19-year-old Manuel moved to Glasgow, where his Scots-born parents had settled after their Coventry home was destroyed in a German bombing raid. Within weeks, he was arrested for housebreaking and, while awaiting trial, he raped an expectant mother and indecently assaulted two other women. He was sentenced to eight years in jail and was released in 1953.

Three years later, Manuel graduated to murder.

His first victim was 17-year-old Annie Knielands, whom he killed in January 1956, and whose body he left on the fifth fairway of a golf course at East Kilbride, near Glasgow. Manuel was questioned and released for lack of evidence. In September 1956, while free on bail over a burglary charge, he broke into a house in Burnside, Glasgow, and shot dead housewife Marion Watt, her sister Margaret, and Marion's 16-year-old daughter Vivienne. Again Manuel was arrested, quizzed and, although he was given 18 months' jail for the earlier burglary, there was insufficient evidence to pin the murders on him.

On his release, Manuel visited Newcastle Upon Tyne for a job interview in early December 1957, where he shot and killed taxi driver Sydney Dunn. Back in

charged with the murder of the Smarts. His father was charged with receiving stolen goods from various burglaries, which, in an attempt to shield his son, he claimed to have bought at a market. Showing remorse for the first time, Manuel offered a full confession in return for his father's release. He led police to the spot where he had thrown two guns into a river and showed them where he had buried Isabelle Cooke.

At his trial, which began in May 1958, Manuel was found guilty of seven murders—although Glasgow police believe he may have killed up to 15 people. The judge commented that 'a man may be very bad without being mad' before sentencing him to death. On July 11, 1958, Peter Manuel was allowed to hear Mass and take Holy Communion before making his final, short walk to the gallows at Glasgow's Barlinnie Jail.

ABOVE: Scottish mass-murderer Peter Manuel smiling during his trial in Glasgow on May 29, 1958.

Glasgow, he struck again on December 27. Isabelle Cooke, aged 17, left her home in Mount Vernon to go to a dance but never returned. Even as police searched for her, three bodies were found in a house just 10 minutes' walk away from Manuel's home. Peter Smart, his wife Doris, and their 11-year-old son Michael had all been shot through the head at close range.

Peter Manuel was arrested on January 14, 1958, and

ABOVE: Manuel is led away by police following his arrest for murder on January 17, 1958.

Robert Maudsley

Robert Maudsley may not be Britain's most prolific serial killer but the jailbird is certainly judged the most dangerous. He committed 'only' four murders—three of them while in prison on a life sentence for the first. His most sickening claim to infamy was taunting jail warders by eating the brains of one of his victims.

Cannibal Killer Ate Prisoner's Brains

Robert **John Maudsley** was born in Liverpool in 1953, one of 12 children of a violent father. He spent his early years in an orphanage run by nuns. As a teenager, he moved to London and became a rent boy to pay for his drug addiction. In 1974, he attacked a laborer who had picked him up for sex, stabbing him, smashing him over the head with a hammer, and garrotting him. He explained that he had become angry when the man showed him pictures of children he had sexually abused.

Maudsley was given a life sentence and sent to Broadmoor hospital for the criminally insane. There, in February 1977, he and another prisoner, David Cheeseman, dragged convicted pedophile David Francis into a room on their ward, barricaded the door, tied him up with flex from a record player and held him hostage. For 10 hours, staff listened to his screams as he was tortured. Eventually the pair came out, holding the garrotted corpse above their heads as a trophy.

Following this Maudsley was sent to Wakefield Prison, in Yorkshire, where, despite the high security, Prisoner 467637's killing spree continued. In July 1978, Maudsley fashioned a knife from a soup spoon and waited for sex offender Salney Darwood to enter his cell. Maudsley plunged the knife into his back and head, then expertly garrotted him. He stuffed the body under a bunk and went in search of another victim.

Next to die was William Roberts, who was lying face down on his bunk. Maudsley stabbed him then smashed his head against the wall. He is then said to have used his homemade knife to prise open the skull 'like a boiled egg' to scoop out the brains. Afterward, Maudsley strode up to the officer in charge and said: 'There'll be two short on the roll call.'

The incident earned Maudsley the media nickname 'Hannibal the Cannibal', although his fellow inmates referred to him simply as 'Spoons'. Deemed too dangerous for a normal cell, he was placed in solitary confinement in a purpose-built Perspex cage with cardboard furniture and concrete bed beneath Wakefield Prison's F-Wing. Over the next quarter century, he allowed his hair to grow long and his fingernails to 'look more like a vulture's talons', according to one newspaper report.

Maudsley, who enjoys poetry, classical music, and art and has a genius-level IQ, once described life in his 10ft (3m) square cell as 'like being buried alive in a coffin'. He wrote: 'I am left to stagnate; vegetate; and to regress; left to confront my solitary head-on, with people who have eyes but don't see, ears but don't hear, mouths but don't speak; consequently I too am left with no voice, nowhere to turn to but inward.'

Ivan Milat

In September 1992, ramblers in the Belanglo State Forest, New South Wales, Australia, discovered a corpse. The following day, police discovered a second body nearby. The corpses were those of two British girls, 21-year-old Caroline Clarke and 22-year-old Joanne Walters, who had been missing since hitch-hiking from Sydney.

Hitch-Hikers Executed By The 'Backpack Killer'

Caroline had been stabbed and shot in the head several times, the angle of the bullets' entry suggesting to forensic scientists that the killer had used her for target practice. Joanne had been stabbed in the heart and lungs, one cut penetrating her spine and probably paralyzing her before the wounds that finally killed her.

The discoveries sparked a hunt for one of Australia's most notorious and evil serial killers: Ivan Robert Marko Milat. Born in 1945, one of 14 children of a Croat immigrant, he became known as the 'Backpack Killer' because of the way he targeted young hikers. Belanglo State Forest seemed to be his favorite 'killing field'.

Other corpses began turning up in the forest. In October 1993, a walker discovered the remains of James Gibson, and his girlfriend Deborah Everist, both 19 and from Victoria, who had disappeared while hitch-hiking in December 1989. Forensics later confirmed that James had suffered the killer's 'trademark' knife wound through the spine, paralyzing him before he was killed.

The same fate had been suffered by Simone Schmidl, 21, whose body was found the following month. The German girl, missing since January 1991, had been sexually assaulted. Clothing found at the scene was not Schmidl's, however, but matched that of another missing backpacker, 20-year-old Anja Habschied. What was left of Anja and 21-year-old boyfriend Gabor Neugebauer was discovered a few days later. Her head was missing, together with two of her vertebrae. She had been decapitated with a sword while alive and in a kneeling position, Gabor had been gagged and strangled. His skull showed six bullet entries.

It was now clear that a ritualistic serial killer was on the prowl. Police received hundreds of calls from worried parents around the world who wanted assurance that their backpacking children were safe. But news of the killing spree also brought the first clue as to the identity of the perpetrator.

ABOVE: The house of the 'Backpack Killer', Ivan Milat, raided by Australian police in 1994.

ABOVE: The scene outside Campbelltown Local Court in May 1994 as Ivan Milat is charged in relation to the Paul Onions case.

British student Paul Onions, 20, had been picked up by a driver in southern New South Wales in January 1990. The man acted so peculiarly that Paul fled and, with his pursuer chasing him gun in hand, Paul flagged down another passing vehicle and escaped. He reported the attack but was told by police that, without the license plate number, there was little chance of tracing the gunman.

Tragically for other, less lucky victims, that proved to be the case. But when Paul Onions repeated his story four years later, police had a description of the 'Backpack Killer'. And when Ivan Milat was subsequently fingered as the prime suspect, Paul was shown a photograph of Milat and was able to identify him straight away.

The final breakthrough came when a woman called to say that her boyfriend worked at a ready-mixed concrete company with a man called Ivan Milat who lived near the forest and was a gun fanatic. Detectives established that Milat had been absent from work on the probable dates of murders, and they pounced on him at his home in Eaglevale while he lay in bed with his girlfriend.

Milat vehemently denied knowledge of the slayings but a search of his house produced items of property belonging to his victims, along with cartridges that matched those found near the backpackers' bodies.

Charged with the seven murders, Milat was finally found guilty on all counts and, in June 1995, was sentenced to life imprisonment. He was taken to a high security jail in Maitland, southwest of Sydney, bragging that he would one day escape. He made one failed escape attempt in July 1995.

Six years later, a closely-guarded Milat was brought from prison to appear at a reopened inquest into the deaths of three girls who had disappeared in 1978 and 1979 in similar circumstances to those surrounding Milat's other victims. The killer refused to cooperate, and the deaths of the girls, aged 20, 17, and 14, remained unattributed. However, Milat is still suspected of being responsible for many other murders.

Over the years, Milat continued to raise appeals against his conviction. Several times, he injured himself in prison, swallowing razor blades, staples, and other metal objects. In January 2009, he cut off his little finger with a plastic knife, planning to mail it to the High Court.

ABOVE: The prison van used to transport Milat to court to face various charges in May 1994.

Herman Mudgett

Herman Webster Mudgett arrived in Chicago in 1886 with two wives, no money, a fake university degree, and a mission: to get very rich very quickly. He had charm, style, wit, and a way about him that women found irresistible—more often than not, to their cost. Mudgett realized that, in this booming, anything-goes, crime-ridden city preparing to host the World's Fair, he had found the ideal environment in which to carry out his nefarious projects. In so doing, he became America's first identified serial killer.

Secret Gas Chambers In Torturer's Castle

Born in 1860 into a prominent family in Gilmanton, New Hampshire, mustachioed Mudgett was intelligent, handsome, and charming. Kicked out of medical school for stealing cadavers, with which he planned to defraud insurance companies, his knowledge of medicine nevertheless enabled him to pass himself off as a qualified physician, 'Dr Henry Howard Holmes', once he had settled in Chicago.

His first job in that city had been more modest. He took a job as a prescription clerk at a drug store in the Englewood district. After a few months, his employer, a widow, and her young daughter disappeared, Mudgett telling any curious customers that they had moved to California after selling him the store. In fact, Mudgett had killed them.

From his newly acquired base, Mudgett launched a series of dodgy ventures. He bottled tap water as an all-purpose 'miracle cure'. He sold a 'sure-fire cure for alcoholism' at $50 a bottle. And he claimed to have invented a device for turning water into domestic gas that won him a research contract from a utility company. As the money rolled in, he purchased a large plot of land across the road at 701 and 703 Sixty-third Street. It was to be the site of what later became known infamously as Holmes Castle, a three-storey labyrinthine edifice of 100 rooms, with secret passageways, false walls, and mysterious trap-doors.

Mudgett completed his mansion in 1888, when he was aged just 28. Over the years, he lured scores of young women to Holmes Castle with the promise of

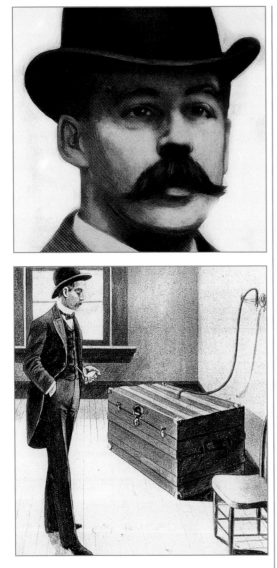

non-existent jobs. There, he would murder his visitors by leaving them in one of the several rooms that were sealed and fed by mysterious pipes. These were his gas chambers. He would then dispose of the bodies in one of two ways—either in his 6ft (2m) wide stove or in barrels of acid.

Mudgett got away with mass murder until September 1894 when he killed a small-time Philadelphia criminal to claim life insurance. A sharp-eyed insurance investigator cast doubt on the claim, and detectives visited the address to where the money was to have been sent: Holmes Castle. What they discovered there is related in a report of the time which describes ordinary bedrooms used for

ABOVE: A contemporary print of a detective looking at a trunk fed by a gas pipe—the 'execution chamber' of some of Mudgett's victims.

ABOVE: An ink sketch published at the time of his arrest showing how the 'Torture Castle' killer disposed of his younger victims.

seduction, alongside windowless rooms fed by gas pipes. More horrifically, police believed that in one asbestos-lined chamber he had devised a means of introducing fire, so that the gas pipe became a blow-torch. The basement contained a medieval-style torture rack—and several women's skeletons from which the flesh had been carefully stripped.

Mudgett went on the run but was traced to Boston, where he was arrested in November 1894 planning to flee the country. He was put on trial in Philadelphia for the murder of the petty criminal, although by then it was known that he had also killed the man's three children. After his conviction but while awaiting

sentence, he sold his story for $7,500 to Hearst newspapers, in which he confessed to 27 murders in Chicago, Indianapolis, and Toronto.

Although estimates of the number of his victims range up to 200, the true count will never be known. Herman Mudgett was hanged at Philadelphia's Moyamensing Prison on May 7, 1896. He took almost 15 minutes to die.

Dennis Nilsen

Dennis Nilsen was a prolific serial killer, preying on men throughout London in the 1970s and 80s. Insisting he had no control of his actions, he claimed to be in a trance throughout and would 'wake up' to find a dead man in his home. While he argued that his murders were the fault of a personality disorder, the sheer ruthlessness of his killings and disposal of the bodies demonstrated a deadly instinct. Nilsen's own efforts to end his rampage would prove to be his downfall.

Killer Boiled Human Head In A Cookpot

Nilsen killed for the first time in 1978. He picked up a stranger in a pub and they slept together. As dawn broke he realized that he could not bear this newfound bedfellow to leave. He used a tie to strangle the sleeping man, then finished him off by plunging his head into a bucket of water.

Nilsen was at first shocked by his own barbarity but he soon overcame any qualms. His compulsion to kill led to bodies being stored beneath the floorboards of his apartment at Melrose Avenue, Willesden. One nameless victim was so physically appealing to Nilsen that it was a week before the body was put underneath the floor. The killer kept him in the room, returning from work to 'chat' with him and have sex with the corpse.

ABOVE: Dennis Nilsen developed a fascination with corpses, aged five, following the death of his grandfather.

ABOVE: Nilsen at Highgate Magistrates Court, London, during his trial for murder.

including the boiled head, were put into black plastic bags. Nilsen had no time to dispose of them, however, because neighbors had decided to resolve the plumbing problems by calling in industrial drain clearers.

When an engineer removed a manhole cover, he found decomposing matter was still evident. Police were called and a forensic scientist confirmed that it was human flesh.

When Nilsen returned home from work on February 9, 1983, detectives were waiting for him. He confessed, showing them the bags containing body parts stored in his wardrobe. He went on to relate a macabre series of murderous crimes committed by one of the most unlikely looking villains ever.

For Nilsen just did not look the part of a serial killer. He seemed just too 'ordinary'. Yet it transpired that his fascination with human corpses had been spawned in him when he was very young…

ABOVE: Nilsen's apartment in Melrose Avenue. Victims were murdered and their bodies stored under floorboards.

Another of his many victims had the misfortune to suffer an epileptic fit outside Nilsen's home. Nilsen tended him and, when the man returned the next day to thank him, he was murdered. Nilsen eventually disposed of his stash of corpses by chopping them up and burning them in backyard bonfires.

When Nilsen moved to an apartment at Cranley Gardens, Muswell Hill, he no longer had access to a garden, so he was forced to dissect corpses more fully, flushing the skin and bone down the toilet. Eventually the plumbing failed and kindly neighbors posted warning signs on his door. Nilsen knew he had to work fast—for if plumbers entered his apartment, they might find the malodorous body of a 20-year-old man killed the previous week and hidden in his wardrobe.

Nilsen laid plastic sheets across the floor of his front room and, with a kitchen knife, dismembered the body and severed the head, placing it in a large cooking pot simmering on the stove. The body parts,

Dennis Andrew Nilsen was born in November 1945 in Fraserburgh, Scotland, the second son of Olav Nilsen, a Norwegian serviceman. Dennis grew up without his father but received enough love and attention from his grandfather, Andrew Whyte, with whom he and his mother lived. When the old man died of a heart attack at the age of 62, he was laid out at home. And it was noted then that little Dennis, just five years old, was fascinated by the corpse. He later admitted that the powerful image of death loomed large in his mind for years.

Aged 16, Nilsen enlisted in the Army, serving as a butcher in the Catering Corps, learning the skills that served him so well during his five-year killing spree. On leaving the Army in 1972, he took up police training but resigned and went on to become a recruitment interviewer. In 1975, he moved into the Melrose Road apartment with another man, although the latter denied

ABOVE: The lack of outside space at Nilsen's apartment in Cranley Gardens led him to flush his victims' remains down the toilet.

ABOVE: Nilsen during his spell in the Army in the 1960s. He worked as a butcher in the Catering Corps.

it was a homosexual relationship. Their friendship lasted two years but when the man left, Nilsen's life began a downward spiral into alcohol and loneliness that culminated in the first murder 18 months later. Nilsen resolved that nobody would walk out on him again—and, for many visitors, that really did mean 'never'.

One visitor who did live to tell the tale was a male model who, during the wave of publicity following Nilsen's arrest in February 1983, told police that he had narrowly escaped death at the hands of the mass killer after meeting Nilsen in a bar and returning with him to his apartment in Cranley Gardens. The model had later awoken gasping for breath, with a swollen tongue and burn marks around his neck. Nilsen had not only tried to strangle him but had also thrust his head into a bucket of water. The would-be victim sought hospital treatment but did not go to the police.

In court, Nilsen's defense counsel tried to persuade

the jury that the killer was mad. Thanks in part to the male model's evidence, the panel at the Old Bailey did not believe it. He was found guilty of six murders and two attempted murders. The full tally was reckoned to be at least 15. On November 4, 1983, still showing not a shred of remorse, Dennis Nilsen was jailed for life.

RIGHT: Nilsen during a police interview. He was found guilty of six murders and two attempted murders and jailed for life.

Paul Ogorzow

In 1940, as German tanks rolled across Europe, a few more acts of savagery would hardly be an issue for the Nazi hierarchy—or so one would have thought. But a few seemingly isolated events in the German capital gave more concern to the authorities than their actual numbers might have otherwise warranted.

Hushed-Up Shame Of Nazi Era Cops

Over the summer months, three women had been stabbed and two others assaulted in the eastern districts of Berlin. Now, as winter approached, women's bodies began turning up. In October, a 20-year-old mother of two was stabbed in the neck and strangled. A month later, a 30-year-old was thrown unconscious from a moving train but survived. In December, a 26-year-old nurse was beaten to death and thrown from a train. On the same day, and only 550 yards (500m) away, a 19-year-old girl had her skull smashed and was raped.

Just before Christmas, a 30-year-old woman was found with a fractured skull. The next victim, a 46-year-old with similar injuries, was found a week later. Another body, of a woman aged 28, turned up in January 1941. Police believed all or most of the victims had been attacked on a train or near a rail track.

The attacker, now labeled 'the S-Bahn (City Railroad) Murderer', brought terror to the capital. While the world recoiled at the mounting death toll of World War Two, Berliners concentrated on the slaughter of innocents closer to home. Not that they had much information to go on...

The Nazi propaganda machine, under Joseph Goebbels, wanted only 'good' news, so the murders were only publicized in brief detail for fear of causing public panic. Other factors hampered Berlin's serious crime force, the Kriminalpolizei, in their hunt for the serial killer. A blackout was being enforced in the city and this had proved a dream for criminals and a nightmare for the police. The blackout also caused numerous travel accidents, with an average of one fatality every day on the railroad system. It was initially difficult to distinguish between an accident and a homicide.

The result of these drawbacks was that there were two more victims. The body of a 39-year-old woman was found in February beside the railroad line, evidently having been thrown from a train, and in early July, the body of a woman of 35 was discovered with similar injuries on waste ground.

Despite the problems caused by wartime restrictions,

the Kriminalpolizei had been tardy in identifying the killer. All evidence had pointed to a railroad employee, yet it took several preventable deaths before detectives finally arrested an S-Bahn signalman, Paul Ogorzow, 28, who lived with his wife and two children close to where four of his victims were found.

Shamefully, the police realized that they had already questioned their suspect after a tip-off but had let him go, and on another occasion when challenged by Kriminalpolizei officers, he had simply fled into the night. The tip-off had come from the killer's railroad colleagues, who had long suspected him because of his loudly voiced hatred of women and his habit of vanishing for long spells while on duty.

Ogorzow was charged with eight murders, six cases of attempted murder, and a further 31 cases of assault. In court, he declared himself a family man, loyal Nazi Party member, and an active street fighter with the SA. But the judge agreed he was 'a killer of a completely cold and calculating nature, with depraved sexual urges'. He was executed by guillotine in Plötzensee Prison.

Anatoly Onoprienko

When police seized Anatoly Onoprienko, otherwise known as 'The Terminator', they locked up the worst serial killer the Ukraine had ever known. Onoprienko, a 37-year-old former forestry student, sailor, and mental hospital outpatient, was arrested in April 1996 at his girlfriend's apartment, where police found a shotgun matching the one used in no fewer than 40 murders. The total number of his victims was 52.

Bloody Trail Of 'The Terminator'

Onoprienko **eventually confessed** to all 52 murders in a six-year killing spree, in which he claimed he was commanded by 'inner voices'. Onoprienko's rampage began in June 1989, when he and accomplice Serhiy Rogozin robbed and killed nine people. They first blasted a couple to death in their car, then wiped out a family of five, including an 11-year-old girl.

Onoprienko spent six years traveling around Eastern Europe, where police believe he may have been responsible for other murders. Onoprienko resumed the known killings in late 1995, and they followed a set pattern. He would choose an isolated house, storm in at dawn, round up the family and shoot them all, including the children, at close range with a 12-gauge shotgun. Any witnesses would also be dispatched.

ABOVE: Anatoly Onoprienko, aka The Terminator, is Ukraine's worst ever serial killer, with a body count of 52.

He would hack off fingers to get at wedding rings and even pull out his victims' gold teeth. He would then loot the house before setting it on fire.

In November 1995, after stealing a shotgun, he began a killing spree that at one stage went into manic overdrive—in just one 20-week bloodbath, he killed and mutilated 43 people in the Lvov region, near the border of Poland. Victims ranged from a 70-year-old pensioner to a three-month-old baby. Panic was so widespread in two villages, Bratkovichi and Busk, that the army was sent in, personnel carriers patrolled the streets and police imposed a security cordon.

A manhunt involving 2,000 police and more than 3,000 troops failed to find 'The Terminator'. In the end, a tip-off about an unlicensed gun led detectives, on April 14, 1996, to an apartment in the garrison town of Yavoriv. Onoprienko was sleeping beside his girlfriend—to whom he had once proposed with a ring he had chopped from the finger of one of his victims only a few hours earlier. Ordered out of bed, Onoprienko furtively withdrew a gun from a cupboard, but handcuffs were clapped on him before he could pull the trigger.

In February 1999, a court in the city of Zhytomyr, 90 miles (140km) west of Kiev, ruled that Onoprienko was mentally competent to answer charges. The 39-year-old killer sat impassively in a metal cage as a woman screamed from the back of the court: 'Let us tear him apart. He should die a slow and agonizing death.' The judge commented: 'He doesn't care about anything—only about himself. He is driven by extreme cruelty.' Onoprienko was sentenced to death, later commuted

ABOVE: During a prison interview, Onoprienko claimed: 'I have never felt sorry for those I killed. No love, no hatred, just blind indifference.'

to life in prison.

Explaining his murderous drive, Onoprienko said in a prison interview: 'To me killing people is like ripping up a duvet. Women, old people, children, they are all the same. I have never felt sorry for those I killed. No love, no hatred, just blind indifference.'

William Palmer

Deep in debt and gambling wildly, Dr William Palmer cheered up somewhat when the friend he was accompanying to the races won more than £2,000—a small fortune in 1855. Palmer, aged 31, watched as the lucky winner, 28-year-old John Parsons Cooke, drained a celebratory brandy and gasped: 'Good God, there's something in it—it burns my throat.' Palmer himself nonchalantly knocked back the few remaining drops in the bottom of the glass. In front of a witness he declared: 'Nonsense, there is nothing in it.'

How Dr Palmer The Poisoner Gambled And Lost

In pain, Cooke left the racecourse at Shrewsbury, Shropshire, and traveled the 40 miles (64km) to the doctor's home town of Rugeley, Staffordshire, where he stayed at an inn, which Palmer's visited regularly to treat his patient. Strangely, the medicine and broths prescribed only seemed to make Cooke worse.

ABOVE: Dr William Palmer on the stand during his trial at the Central Criminal Court in London, in May 1856.

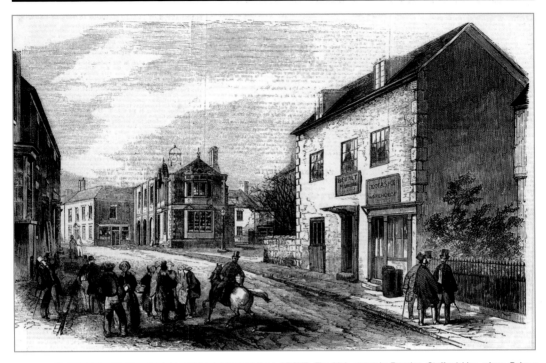

ABOVE: The high street in Rugeley, Staffordshire, where Palmer murdered his 'friend' John Parsons Cooke.

Only when the bookmakers had paid out Cooke's winnings, swiftly pocketed by Palmer, did the doctor finish him off. After suffering convulsions for several days, Cooke went rigid in spasms and finally suffocated—the symptoms of strychnine poisoning.

Cooke, it transpired, was far from being Palmer's first victim in a medical career that was disgracefully blighted. By the time he was 17, he had already been dismissed from two pharmacy apprenticeships, once for taking cash and the second time for running an illegal abortion service. He finally qualified as a doctor in London in 1846 and the following year married Anne Brookes, the heiress daughter of a wealthy widow.

LEFT: A period sketch of Dr Palmer at the horse races. He was known as the 'Prince of Poisoners'.

Palmer paid little heed to his family or to his doctor's practice, instead spending his days at racecourses. As his debts mounted, however, a string of deaths occurred in his family. First, Palmer's rich mother-in-law died, followed by his wife, who had been heavily insured. Palmer's brother, four children, an uncle, and several more of his creditors met similar ends.

Palmer became both greedy and impatient. And it was his blatant poisoning of his friend Cooke in 1855 that ended his one-man crime wave. Arrested and brought to trial at London's Old Bailey, he heard medical evidence that only strychnine poisoning could have produced such symptoms—and that the day before his friend's death, the doctor had bought a bottle of strychnine from a local chemist.

The jury was out for only 100 minutes before returning a guilty verdict and Palmer was sentenced to be hanged at Stafford Prison. Interviewed there by the governor, the condemned man replied: 'I have nothing more to say than this—that I am quite easy in my conscience and happy in my mind.' To the very end, he refused to confess. He insisted he had been unjustly convicted of murder by strychnine—though lawyers believed this was his way of hinting that he had killed his friend by some other means. Indeed, his last remark made to the priest who visited him before his execution was: 'Cooke did not die from strychninia.'

Such was the sensational nature of the case that an estimated 25,000 people flocked to Stafford by road, rail, on horseback, and on foot to cheer the evil doctor's hanging at eight o'clock on the morning of June 14, 1856.

Carl Panzram

Carl Panzram wrote from his cell on Death Row in Leavenworth Prison, Kansas, in 1929: 'In my lifetime, I have murdered 21 human beings. I have committed thousands of burglaries, robberies, larcenies, arsons and, last but not least, I have committed sodomy on more than 100 male human beings. For all these things I am not in the least bit sorry.'

'I Hate The Whole Damned Human Race'

Born of Prussian immigrant parents in Warren, Minnesota, in 1891, Panzram had been in trouble with police from the age of eight, when he was arrested for being drunk and disorderly! Three years later, a string of burglaries landed him in reform school—which he tried to burn down, with some success. Freed at the age of 13, he had already gained the knowledge he needed for his life of crime: 'how to steal, lie, hate, burn and kill,' as he later wrote in his autobiography.

Panzram joined the US Army at 16 but was so rebellious that he was court-martialed and jailed for three years—the first of several terms in prison. He went on to murder indiscriminately all over the world, but his principal areas of operation were West Africa, Mexico, California, Montana, and Washington DC.

His two most infamous crimes were committed in the 1920s. Panzram bought a yacht, the John O'Leary (which was also one of his aliases) and lured 10 crewmen aboard with the promise of unlimited bootleg liquor. The men were given alcohol until they were senseless, then were raped and murdered, their bodies thrown overboard. Later, in Portuguese West Africa, he hired 10 locals to accompany him on a crocodile hunt. He killed them all, sodomizing their corpses before feeding them to the crocs.

In 1928 he was jailed at Leavenworth for 20 years for another murder. He told the warden: 'I'll kill the first man who crosses me'—and carried out his threat by battering to death a civilian employee with an iron bar.

He was sentenced to death, spurning attempts at a reprieve by telling liberal campaigners: 'I believe the only way to reform people is to kill them.'

He went to the gallows on September 5, 1930, berating his executioner: 'Hurry up, you bastard, I could hang a dozen men while you're fooling around.' The remorseless killer left behind an autobiography in which he summed up his philosophy in three defiant sentences: 'I don't believe in Man, God nor Devil'; 'I hate the whole damned human race, including myself', and 'I wish the whole world had but a single throat and I had my hands around it.'

Elaine Parent

Elaine Antoinette Parent traveled the world under at least 20 stolen identities and eluded investigators for 12 years. Although hunted by police for killing and mutilating one female victim, she is feared to have murdered and stolen the identities of many more.

The 'Chameleon' Who Stole Other People's Lives

New York-born Parent, nicknamed 'The Chameleon', was an expert con-artist; bisexual, beautiful, clever, and deadly. This is how she operated…

In early 1990, lonely bank employee Beverly McGowan, 34, placed a newspaper advertisement for someone to share her Miami condominium. A woman in her late 40s, calling herself 'Alice', answered the advert, and swiftly moved in. Beverly told her brother, Steve, about her charming new roommate and said she felt her life 'had turned around'. Indeed, it was about to.

Pretending to be an expert on numerology, and promising to predict a rosy future for her, the newcomer convinced Beverly to part with her date and time of birth and her credit card and driver's license numbers.

On July 8, someone using the name Beverly McGowan called her place of work to take a day off sick. A day later, brother Steve received a goodbye letter supposedly from Beverly, saying that she was leaving home for a while. Knowing this to be uncharacteristic behavior, he called at his sister's condo and, finding her missing, stopped her credit cards.

At about the same time that Steve arrived at her front door, however, a mutilated and decapitated corpse was being recovered from a remote canal bank in southern Florida. The female's head and hands had been hacked off at the wrists with a chainsaw to delay identification, a hole in her stomach had been gouged out to eradicate the identifying tattoo that lay there, and only five teeth and half a jaw remained. But the killer had missed the tattoo of a rose on the woman's ankle and police were able to identify the body as Beverly McGowan's.

A few days later, 'Alice' tried to use Beverly's canceled credit card to book a flight to London and rent a car. Nobody by the name of Alice or Beverly McGowan turned up at Heathrow Airport, and when the credit card transactions failed, the investigation became an international manhunt. 'Alice', however, disappeared.

Six years later, after reinvestigating the manifest for the 1990 flight to London, detectives concentrated on a passenger listed as 'Sylvia Ann Hodgkinson'. They found that Hodgkinson was a deceased British citizen and had three other identities linked to her: Charlotte Rae Cowan, Ann Tremont, and Elaine Antoinette Parent.

Inquiries back in Florida revealed that Parent, using the alias Ann Tremont, had befriended a woman in a bar in Orlando in 1989 and, using numerology to obtain vital information, had stolen her identity. A modus operandi was emerging that made Elaine Parent prime suspect for the murder of Beverly McGowan.

Forensic investigators now re-examined the writing pad supposedly used by Beverly in her 'goodbye' letter. Impressions on the pad revealed hidden correspondence in Parent's handwriting—the content being angry threats to an ex-lover living in London, where Parent had fled in 1990. The lover, a businesswoman, told police of Parent's violent mood swings. Another ex-lover revealed that she was sometimes so frightened of Parent that she would drive 80 miles (128km) to a friend's house to escape.

In April 2002, Parent, then aged 60, was finally tracked down to a house in Panama City, Florida, where she was using the name 'Darlene Thompson'. When police called to arrest her, she asked if she could change her clothes. She went back into the bedroom—and fired a shot through her heart with a .375 Magnum.

To this day, police still don't know how many identities Elaine Parent acquired, and they fear several more women suffered the same fate as Beverly McGowan. The full extent of secretive Parent's homicidal history may never be known.

Leszek Pekalski

When Leszek Pekalski confessed to 70 murders, he became infamous as Poland's most prolific serial killer. Whether he really did slaughter so many is unlikely, and the true figure may never be known, for Pekalski later retracted his confession. But police believe that a tally of 17 butchered and abused female victims is a sad certainty.

'I'm Just A Weak Man' Claims Killer

Born in 1966 at Osieki near Bytów, Poland, Pekalski was deserted by his father and abused by his mother before she also abandoned him. Raised by nuns, he was never able to form a normal relationship and instead discovered that by attacking women, he could control them—beating, stabbing or strangling his victims in order to have sex with them.

Pekalski first killed when, at the age of only 16, he pounced on a 13-year-old girl playing in the countryside on a school outing. It launched him on a reign of terror lasting a dozen years as the misfit became a wanderer, traveling the length and breadth of his homeland.

A detective later said: 'We couldn't find his trail. He never followed a regular pattern. There was no typical victim or a repeated killing method. He would hit with a wooden cane or would strangle his victim with a belt.'

Yet a chance to stop Pekalski was lost in 1990 when he was arrested on suspicion of rape and positively identified by the victim. The investigating officers merely ordered that he attend a psychiatric examination. He was finally given a two-year suspended sentence—and the killing spree continued.

Now labeled the 'Vampire of Bytów', he went on to beat a 17-year-old girl to death with a metal post in woods near her home. The sick killer watched from a hideout as the girl's devastated father discovered the body. Pekalski spoke too openly about the killing, however, and in 1992 police interviewed him as a suspect. He made a handwritten confession, claiming he had committed 70 murders, but, by the time he appeared in court in the northern city of Slupsk, he had changed his mind.

He told the magistrate: 'I'm a gullible man and I was easily persuaded by what the officers had told me. I'm mentally weak and if somebody pushes me I break down. Then I admit to things I have never done. I have never killed anyone. I'm so scared.'

The accused man struck a pitiful pose in the dock and, to the anger of the dead women's families, the magistrate said he could not 'help feeling vaguely sorry for him'. The case faltered when DNA evidence was ruled to be 'contaminated'. However, police witnesses insisted that Pekalski's confession included details of crimes that no one but the killer could have known.

The trial dragged on for eight months. Victims' families were furious when, in 1994, the 17 murder charges against him resulted in only one conviction for a single killing. He was cleared of the others on the grounds of insufficient evidence. Pekalski was sentenced to 25 years in a psychiatric institute, where an initial report judged him, not unexpectedly, to have 'an abnormal sex drive'.

Marcel Petiot

When Dr Marcel Andre Felix Petiot became mayor of Villeneuve-sur-Yonne, in Burgundy, he seemed a paragon of respectability. Yet strange events began to occur in the French town. In 1928 the mayor's pregnant housekeeper vanished without trace. Two years later a woman patient was murdered. A friend who pointed the finger of blame at the doctor also mysteriously fell ill and died. Petiot signed the death certificate.

Treacherous Doctor Death Dies By The Guillotine

How Petiot ever got to become mayor in the first place is as astonishing as his becoming a doctor. Born in Auxerre, 100 miles (160km) south of Paris, in 1897, the young Marcel was expelled from school for circulating obscene photographs to other children. He also enjoyed torturing animals to death.

An early career of petty crime was foreshortened when, in January 1916, with World War One in progress, he was drafted into the French infantry. He was discharged in 1917 with the recommendation that he enter an asylum. Instead, he took advantage of an education program for war veterans, trained as a doctor and, amazingly, qualified.

Petiot began a practice in the town of Villeneuve-sur-Yonne, where he married, had a son and eventually became mayor. He stole from the townspeople, overcharged his patients, and cheated on his wife,

ABOVE: Marcel Petiot speaks from the dock during his trial at the Palais de Justice in March 1946.

ABOVE: Petiot in the dock, with his lawyer Dr Fleuriot, in the foreground.

having an affair The charges had to be an affair with a young woman whose dismembered body was found in a river. When his housekeeper died in mysterious circumstances, Petiot was accused of her murder. The charges had to be dropped, however, when the case files disappeared.

Petiot and his family moved in 1933 to Paris, where he set himself up in a practice on the Rue Caumartin. He thrived by supplying drugs to addicts and carrying out illegal abortions until, charged with stealing from a dead patient, he pleaded insanity and was sent to a mental hospital.

Released in time for the outbreak of World War Two, Petiot pretended to be a member of the French

RIGHT: Charged with multiple counts of murder, crazed Petiot claimed he was in fact a hero of the French Reistance.

Resistance and offered to aid refugees, mainly Jewish, who were trapped in Paris when the Nazis took the city in 1940. Instead, he robbed and murdered them.

The bodies of dozens of these unfortunates were found in his cellar when firemen were called to his elegant house at Rue Lesueur, in the fashionable Etoile district, in March 1944. Neighbors had complained of thick, black, foul smelling smoke spewing from the chimney. Firemen soon discovered the cause—the flames of a coal burning furnace consuming human arms, legs, and torsos in every state of dismemberment. In an outhouse were several corpses covered with lime. Petiot fled and really did join the Resistance, using the name 'Henri Valery'. Finally arrested in October 1944, he put up an outraged defense, passing himself off as a

hero of *La Liberation*. At his trial at the Palais de Justice in March 1946, the jury were initially sympathetic—until they heard how the doctor had injected an entire Jewish family 'for typhoid' then watched through a peephole as they died in agony.

Petiot admitted killing 19 of the 27 victims found at Rue Lesueur but denied any knowledge of a further 44 identified victims. Sentenced to death by guillotine, he cried out to his wife Georgette: 'You must avenge me.' Her appeals for presidential clemency failed, however, and the evil doctor's head was laid on the block of the guillotine early in the morning of May 25, 1946.

ABOVE: The jury at Petiot's trial learned how the evil doctor had administered lethal injections to an entire Jewish family.

Paul and Herman Petrillo and Morris Bolber

A bogus medic specializing in potions to curb husbands' sexual urges was just one member of an extraordinary syndicate of crooks, charlatans, and cheats operating in Philadelphia in the 1930s. He was 'Doctor' Morris Bolber, and it was a visit by a grocer's wife that turned the phoney physician into a murderer. He helped kill the wife's husband with poison after persuading her to take out life insurance on him.

Poison Gang Disposed Of Husbands By The Dozen

Bolber decided there were riches to be made in relieving unhappy wives of their husbands. He teamed up with Italian cousins Paul and Herman Petrillo, who were already long-term criminals, Herman being an expert counterfeiter and Paul running insurance scams. A principal partner was enrolled: Carino Favato, nicknamed the 'Philadelphia Witch', who, having poisoned her own husband, provided the names of further potential victims through her contacts in the murky world of contract crime.

Together, they formed what would become known as the 'Philadelphia Poison Gang', led by the Petrillos and eventually employing more than a dozen calculating killers. Although initially tending more to the underworld of gangsterism, the group's activities soon qualified them for inclusion in the category of serial killers.

The gang's 'front' was a business advertising itself as a marriage agency. They made a play of helping recently-widowed women move on with their lives, find new romance and remarry—always taking out life insurance policies for their new husbands. In reality, the agency was an elaborate cover for collecting insurance payouts as soon as Husband Number Two had been dispatched to join Husband Number One in the afterlife.

In a typical case, a gang member would impersonate a soon-to-be-murdered husband and take out a policy on his life, leaving his widow a handsome sum to share with her partners in crime. The Petrillos, Bolber and their ever-widening band of cohorts progressed from contrived 'accidents'—one of their victims was pushed

ABOVE: Paul Petrillo, one member of the 'Philadelphia Poison Gang', in court on February 11, 1939.

ABOVE: Morris Bolber (right) shown before magistrate Thomas A. O'Hara on May 11, 1939, during the Poison Gang's trial.

off a building site roof—to death by 'natural means': Victims would be dealt heavy blows with canvas bags full of sand so that there would be no signs of violence.

The normal method of disposal, however, was poisoning. Police had heard rumors of an arsenic killing spree in the city, the victims usually being Italian immigrants, and the death toll was said to be as high as 70. But rumors were one thing, proof another.

The Petrillos' murderous business began to fall apart in February 1939 after Herman bragged to a loose-tongued friend about his sure-fire insurance scam. He, cousin Paul and Mrs Favato were arrested, along with another recent widow, Mrs Stella Alfonsi. The bodies of their spouses as well as those of several other victims were exhumed and found to have traces of arsenic in their systems.

Each eagerly blamed other members of the gang, and the trail soon led to Morris Bolber, now known in the criminal fraternity as 'the Rabbi', and to his secretary Rose Carina, alias 'Rose of Death'. She was found to have had five husbands, three of whom were dead.

At their trials, which stretched through 1939, no fewer than 14 people were found guilty of murder. Of the principal conspirators, Bolber and Favato escaped the ultimate penalty and were sentenced to life imprisonment but the Petrillos met their deaths in the electric chair.

Alexander Pichushkin

Alexander Yuryevich Pichushkin lured his victims to Moscow's vast, wooded Bitsevsky Park with the promise of a bottle of beer or a shot of vodka. Occasionally, he would suggest a game of chess. And after bludgeoning each victim to death, he would place a coin or vodka bottle stopper on one more square on the chessboard in his apartment. That is the way the notorious serial killer recorded his grisly crimes, attaching a number to another square of the board every time he struck. By the time he was caught, Pichushkin had filled in 62 of the 64 squares.

Woodland Victims Drowned In A Pit Of Filth

The 'Chessboard Killer', as Pichushkin came to be known, first struck in 1992 when he was just 18 years old, murdering the boyfriend of a neighbor he had fallen in love with. He later killed the girl, whose body

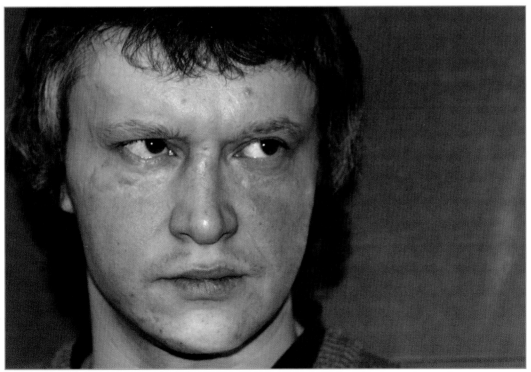

ABOVE: At one point during 2005, Alexander Pichushkin, 'The Chessboard Killer', was committing one murder a week.

was found in Bitsevsky Park, near to the apartment block where Pichushkin lived with his aged mother.

Subsequent murders were sporadic but in 2005 the supermarket shelf-stacker embarked on a killing spree. At one stage, police were uncovering one body every week—all having the serial killer's hallmark of a smashed skull, with the neck of a vodka bottle thrust into the gaping wound.

Most of his victims were homeless drifters or drunks. Those who were not killed instantly ended their agonies by drowning after Pichushkin threw them into the sewers that ran beneath the park. Others were strangled or killed with a blow to the skull from a hammer or blunt object. He would always attack from behind in order to stop blood from soaking his clothes, and finally he would stick the neck of a vodka bottle into his victims' skull, ensuring that they did not survive.

Three of his victims were women and one a child, a homeless nine-year-old boy. The body of one woman was found with tiny stakes hammered into her skull and around her eyes. His final victim, a female colleague from the supermarket where he worked, caused Pichushkin's capture. Before accompanying the killer to the park, she had left a note with her son telling her who she was meeting. CCTV cameras also caught them strolling toward the park shortly before she was murdered there in June 2006.

Under arrest, 32-year-old Pichushkin confessed: 'I liked to watch their agony. For me, a life without murder is like a life without food for anyone else. I felt like the father of all these people, since it was I who opened the door for them to another world.'

A psychologist who analyzed the killer prior to his trial in September 2007 reported that his love of chess, which ironically he couldn't play, was a clue to his character. Pichushkin, it was said, 'is detached from human beings, who are no more than wooden dolls—like chess pieces to him'.

At his trial, the prosecution claimed that Pichushkin 'dreamed of going down in history by surpassing Andrei Chikatilo'—the so-called 'Rostov Ripper' who was Russia's previously most notorious serial killer, executed in 1994 for murdering 52 women and children (see page 43). Pichushkin wished to confess to 62 slayings but there was sufficient evidence for only 48 charges of murder. With the death penalty

ABOVE: The 'Bitsevsky Maniac' is escorted into the Moscow City Court on August 13, 2007.

no longer in force, he was jailed for life, with the first 15 years in solitary confinement.

Robert Pickton

Pig farmer and serial killer Robert 'Willie' Pickton is currently serving the longest sentence available under Canadian law for murdering six women; feeding their remains to his pigs and hanging and skinning one victim on a meat hook. The women, who disappeared between 1997 and 2001, are only a fraction of the total number Pickton is thought to have slaughtered, as the six cases were the only ones where adequate body parts survived.

Women Were Butchered And Fed To The Pigs

Pickton, born in British Columbia on October 24, 1949, was well-known for the parties he threw for prostitutes and bikers. He lured the women to his farm in Port Coquitlam, just outside Vancouver, with the promise of money and drugs.

Most of his victims were prostitutes and drug addicts from Vancouver's Downtown Eastside, and police were accused of paying insufficient heed to these 'missing persons' cases over the course of the past 20 years. But in February 2002, they raided Pickton's scruffy pig farm in an unrelated investigation into illegal firearms and discovered property and identity cards of some of the women listed as missing.

In the farm's slaughterhouse, they dug up human remains—from body parts to minute traces of DNA—until the count came to 30. Four could not be identified but the other 26 were among the names of 67 women

ABOVE: Robert Pickton was convicted of six murders, but the remains of many other nameless victims were fed to his pigs.

ABOVE: The common-law husband of Mona Wilson holds a photograph of his partner. She died at the hands of Robert Pickton.

ABOVE: A police forensic officer searches for evidence. Various human remains were found in the farm's slaughterhouse.

who had disappeared from the Downtown Eastside.

In the freezers, they found skulls of two women among the most recently reported missing. Some carcasses were cut in half, like slaughtered pigs, with hands and feet stuffed inside. The remains of one victim was in a garbage bag and her blood-stained clothing was found in the trailer in which Pickton lived. Part of another victim's jawbone and teeth were found in the ground beside the slaughterhouse. Much of the evidence, however, had been devoured by pigs long before the police search.

At Pickton's trial in January 2007, a former farm employee, Scott Chubb, testified that Pickton told

ABOVE: Police trailers set up in April 2002, during the extensive on-site murder investigation at Pickton's farm.

ABOVE: A spokesman for the Crown Counsel speaks outside court following a preliminary hearing during Pickton's murder trial.

ABOVE: An artist's impression of Pickton's trial in January 2007. He was sentenced to life imprisonment.

him the way to get rid of 'junkies' was to inject them with a syringe filled with windshield washer fluid. A syringe with the fluid was found in Pickton's trailer. Another witness, Andrew Bellwood, testified that Pickton demonstrated how he killed the women. He produced a pair of handcuffs, a leather belt, and a thin wire with loops on the end and showed him how he strangled the women while having sex with them.

The most disturbing story the jury heard from a witness was told by Lynn Ellingsen. After waking up from a crack binge at the farm one night, she had gone outside to the barn because she saw a light on. When she opened the door, she saw a body hanging from a chain. Beside the body was a bloodied Pickton, who

RIGHT: Crown prosecutor Michael Petrie (center) walks with his team as they arrive for the start of the trial on January 22, 2007.

warned her that 'she'd be next' if she said anything.

Further damning evidence at the trial came from a conversation Pickton had with an undercover police officer posing as a cellmate, in which he confessed to 49 murders. He told the officer that he wanted to kill another woman to make it an even 50, and that he was caught because he was 'sloppy'.

In the largest serial murder case in Canadian history, the jury of seven men and five women took 10 days to reach a verdict. In December 2007, Pickton received a mandatory life sentence, with no possibility of parole.

Jesse Pomeroy

When a number of children were abducted and sadistically tortured in the backstreets of 19th-century Boston, Massachusetts, few could believe that the foul sexual assaults could have been committed by anyone but a sick adult. Yet the culprit was found to be a 12-year-old boy: Jesse Pomeroy, a gangling child with a hare lip, one completely white eye, and extremely low intelligence.

The Ugly Kid Who Killed 27 Times

Jesse, born in 1860 and raised in a South Boston slum tenement, was shunned by other children because of his obvious disabilities and unprepossessing appearance. His revenge for being ostracized was a terrible one. Between December 1871 and September 1872, a number of children were snatched from the streets, sadistically tortured with whips, knives, and pins and left unconscious.

Jessie was sent to West Borough Reform School but was handed back into the care of his mother two years later. The 14-year-old sadist immediately sought fresh victims, both male and female.

In March 1874, he murdered nine-year-old Katie Curran, whose body he buried in the basement of his mother's dressmaking store. Five weeks later, the body of four-year-old Horace Mullen was found on a Boston beach. He had been beaten, stabbed 15 times and his throat cut.

The ensuing manhunt turned into a boy-hunt when the evidence pointed toward Pomeroy. When police asked him if he had killed the little boy, whose body

ABOVE: Child killer Jesse Pomeroy as a much older adult. He spent more than 40 years of his life sentence in solitary confinement.

was the first to be found, Jesse replied: 'I suppose I did.' Shamed by the arrest of her son, Jesse's mother moved house—and the new owners found 12 corpses buried in her trash-strewn yard. He eventually confessed to torturing to death 27 youngsters.

At his trial in December 1874, Jesse Pomeroy was accused only of the single murder of Horace Mullen. He pleaded insanity but was found guilty and sentenced to death. There were appeals for mercy to be shown to such a young offender and the sentence was commuted to life imprisonment—but to be spent entirely in solitary confinement.

Pomeroy began his solo existence on September 7, 1876, when he was transferred from the Suffolk County Jail to a single cell at the State Prison at Charlestown, and began his life in solitary. He was 16 years and 10 months and would spend more than 40 years entirely alone in his cell before finally being allowed to mingle with other convicts. He had used his lonely decades in solitary to study and he ended up writing his autobiography which chronicled his early life and terrible crimes. In 1929, in frail health, he was transferred to Bridgewater Hospital for the Criminally Insane, where he died on September 29, 1932, at the age of 73.

Dennis Rader

To his neighbors, he was a pillar of the community, a churchgoer, a scout leader, a respectable family man. What they failed to see in him was the sickening serial killer who managed to evade justice for 30 years. His name was Dennis Rader, but he was better known by his nickname 'BTK' because of his method of murder: Bind, Torture, Kill.

'BTK' Was His Nickname. It Stood For 'Bind, Torture, Kill'

His sick crime spree left 10 dead. He strangled four members of one family, hanged an 11-year-old girl from a sewer pipe to watch her die, photographed the bodies of his victims and taunted police by sending them trophies taken from the corpses.

Yet, to most who knew him, father-of-two Rader seemed 'an ordinary guy'. A US Air Force veteran, he was an attentive parent who took his children on camping and fishing expeditions. He ran his son Brian's scout troop. He was an usher at his local church in Wichita, Kansas, where he worked as a 'code compliance officer', enforcing petty rules for the city authority.

ABOVE: Dennis Rader was an apparent pillar of the community, but behind the facade he was a serial killer who claimed 10 lives.

ABOVE: A news conference outside the Sedgwick County Courthouse in Wichita, Kansas on March 1, 2005.

He was, however, a secret sadist, with the classic serial-killer background of torturing small animals. His depths of evil finally found full expression in 1974 when, at the age of 28, he burst into the home of the Otero family, held them at gunpoint, bound, and gagged them. Joe Otero, 38, his wife Julie, 34, and nine-year-old son Joey were strangled one by one. But it was the fate of 11-year-old Josephine 'Josie' Otero that was to send a wave of revulsion through the Kansas town.

Josie's body was found hanging from the basement sewer pipe. Her hands were bound behind her back and she wore nothing but socks and a sweater. The rest of her clothes were in a pile by the foot of the stairs, left by her killer before he carried out a sex act on her corpse.

His next victim was 21-year-old student Kathryn Bright, who returned home with her younger brother Kevin to be confronted by a gun-toting intruder

ABOVE: Police work in front of Dennis Rader's house in Park City, Kansas, following his arrest in February 2005.

wearing a black stocking cap, camouflage jacket, and black gloves. Rader tied them up and stabbed Kathryn to death. Kevin was shot in the head but survived.

Police at first failed to link the attack to the Oteros massacre—but Rader seemed to want recognition for his crimes and wrote to the *Wichita Eagle* newspaper, claiming to be 'BTK', bragging about the slaughter and promising to kill again. He did not do so for three years. Then, in March 1977, mother-of-three Shirley Vian, 24, was found bound and strangled in her Wichita home. A plastic bag had been placed over her head and her panties had been removed as a trophy.

Nancy Fox, a 25-year-old secretary, was next. Rader

broke into her home, handcuffed her and stripped her, before assaulting her and finally throttling her with a belt. To ensure recognition for the crime, Rader rang police from a payphone to report the murder. As 'BTK', he later sent letters to local media asking: 'How many do I have to kill before I get some national attention?'

'BTK' then went to ground for almost eight years and police assumed he had died. But in April 1985, his urge to kill returned and he murdered his 53-year-old neighbor, Marine Hedge. Rader took her body to the Christ Lutheran Church where he was congregation president, placed the corpse on the altar and took bondage photos before dumping it in a ditch.

The following September he entered the home of Vicki Wegerle, 28, after posing as a telephone repairman and strangled her. His final victim was Dolores Davis, 62, abducted and strangled in 1991. He dumped her body under a bridge—then returned to place a mask over the corpse's head and take photographs. As always, he performed a sex act at the scene.

Police failed to link the latest deaths to the earlier 'BTK' murders until, in 2004, Rader again wrote to the local media, sending them and the police trophies from his crimes. They included pictures of Vicki Wegerle's body, Nancy Fox's driving license, and a doll symbolizing Josie Otero's murder.

'BTK' was finally captured in February 2005 when a floppy disk he sent to a TV station was traced to Rader's church. Confronted with a DNA test that matched him with a sample found in Josie Otero's body 31 years earlier, Rader admitted all 10 murders.

In a written confession, he said: 'Josephine, when I hung her really turn(ed) me on. Her pleading for mercy…then the rope took (hold); she helpless; staring at me with wide terror fill(ed) eyes, the rope getting tighter-tighter.'

At his trial in August 2005, the bespectacled 60-year-old looked relaxed as he admitted planning further murders, adding: 'I was thinking about it but I was beginning to slow down.' Since the crimes were committed before Kansas reintroduced capital punishment, the judge handed down the maximum prison sentence he could deliver: 175 years with no chance of parole.

ABOVE: A manacled Rader, flanked by police officers. The evil killer was sentenced to 175 years in prison.

Richard Ramírez

The spooky killer known as the 'Night Stalker' was an avowed Satanist who terrorized the streets of Los Angeles for 13 months from 1984–85. Richard Ramírez would creep into a house at night, shoot or strangle any adult males and then subject women and children to sadistic rape and mutilation. Occasionally he would leave his mark as the 'Devil's Disciple'—an inverted pentagram scrawled on a mirror or wall. He also used to draw occult signs on the victims' bodies.

Fan Mail Galore For The 'Night Stalker'

ABOVE: A police mugshot of Richard Ramírez. The Mexican was fascinated by death from an early age.

Ricardo Múñoz Ramírez was born in El Paso, Texas, the son of Mexican immigrants. At an early age, he was fascinated by death and would spend nights in cemeteries. At 12, he fell under the influence of a cousin, a Vietnam War veteran who told tales of killing and torturing civilian women. According to later testimony, the cousin murdered his own wife while Ramírez was in the same room.

In his teens, Ramírez turned to crime and drugs.

ABOVE: Ramírez, appearing to revel in his notoriety, wears sunglasses during a court appearance.

ABOVE: After his conviction the killer proclaimed: 'I will be avenged. Lucifer dwells within all of us.'

A police profile described him as 'a confused, angry loner who sought refuge in thievery, drugs, the dark side of rock music, and finally murder and rape'.

Upon moving to Los Angeles, Ramírez committed his first 'Night Stalker' murder in June 1984 when, high on cocaine, he crept into the apartment of a 79-year-old woman, stabbed her repeatedly, almost decapitating her, then sexually assaulted her. He was responsible for at least 18 further killings, his victims' ages ranging from the early 30s to the 70s. The methods he used were varied but included shooting, bludgeoning, throat cutting, and battering to death. Although the attacks satisfied Ramírez's sadistic sexual urges, he also stole from those he killed.

RIGHT: Ramírez in court with one of his calling cards, an inverted pentagram, drawn on his left palm.

Police finally got lucky in August 1985 when they found a fingerprint in a getaway car used for one of the attacks and matched it to Ramírez, then aged 25 and a known petty criminal. His photograph was circulated to the press—and had an instant result. Ramírez was recognized as he tried to drag a woman out of her car in a Los Angeles suburb. He was attacked by the woman's husband and by a gathering mob, who turned him over to the cops bruised and bleeding.

After one of the lengthiest murder trials in American history, Ramírez was found guilty in September 1989 of 13 murders, five attempted murders, 11 sexual assaults, and 14 burglaries. He was sentenced to death in California's gas chamber and, as he left the courtroom for San Quentin's Death Row, he snarled: 'You maggots make me sick. I will be avenged. Lucifer dwells within all of us.' Of the death sentence he joked: 'Big deal. Death comes with the territory. See you in Disneyland.'

Inexplicably, the 'Night Stalker' trial had generated an amazing amount of fan mail for Ramírez. One besotted woman, Doreen Lioy, who wrote him 75 letters, won a proposal of marriage. With California's death sentences seemingly permanently stalled, the couple were wed in San Quentin in 1996.

David Parker Ray

David Parker Ray is the serial killer who was never convicted of a single slaying, although his tally of female victims may be as high as 60; they died in the most horrific circumstances after kidnap, captivity, abuse, rape, and torture. Yet he escaped the full weight of justice, dying in 2002 of heart failure after just three years in prison on charges that all fell short of murder.

How Many Innocents Lured To 'Satan's Den'?

Ray was a loner with four failed marriages who built a torture chamber in a trailer at the back of his home. There, in what he referred to as his 'Satan's Den' or 'The Toy Box', his victims were drugged and chained to a gynecological chair fitted with straps and surrounded by an array of torture instruments and sex toys.

Ray's reign of terror ended in March 1999 when one of his victims, Cynthia Vigil, escaped from him and ran through the streets of Elephant Butte, New Mexico, naked, with a metal collar around her neck and trailing a chain. The sobbing 21-year-old had been held captive for three days and subjected to a terrifying ordeal of rape and torture.

Police arrested Ray, a 59-year-old park warden and mechanic, and searched his home and backyard den. A policeman said: 'There were sadistic pictures on the walls, straps and chains, a bar he'd labeled "ankle stretcher", sex toys attached to power drills, dildos with nails embedded in them. Everything in that trailer denoted pain.'

Officers found a tape recording in which Ray explained to his victims what he was about to do to them, saying that he had 'no qualms about slitting your throat' because 'you're a piece of meat to me'. On the tape, he talked of 37 previous abductions.

Police also examined videotapes containing footage of one of Ray's victims strapped to the chair. Apparently drugged, she could be identified only by an unusual tattoo on her leg. When the tattoo was shown on TV, a 25-year-old woman, Kelly Van Cleave, identified herself but said she was confused because she had no memory of being held captive. It was only under police questioning that her memory partially returned and, horrified, she realized that the nightmares she had been suffering were of real events and that she had been drugged to prevent her from recalling the horrors of her captivity.

Police suspected that Ray may have slain as many as 60 women but, when a search of the area revealed not a single body, prosecutors decided a murder charge was impossible. Instead, Ray was charged with kidnapping, rape, and torture.

He almost escaped justice entirely, because the two principal witnesses were deemed potentially unreliable, Kelly Van Cleave still having only partial memories of her experience and Cynthia Vigil being a heroin-addicted prostitute. Moreover, at Ray's trial in July 2000, the judge ruled that the incriminating tape recording was inadmissible. The trial ended in a hung jury.

A retrial nine months later produced a different verdict. On April 16, 2001, the jury were unanimous. David Parker Ray was jailed for 224 years, less the two and a half years he had already spent in prison. On May

ABOVE: The smart appearance of Ray during his trial belied a man capable of remorseless evil.

28, 2002, just eight months into his sentence, David Parker Ray died of heart failure.

Earlier, in other trials, three of Ray's accomplices received lesser sentences after plea deals involving giving evidence against him. Dennis Roy Yancy confessed to strangling to death another kidnap victim, 22-year-old Marie Parker, whose body was never found, and was jailed for 20 years. Ray's live-in girlfriend Cynthia Hendy confessed to being an accessory and received 36 years. Ray's daughter Jessy was convicted of helping her father kidnap and torture Kelly Van Cleave but was released with five years' probation under a deal that her father forewent his right to appeal.

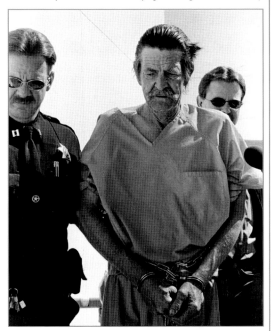

ABOVE: David Parker Ray, shackled by police officers after his arrest. He was later sentenced to 224 years in jail.

Gary Ridgway

Gary Ridgway pleaded guilty to 48 murders in November 2003, making him the worst, confirmed serial killer in America's history at that time. In a statement read in court, he said he killed so many women that he had a hard time keeping count. By way of explanation, he said he hated prostitutes and did not want to pay them for sex.

48 Fell Victim To 'The Green River Killer'

ABOVE: Gary Ridgway was a frequent user of prostitutes, but rather than pay them for sex he murdered them instead.

The so-called 'Green River Killer', named for the river south of Seattle where the first victims were found, had confounded detectives for two decades. The remains of scores of women, mainly runaways and prostitutes, turned up near ravines, rivers, airports, and freeways from the early 1980s. Ridgway had been a suspect ever since 1984, but it was 16 years before advances in DNA technology linked him to the bodies of four of his earliest victims.

Gary Leon Ridgway was born in Utah in February 1949 but grew up south of Seattle, where the household was dominated by his violent mother who discouraged him and his two brothers from mixing with friends. At the age of 13, Ridgway was still a bed-wetter. He was of low intelligence and did badly at school. At 16, he lured a six-year-old boy into woods and stabbed him. The victim survived and recalled Ridgway walking away laughing and saying: 'I always wondered what it would be like to kill someone.'

Ridgway got a job as a painter at a trucking company. He was married three times and fathered one child.

ABOVE: Investigators search for the remains of one of 'Green River Killer' Gary Ridgway's victims at an unknown location.

At the time of his arrest, his third wife was still with him. His first two told police he liked sex outdoors—and detectives were intrigued to discover that these couplings took place at or near where victims' remains were found.

The hunt for the murderer began in July 1982 when the body of a 23-year-old woman was found on the bank of Green River in King County, Washington. Only one month later and half a mile away, the body of a 16-year-old was discovered.

Throughout the rest of the 1980s and 1990s, the 'Green River Killer' murdered 48 or more women in and around Seattle and Tacoma. Most of the victims were either prostitutes or teenage runaways picked up along Pacific Highway South and strangled.

Their bodies, usually naked, were often dumped in clusters, sometimes posed. Ridgway would often scatter items he had collected from others, such as cigarettes, receipts, and gum, around the sites to confuse police.

It had long been a mystery to detectives as to why so many women should so trust the killer that they would accompany him to wild areas. It transpired that Ridgway carried in his pickup truck toys belonging to his son, and would show the boy's photograph to victims to put them at ease. He even took some victims to his house and showed them his son's room to demonstrate they had nothing to fear.

An FBI profile of the killer indicated that he had a deep hatred of women, was possibly a married man

ABOVE: With strong evidence of his guilt in 48 murders, there was little chance of Ridgway escaping justice.

ABOVE: The Washington police forensic investigation centered on land adjacent to the state's Green River.

ABOVE: When Ridgway's court case opened the first eight minutes were spent reading out the names of his many victims.

who came from a broken home and probably hated his mother. It also suggested that the killer would be aged between 20 and 40, white, a heavy smoker who liked to drink and someone with a background of sexual crime. It was an accurate portrait of Gary Ridgway.

The killer's arrest in 2001 was due to improved DNA testing. Ridgway had provided a DNA sample during a 1984 investigation into the murders. That sample now linked him directly with four of the Green River victims from that period. These were the four murders Ridgway was initially charged with. When the case finally came to court in November 2003, however, it took eight minutes to read out the names of all 48 victims with whose murders he was charged.

Ridgway successfully plea-bargained to escape the death penalty and instead, in December 2003, heard King County Superior Court Judge Richard Jones hand out 48 life sentences with no possibility of parole. He was also sentenced to an additional 10 years for tampering with evidence for each of the 48 victims, adding 480 years to his 48 life sentences.

In 2004, prosecutors released videotape of Ridgway's confessions to them. In one, he admitted responsibility for the deaths of 65 women, and in another claimed to have murdered 71. He also confessed to having sex with victims' bodies—but said he began burying the later victims so that he would resist the urge to revisit them.

Joel Rifkin

Joel Rifkin was a landscape gardener who murdered and dismembered at least 17 prostitutes between 1989 and 1993 sometimes storing their bodies in the suburban home he shared with his adoptive parents.

Man Who Kept Clippings On Killers

Born in 1959, the son of unwed teenage parents, Joel was adopted by Ben and Jeanne Rifkin at three weeks of age. They settled in the New York suburb of East Meadow, Long Island, where Joel, despite a high IQ, did badly at school, attributed to the constant bullying of the loner by his classmates who called him 'The Turtle' because of his shy, awkward manner and habitual slouch.

As a teenager, he visualized himself as a knight in shining armor, as this adolescent poem suggests: 'A siren temptress calls me near / a stranger beyond darkness haze / pleading from within the shadows / and though I be helpless to help her / help her I must.'

But his dreams of heroism dissipated in a failed college course and a string of short-term jobs. His only girlfriend over the next decade described him as 'depressive'. Instead, Rifkin turned to prostitutes for comfort, picking them up in Brooklyn and Manhattan.

In 1987, his adoptive father committed suicide to end the pain of cancer, thereby increasing Rifkin's depression. He became increasingly obsessed with violence, collecting books and press clippings on serial killers of prostitutes, including Gary Ridgway (see page 178) and New York's Arthur Shawcross (see page 185).

He began emulating their brutal crimes in 1989. Rifkin's first two victims have never been found or identified. He killed one prostitute in 1989 and another in 1990, dismembering their bodies and dropping the pieces into rivers or canals. Over the next four years, he is believed to have killed 15 more, sometimes taking them back to East Meadow, on other occasions killing them in his car.

Bodies were turning up in a variety of locations. One girl he strangled was found in a plastic bag, another inside a trunk in the East River. Four victims were found wedged into oil drums

ABOVE: Rifkin at the Nassau County Courthouse in Mineola, NY, in December 1993 for a pre-trial hearing.

ABOVE: A bound Joel Rifkin is transferred to District Court on June 29, 1993 in Farmingdale, New York after confessing to murder.

which were then rolled into creeks. Some bodies were found in the countryside, but one dead prostitute was dumped in a vacant lot at JFK airport.

Rifkin was finally caught in June 1993 when police spotted his pickup truck with no license plates. After a high-speed chase, he crashed into a utility pole directly in front of the courthouse in which he would eventually stand trial. In the back of the truck was the dead body of his latest victim, aged 22. A search of his home recovered dozens of items of personal effects of the dead girls—plus a chainsaw stained with blood. Rifkin was found guilty of nine murders in 1994 and sentenced to life.

Danny Rolling

Danny Harold Rolling was born in Shreveport, Louisiana, in 1954 to a police officer father who was abusive to both him and his mother. After leaving school, he failed to hold down a steady job and slid into a life of crime, being jailed for robberies. During yet another argument with his father, Rolling attempted to murder him before fleeing to the university town of Gainesville, Florida, where he was to commit some of the most gruesome murders America has known.

Campus Carnage Of The 'Gainesville Ripper'

He was tagged the 'Gainesville Ripper' in August 1990 after attacking students Christina Powell, 17, and Sonja Larson, 18, whom he savagely killed as they slept in their shared house. He placed tape over their mouths to stop them from screaming. He stabbed Sonja repeatedly and then went downstairs to rape and knife Christina before pouring washing-up liquid over her body in an attempt to destroy any DNA evidence that could identify him.

His next victim, Christa Hoyt, 18, met the same grisly end. She too was raped and her body sliced from throat to stomach and then washed in caustic cleanser, leaving a complete absence of blood.

The cleansing of the bodies became the killer's 'signature', along with the rearranging of the bloodied corpses in such a way as to highlight the carnage in the rooms. In the case of Christa Hoyt, he decapitated her and set her head on a shelf, surrounding it with carefully arranged mirrors—one positioned to reflect the grisly scene out to anyone passing by her window.

Next victim was Tracey Paules, 23, and her roommate,

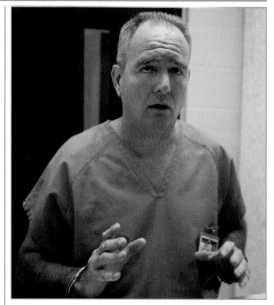

ABOVE: After 15 years in maximum security prison, Danny Rolling was executed by lethal injection in October 2006.

ABOVE: Rolling, the 'Gainesville Ripper', is led into court to answer for his crimes on May 31, 1991.

23-year-old Manuel Taboada, a strapping 6ft (1.83m), 210lb (95kg) football star. They were both taken off-guard and stabbed to death 30 times. Later the same day, Rolling robbed a bank using a 9mm pistol, which police found soon afterward at a campsite where he had been hiding out. Rolling stole a car and carried out a series of thefts until he was caught after holding up a supermarket.

When police ran a check on the small-time thief, a violent past was revealed. Not only did the attempted murder of his father come to light but there were similarities between the Gainesville murders and a triple murder in the previous year, 1989, in Rolling's home town. In that case, 24-year-old Julie Grissom had been stripped, murdered, and her body posed. Her father William, 55, and eight-year-old nephew Sean, who had also

ABOVE: A spokesman for the Florida Department of Corrections briefs the media about Rolling's imminent execution in October 2006.

been stripped, murdered, and her body posed. Her father William, 55, and eight-year-old nephew Sean, who had also been in the house, had been killed, too. Tape had been used to bind them and their bodies had been cleaned.

Rolling was charged in September 1991 with several counts of murder. He pleaded guilty in court and was subsequently convicted and sentenced to death. The 52-year-old serial killer lodged a last-ditch appeal which was rejected by the US Supreme Court.

Rolling was executed by lethal injection on October 25, 2006, and pronounced dead at 6:13pm. He had showed no remorse and had refused to make any comments or offer any apology to the relatives of his victims, several of whom were present at his execution as witnesses.

Efren Saldivar

By their own nature, it is notoriously difficult to apportion blame in the case of hospital killings. Leading forensic scientist Henry Lee, speaking in Los Angeles after one particularly horrifying case, said murders by nursing staff were the most difficult serial killings to detect and on which to obtain a conviction. 'You have to figure out who the victims were long after they were buried,' he said. 'Then you have to link them to the suspect. Prepare to fail.'

Rookie Nurse Killed From The Age Of 19

The case the scientist was referring to was that of Efren Saldivar, by then known as the 'Angel of Death', who confessed to murdering 50 patients while working as a respiratory therapist in a Los Angeles hospital. Texas-born Saldivar had got the job at the Glendale Adventist Medical Center after graduating from a brief course at North Hollywood medical college in 1988. He worked the night shift, when there were fewer staff on duty, killing his patients by injecting a paralytic drug which led to respiratory or cardiac arrest.

His 10 years of quiet killing came to an end in 1998 when, acting on a tip-off from another member of staff, phials of muscle relaxant were found in Saldivar's locker. The 32-year-old nurse was taken to the local police station, where he made a confession. He said he had killed his first patient a decade earlier when he

RIGHT: Sick respiratory therapist, Efren Saldivar confessed to killing 50 patients at a Los Angeles hospital between 1988 and 1998.

was 19 and fresh out of training. The victim, an elderly woman terminally ill with cancer, had been suffering, so Saldivar suffocated her.

He claimed his next victim by introducing a lethal drug into her intravenous drip tube. His first lethal injection was in 1997. After that, he injected more and more elderly patients—according to him, picking only those who were under a 'Do not resuscitate' order. The drugs he used were Succinylcholine and Pavulon.

The case against Saldivar seemed in doubt when he suddenly recanted his confession. To gain a conviction, 20 of the most recently buried patients had to be exhumed—and six of those bodies contained large amounts of Pavulon. Presented with this evidence, the fickle nurse confessed all. He said he had killed the patients because there were too many of them and his department was understaffed.

Apart from the pathology evidence, there were two key witnesses who clinched the case against Saldivar.

A fellow respiratory therapist was granted immunity in exchange for testifying that she had given him the Pavulon and knew the use to which he was putting it. A second witness, who had been a patient at Glendale in 1997, told how she had inexplicably blacked out for some hours after Salvidar had attended her.

Although his confession to 50 killings was considered to be an underestimate—some authorities putting his tally at over 100—Salvidar was charged with only six counts of murder. In court in March 2002, he pleaded guilty, having been told that he would escape the death penalty if he confessed. He also apologized to the families of those he had killed. He was given six consecutive life sentences.

Arthur Shawcross

Known also as the 'Genesee River Killer' after the place many of his victims were found, Arthur John Shawcross was convicted of some of the most savage slayings and cannibalistic perversions that America had known in recent years. And the fact that he was able to kill and kill again was largely down to a tragic blunder—for he claimed most of his victims after being paroled early following the murder of two children.

Cannibal Returned To Eat Rotting Corpses

Born in 1945 in Kittery, Maine, Shawcross's parents moved to Watertown, New York State, where he was a surly, aggressive child with a particularly low IQ. As a teenager, Shawcross had a tendency toward bullying and violence, and received several probationary sentences for minor crimes. In 1967, he was drafted to Vietnam, where his sadistic tendencies seem to have flourished. According to his own accounts, he raped, slaughtered, and cannibalized two Vietnamese peasant girls during a combat mission on his tour of duty.

Back on United States soil, Shawcross was well into his third violent marriage when, in May 1972, a neighbor's son, 10-year-old Jack Blake, disappeared from his home in Watertown, New York. It would be five months before the boy's body was finally located. He had been sexually assaulted and suffocated. Four months later, the body of eight-year-old Karen Hill was found under a bridge. She had been raped and murdered, and mud, leaves, and other debris had been forced down her throat and inside her clothing.

Witnesses linked Shawcross to the two murders and, in October 1972, he pleaded guilty to manslaughter. Due to lack of evidence tying him to Jack Blake's death, Shawcross was charged only with Karen Hill's killing. He received a 25-year jail sentence, of which he served 15 years.

ABOVE: A police mugshot of Arthur Shawcross taken in January 1990. Later that year he was convicted of killing 10 women.

but now he preyed primarily upon prostitutes. In the spring of 1988, mutilated corpses started turning up in woods and marshland, under ice and floating in streams near the Genesee River. The women had been either strangled or battered to death and most, as in the case of his first victim, 27-year-old prostitute Dorothy Blackburn, had undergone a vicious attack revealed by bite marks in the groin area.

As more bodies turned up in similar condition, detectives knew that this was the work of a serial killer, and one that indicated previous criminal or possibly military experience. Yet as Shawcross' criminal records had been sealed, he was not a suspect. Eleven victims were found dead or went missing in the space of less than two years before police finally caught up with the killer.

ABOVE: Shawcross after pleading guilty on first degree manslaughter in the deaths of two children, in October 1972.

Released on parole in March 1987, he settled in Binghamton, NY, but angry citizens learned of his bloody history and ran him out of town. After two other communities turned him away, desperate parole authorities finally smuggled the homicidal pedophile into Rochester, NY. Neglecting to alert the police and sealing Shawcross's criminal record to avoid further public outcry seemed the only way to keep him from being uprooted again, but this gross incompetence would later cost more victims their lives.

It wasn't long before Shawcross began killing again,

ABOVE: A painting by Shawcross from 2001 entitled 'What Dreams Are Made Of'. It was part of a display of inmate art at the New York Legislative Office Building in Albany.

In January 1990, the body of a 34-year-old prostitute June Cicero was discovered by aerial surveillance in the Rochester area. Quite by chance, as the helicopter flew above, Shawcross was reliving the pleasure of the attack by masturbating at the bridge above where the body lay on the frozen river. His vehicle license plate was noted and he was later arrested.

Shawcross confessed to all the murders after a piece of jewelry given to his fourth wife was traced back to one of his victims. In his confession, he stated that he killed one woman because she bit him, another for trying to steal his wallet, a further was murdered because she called him 'a wimp' and one simply because she made too much noise during sex.

He admitted that he would sometimes return to his victims' decomposing remains weeks after the murder to cut out and eat pieces of the corpses, and he bragged of doing similarly disgusting things to young Jack Blake's body after killing the boy.

In December 1990, Shawcross was convicted of killing 10 of the women. His lawyers' attempts to obtain a lighter sentence—citing mental illness and blaming a supposedly abusive upbringing and a traumatic spell in Vietnam—were rejected and he was given 10 life sentences. Three months later, Shawcross pleaded guilty to strangling a further woman whose body had been found in November 1989, in woods in neighboring Wayne County and he received a further life sentence.

While serving time at the Sullivan Correctional Facility in New York for the murder of the 11 women, Shawcross complained of pains in his leg and later died from a massive coronary on November 10, 2008.

Lydia Sherman

In her sick and twisted mind, Lydia Sherman was taking care of her family and doing her very best for them. By the time her atrocities had been discovered, she had aided three husbands, six of her own children, and two step-children through agonizing deaths to their merciful ends.

How 'Black Widow' Diposed Of Family

Born in Burlington, New Jersey, in 1824, Lydia was married at the age of 17 to a 40-year-old New York policeman, Edward Struck, and the couple had six children in quick succession. All was well until the cop was dismissed from the force, accused of cowardice. He fell into a deep depression. Lydia could not bear to see him in such a state, and so purchased a few cents' worth of arsenic to 'put him out of the way'. He died in 1864, the doctors thought of consumption.

Finding herself a widow with six children to support—and, according to her twisted logic, having considered the best course of action for all the family—she poisoned her three youngest children. Baby William, four-year-old Edward, and six-year-old Martha Ann all died on the same day. Next of her offspring to meet an agonizing end was 14-year-old George. Having lost his job bringing in $2.50 a week, she didn't want him to become a burden on the rest of the family.

When little Ann Eliza, aged 12, took ill with fever and chills, she laced her medicine with arsenic. It took her four days to die, the cause of death being declared as 'typhoid'. Two months later, her elder daughter, also named Lydia, was struck down with fever and died in convulsive agony, again diagnosed as 'typhoid'.

With nothing to keep her in New York, Lydia moved to Connecticut and was quickly married to an elderly widower, Dennis Hurlburt. Within a year, Lydia was a widow again, a very wealthy one this time, having poisoned him, too.

In September 1870, she married Horatio Sherman,

himself a widower with four children. Just two months after the wedding, Lydia dispatched baby Frankie, and the following month pretty 16-year-old Ada. The sudden death of two of his children devastated Sherman and he took to the bottle. Lydia tolerated his drunkenness for a few months but her patience ran out in May 1871, and Sherman took to his bed with stomach pains and diarrhea. He was dead within a week.

Given the frequency of tragic deaths in Lydia's past, foul play was suspected and a post-mortem was carried out, revealing a liver saturated with arsenic. Lydia's relentless murder spree was over. The 'Black Widow', as she was called, stood trial in 1872 and, convicted of second-degree murder, was sentenced to life imprisonment. She died in jail in 1878.

Harold Shipman

A jubilant cry of 'Yes!' rang out from one of the deceased's relatives after the guilty verdict was announced in the case against Dr Harold Shipman. Britain's 'Doctor Death' was going to prison for life. That day, January 31, 2000, ended a chilling chapter in criminal history. For Shipman's 24-year-long trail of corpses made him the country's most prolific serial killer ever.

'Doctor Death': Britain's Most Prolific Serial Killer

The doctor was convicted of murdering 15 patients. A year later, a government report put the number of his victims at 236, of whom 218 could positively be identified. That immediately placed him just behind recent history's most prolific serial killer, Colombian Pedro López, dubbed the 'Monster of the Andes' (see page 134).

Shipman hid his murders behind the mask of a respected suburban doctor. His victims tended to be elderly females, although the 20 percent who were males included his youngest, aged 41. The doctor hoarded lethal drugs like candy and often caringly patted his victims' hands as he injected them with heroin along with an assurance that it would cure their illness or at least ease their suffering.

Dr Harold Frederick Shipman graduated from Leeds School of Medicine in 1970 when he was aged 24.

RIGHT: Harold Shipman hid behind a mask of caring GP to murder at least 236 of his patients over a 24-year period.

ABOVE: 'Doctor Death' ended his own life while in Wakefield Prison, hanging himself in his cell in January 2004.

In 1976, while practicing in West Yorkshire, he pleaded guilty to forging prescriptions and stealing drugs, and asked for 74 other offenses to be taken into consideration. He next got a post conducting baby clinics in County Durham but was supervised throughout because of his past criminal record. By the end of 1977, he was considered to have sufficiently rehabilitated himself to be allowed back into general practice and moved to Hyde, Greater Manchester, where he worked as a GP through the 1980s and 1990s. But Shipman was far from rehabilitated.

Shipman's first murder victim in Hyde was believed to have been a 76-year-old who visited him in September 1984 complaining of a cold. On a follow-up home visit,

he said he found her 'lying dead on her bed'. There was then an average of one suspicious death a year until Shipman left the Hyde group practice where he was working until 1992 and founded his own surgery in 1993. Then the number of deaths escalated—eight that year, starting with a 92-year-old who was found dead within hours of a visit by Shipman.

It was neither suspicious police nor worried patients who brought Shipman's deadly bedside manner to a close. It was the intervention, in March 1998, of a 28-year-old local undertaker, Deborah Bamroffe, who decided 'there were just too many deaths for a one-doctor surgery'. She voiced her suspicions to one of the doctors who had been countersigning Shipman's

ABOVE: Elaine Oswald, believed to have been the first intended victim of the serial killer in 1974, arrives to give evidence against him.

deaths for cremation purposes. Within days, coroner John Pollard was briefed and he called in Greater Manchester Police. However, Shipman still managed to kill three more patients before his arrest.

One of them was a fit and active 81-year-old, Mrs Grundy, who was found dead at her home in June 1998. Shipman gave the cause of death as old age—but when it was discovered that her will left her entire £386,000 estate to the doctor, her daughter contacted police. The will had been typed on Shipman's typewriter and had his fingerprints on it. Mrs Grundy's body was exhumed and lethal levels of morphine were found.

Shipman, by then a 52-year-old married father of four, was arrested in September and brought to court in Preston the following October, when he denied one charge of forging the will and 15 charges of murdering old ladies. 'All of them died most unexpectedly,' said the prosecuting counsel, 'and all of them had seen Dr Shipman on the day of their death.' He added that Shipman's drive to kill was fed by a God-like belief that

he had power over life and death.

After the jury returned guilty verdicts, the judge, Mr Justice Forbes, told Shipman: 'These were wicked, wicked, crimes. Each of your victims was your patient. You murdered each and every one of your victims by a calculating and cold-blooded perversion of your medical skills. For your own evil and wicked purpose, you took advantage and grossly abused the trust each of your victims put in you. I have little doubt each of your victims smiled and thanked you as she submitted to your deadly administrations. None of your victims realized that yours was not a healing touch.'

Shipman was jailed in top-security prisons and told he would never be released. He carried out his own death sentence, hanging himself in his cell at Wakefield Prison, West Yorkshire, on January 13, 2004.

Joseph Smith

George Joseph Smith, born 1872, became known as the 'Brides In The Bath Murderer' because of the manner in which he disposed of three of his five wives. The first of these spouses, Caroline Thornhill, whom he married in 1898, was a petty thief, just like her husband. They fell out, however, and she tipped off police about his crimes, resulting in a jail sentence. Once free, he sought revenge but Caroline survived by emigrating to Canada.

Wooing Ways Of 'Brides In Bath' Murderer

Smith, of Bethnal Green, London, then used a series of pseudonyms for his subsequent, bigamous marriages. Beatrice Mundy died by drowning in July 1912 still clutching a piece of soap in her hand. Alice Burnham left a large clump of hair in her death bath. Smith had taken out insurance policies on the lives of his wives and he lived well on the proceeds.

The murder of Smith's final victim, Margaret Lofty, followed an identical pattern. A clergyman's daughter, he established that she already had a nest egg and wooed her under the alias 'John Lloyd'. With a £700 policy on her life and a freshly written will safely in his hands, Smith married her on December 17, 1914. On the evening of the very next day, their landlady heard splashing noises from the bathroom and, true to form, the latest bride was found 'accidentally' drowned.

But Margaret's murder proved literally a fatal mistake for Smith. Margaret had been a bride for only one day, and her death therefore made front-page news, revealing suspicious similarities with the previous deaths

ABOVE: Joseph Smith was hanged in August 1913. He drowned three of his five wives in a bath tub.

filled with water so that a female volunteer could demonstrate how easy it would have been for a killer to drown a victim in it. She performed the task so convincingly that she passed out and had to be revived. Smith's behavior in court was outrageous, attacking the judge, jury, and his own lawyers. 'It's a disgrace to a Christian country,' he screeched at the judge. 'I might be a bit peculiar but I'm not a murderer.' The jury disbelieved him. Smith was found guilty and, quaking with fear, he was hanged at Maidstone Prison on August 13, 1915.

ABOVE: Smith with Beatrice Mundy, his first victim in July 1912. She was found dead, still clutching a piece of soap.

'Bride's tragic fate on day after wedding' ran one headline; another read 'Bride found dead in bath'. The reports were seen by relatives of his previous victims and police were waiting for 'John Lloyd' when he turned up at a solicitor's office to collect the money from his murdered wife's insurance policy.

The bodies of Beatrice Mundy, Alice Burnham, and Margaret Lofty were exhumed but Smith was charged with only one murder, that of his first victim. The courtroom drama was played out at the Old Bailey against the backdrop of news pouring in from the battlefields of the Western Front. One odd aspect of the case was the appearance of a bathtub which was

Richard Speck

Corazon Amurao opened the door of a South Chicago nurses' home late one night in July 1966 and found a man with a pockmarked face brandishing a gun. He forced his way in, telling her and two other nurses: 'I'm not going to hurt you.' Scouring the hostel, Speck found three more student nurses asleep in their beds and forced them into one room. Another three nurses returning after a night out were also rounded up.

Sole Survivor Of The Pockmarked Killer

BELOW: Richard Speck in handcuffs. He murdered eight young nurses in their Chicago hostel in July 1966.

The attacker, 25-year-old Richard Speck, bound all nine girls together while he stole money and jewelry from their rooms. High on a mixture of drink and drugs, Speck then set about systematically killing his captives, all in their early 20s.

He led his first victim to another room, where he stabbed and strangled her with a strip of sheet. Two more girls were taken into a bedroom, where one was stabbed in the heart, neck, and eye, while the other suffered 18 knife wounds and was raped as she lay dying. The next five victims were all stabbed and then strangled. He raped two of them. Midway through the 20-minute frenzy, Speck calmly walked to the bathroom to wash his hands.

In his befuddled state, Speck failed to keep tally of the nurses. Corazon Amurao, the 23-year-old who had first opened the door to him, squeezed herself under a bed petrified as her friends were murdered. It was several hours before she could muster up courage to drag herself out, open a window and cry for help.

Corazon told police that the killer had a 'Born to Raise Hell' tattoo on his arm. Detectives also deduced that the knots binding the nurses' wrists had been tied by a seaman and, with the help of the Seamen's Union, Speck was identified as Chicago's 'most wanted'. He was arrested in Cook County Hospital two days after the murders, having slashed his wrists in a failed suicide bid.

Speck's long police record revealed that he had been born in Kirkwood, Illinois, in 1941, had worked as a garbage collector, had wed a 15-year-old bride when he was aged 20, and that the couple had split in 1966. Speck had been arrested 37 times, on charges ranging from drunkenness to burglary, his most serious offense being an assault on a woman while holding a knife to her throat. The semi-literate drifter had become addicted to drugs and was on a deranged drinking spree when he committed the nurses' home massacre.

In April 1967, a court in Peoria, Illinois, found Speck guilty on eight counts of murder and he was sentenced to die in the electric chair. The ultimate penalty was later waived by the Supreme Court, which replaced it with a record jail term of between 400 and 1,200 years.

Speck died of a heart attack in 1991 without ever cooperating with police over their suspicions that he was responsible for the murders of four other women in the months before the nurses' slaughter. A barmaid who had rejected his advances was found dead in April 1966, and three months later three girls disappeared from Illinois Beach State Park, where Speck had been sighted. Their bodies were never found.

Lucian Staniak

Nicknamed the 'Red Spider', Lucian Staniak murdered at least 20 Polish girls in the mid-1960s. His modus operandi was particularly horrific: he would rape his victims before killing them, mutilating and often disemboweling them. And frighteningly, he often chose public holidays, when his targets would be particularly carefree.

Inky Scrawl Of The 'Red Spider'

His first victim, a 17-year-old girl, was raped and murdered at Olsztyn on the 1964 anniversary of Poland's liberation from Nazi occupation. The 'Spider' followed up his attack with a sinister threat to police: 'I picked a juicy flower in Olsztyn and I shall do it again elsewhere, for there is no holiday without a funeral.'

It was just one of several taunting letters, written in spidery red script, advising police or newspapers where the latest body was to be found. One read: 'There is no happiness without tears, no life without death. Beware, I am going to make you cry.'

It was the red ink—in reality, artists' paint—used by the 'Spider' in his notes that proved to be his undoing. In 1967, police identified the mutilated body of a 17-year-old girl found on a train in Krakow and realized that she was the sister of a 14-year-old murdered in Warsaw two years earlier. Both had belonged to an amateur artists' club, and detectives set about tracing its fellow members.

One of them was Lucian Staniak, a 26-year-old translator from Katowice, whose job with a Krakow publishing firm took him to all parts of the country. When police visited the club and asked to see some of his work, they realized they had found the 'Spider'. His favorite color was blood-red, one of his paintings depicting a disemboweled woman with a bunch of flowers in her stomach cavity.

The police had found their man—but not soon enough. Before they arrested Staniak, he murdered a young student, found dead at Lodz railroad station. A few hours later, on his way home from his last slaying on February 1, 1967, they seized him. Under interrogation, he told detectives that he had begun killing by way of vengeance after a court freed a woman driver who had mown down and killed his sister and parents. His first victim was chosen for her likeness to the hit-and-run driver.

Staniak admitted 20 murders and was tried for six of them. He was sentenced to death but later judged to be insane and ordered to be committed to an asylum for life.

Peter Stump

One of the most extraordinary trials in history was that of Peter Stump. A peculiarity of the case is the wide number of names under which he is known: Peter Stumpp, Stubbe or Stumpf and Abal, Abil or Ubil Griswold. The other oddity is that he was a werewolf! At least, that is what he confessed to when he was dragged into court in Germany in 1589.

Wolfman Who Sold His Soul To The Devil

Stump, a wealthy farmer, was accused of selling his soul to the Devil for the ability to transform himself into a wolf. He had, for 25 years, roamed the countryside around the village of Bedburg, near the ancient city of Cologne, tearing innocent victims to shreds to satisfy his bloodlust. According to a contemporary assessment of his foul deeds, once he had tasted human flesh, 'he took such pleasure and delight in the shedding of blood that he would night and day walk the fields and perform extreme cruelties.'

His favored victims were young girls, whom he captured and raped before 'changing into a wolf' to tear them apart. In just five years, according to his German biographer, he murdered 15 women and children, including two girls who were pregnant. In some cases, he tore out their hearts and ate them 'panting hot and raw'.

Stump was aided and abetted in his savagery by his mistress, Katherine Trompin, and by his daughter, Beele or Beell, with whom he was committing incest. She bore him a son but such was his stomach-churning depravity that he ate the infant—and declared the brains as 'a most savory and dainty delicious' meal.

Until his capture, limbs of his victims were found almost weekly in the fields around Bedburg, whose villagers dared not leave their homes unless armed or protected. Stump's rampage of terror finally ended when, ironically, a pack of hunting dogs led their

ABOVE: Woodcuts depict the capture and trial of the Cologne wolfman, Peter Stump.

ABOVE: The manner of Peter Stump's death was a grisly as the demise of his many victims.

masters to him in their search for what they believed to be a real wolf. According to legend, when tracked down he was 'still in the guise of a werewolf'. According to the superstitious witnesses, he made a desperate last attempt to resume his human shape as he hid behind a bush. But he was spotted removing his 'Devil's Girdle' (a supposedly false skin) and seized.

The tortures and punishment finally endured by Stump following his capture are terrible to record. After being stretched on the rack, he confessed to having practiced black magic since he was 12 years old. In court in Cologne, he was predictably found guilty, and his fate matched in horror that of his victims.

The judge ordered: 'His body shall be laid on a wheel and, with red hot burning pincers, in several places to have the flesh pulled off him from the bones. After that his legs and arms to be broken with a wooden hatchet, afterwards to have his head struck from his body, then to have his carcass burned to ashes.' After being forced to watch the burning of Stump's headless corpse, his mistress and daughter were also burned at the stake.

RIGHT: A depiction of Stump as the 'Beast of Bedburg', a guise he was able to adopt after selling his soul to the devil.

Peter Sutcliffe

The hunt for the 'Yorkshire Ripper' began with the grisly discovery of the half-naked and viciously stabbed body of 28-year-old prostitute Wilma McCann on a Leeds playing field on the morning of October 30, 1975. The manhunt, dogged by blunders and slip-ups, lasted five years until, 13 murders and seven attempted murders later, Peter William Sutcliffe was finally caught in a routine motoring check. In his car, he had the luckiest prostitute in Yorkshire, along with a Phillips screwdriver and a ball-peen hammer.

Police Blunders Left 'Yorkshire Ripper' Free To Kill

Following the **Wilma McCann killing,** Sutcliffe's next target was prostitute Emily Jackson, 42, whose body was found in the Chapeltown red-light district of Leeds. Her post–mortem revealed more than 50

ABOVE: A photofit image of the man Yorkshire police failed to capture for five years.

ABOVE: Peter Sutcliffe on his wedding day in August 1974. He began murdering women a year later.

ABOVE: Six of the Yorkshire Ripper's victims. Top left to right; Vera Millward, Jayne MacDonald, and Josephine Whittaker. Bottom left to right; Jean Royle, Helga Rytka, and Barbara Leach.

stab wounds inflicted with a Phillips screwdriver, the imprint of a size-seven Dunlop boot on her thigh and two heavy blows with a hammer to her head, the cause of her death.

Prostitute Number Three was also attacked with a hammer and, having masturbated over her semi-conscious body, Sutcliffe left her with £5 and a warning not to tell. Her description was found to be very accurate but, in a series of police errors, was largely ignored.

His next three victims in 1977 all bore similar

horrific injuries: bodies face down, hammer blows to the skull, and frenzied stabbing to the stomach. Victim Number Seven in July that year survived the Ripper's attack and, following emergency surgery, was able to give a poor description.

The Ripper knew the police were scouring Leeds and Bradford and so found new hunting grounds. In October he murdered Jean Jordan, a 21-year-old prostitute in Manchester. Her body lay undetected for over a week, but he left a vital clue: a brand new £5 note, which had been issued to only 6,000 employees, among them those of the firm that employed Sutcliffe as a lorry

ABOVE: The bus stop outside the Arndale shopping center in Leeds, where Jacqueline Hill was last seen alive.

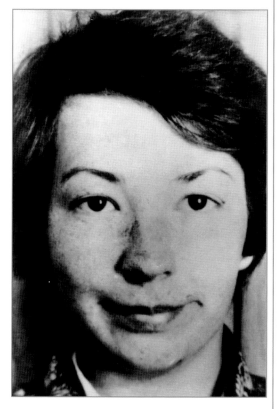

ABOVE: Student Jacqueline Hill, 20, was the Ripper's 13th and final victim, murdered in Leeds in November 1980.

driver. He was interviewed but police failed to pick up on his criminal record, which recorded his arrest in 1969 for 'going equipped for theft' with a hammer.

Following his next attack, in December that year—during which he screamed, 'You dirty prostitute' at his surviving victim—Sutcliffe killed again twice in 10 days. He hammered and stabbed Yvonne Pearson to death in January 1978, returning to her body before its discovery some two months later to inflict more macabre wounds. His next victim, an 18-year-old, was the only one he had sex with. Three more killings followed that summer, all victims receiving similar horrific wounds, including savage hammer blows to the head and the slashing to the stomach.

Sutcliffe lay low for almost a year without any further murders. More than 250 officers were working

ABOVE: Yorkshire police chiefs look satisfied with Sutcliffe's conviction. But for their blunders, he would have been stopped sooner.

full-time to try and catch him, their attempts plagued by hoaxes. The police concentrated on suspects with Geordie accents following an audio tape supposedly from the Ripper.

With his final two victims, Sutcliffe changed his modus operandi in a bid to throw police off the scent. The second of these was lucky; a passing police car disturbed Sutcliffe. A 20-year-old student from Leeds was not so lucky, however, and became his next murder victim in November 1980.

LEFT: Police hold back crowds outside Dewsbury court during an appearance by Sutcliffe on murder chages in January 1981.

Up until the time of his capture, Sutcliffe had been interviewed five times by police. He was known to frequent red-light districts. He had a previous record for possession of a hammer. Yet, as he didn't have a Geordie accent, he was never marked as a prime suspect.

Following his confession, Sutcliffe was tried at the Old Bailey and, on May 22, 1981, was sentenced to life, with a recommendation that he serve at least 30 years. Since then, he has been held in Broadmoor Hospital for the criminally insane. The reason for his crimes? According to his brother Carl, Peter Sutcliffe felt he was just 'cleaning up the streets'.

RIGHT: Multiple killer Peter Sutcliffe is bundled into Dewsbury court under a blanket on January 6, 1981.

Joseph Swango

Born Joseph Michael Swango, he shone at school, studying music and then biology before going on to Southern Illinois University where he graduated in medicine in 1983, at the age of 28, winning a year-long internship in general surgery at the Ohio State University Medical Center. But in January 1984, it was first noted that the former prize pupil was acting suspiciously. A nurse saw him checking on a patient and shortly afterward found the woman turning blue and suffocating. Emergency treatment managed to save her but a week later she was dead. Swango had been the last person to attend to her.

How Many Did The 'Doughnut Poisoner' Murder?

Similar occurrences rang alarm bells with anxious nurses who, comparing notes, discovered that at least six other patients, all evidently making good progress, had suddenly died. Their ages ranged from 19 to 47. Swango had been the duty intern at the time each of them had succumbed. Incredibly, although an investigation was carried out, none of the nurses who had raised the alarm were interviewed.

The high number of deaths whenever Swango was around continued, however, and the hospital terminated his employment. Swango returned to his hometown of Quincy, Illinois, where he joined the Adams County Ambulance Corps. On one occasion, an entire paramedic crew became ill after eating doughnuts bought in by Swango. His colleagues decided to investigate the newcomer a little further—and found arsenic in his locker. When alerted, police searched the poisoner's apartment and discovered a hoard of phials, bottles, syringes, and a library of books on murder.

there was also a selection of guns and knives.

Dubbed the 'Doughnut Poisoner', Swango was arrested and charged with seven counts of aggravated battery. In April 1985, a court sentenced him to five years' imprisonment. He was released for good behavior only two years later.

Happily for hospital staff and patients, Joseph Swango spent the next few years in various jobs away from medicine. He also had a girlfriend, Kirstin Kinney, a 26-year-old nurse who moved with him to South

Dakota in 1992 when Swango accepted a position as emergency doctor at the Veterans Affairs Medical Center in Sioux Falls. Both he and Kirstin were considered dedicated staffers.

The love affair ended, however, when a program about the notorious 'Doughnut Poisoner' was shown on television. Swango was dismissed. Kirstin, who realized the migraine headaches she now repeatedly suffered seemed to disappear whenever she was away from her boyfriend, fled home, wrote a note to her parents and shot herself.

With the fake references that he had become expert in forging, Swango moved to New York State in 1993 and got a job at the Internal Medicine Department at the Veterans Administration Headquarters, Northport, Long Island. His first patient died within hours of his arrival. Others were also to die in his 'care', all suffering heart failure in the dead of night.

It was not good police work or the vigilance of hospital authorities that finally halted Swango but Kirstin Kinney's parents, who could not forgive him for driving their daughter to suicide. They alerted the Long Island hospital and he was fired, the hospital authorities writing to every medical school in America warning them about him.

Swango disappeared, surfacing again in Zimbabwe at the Mnene Lutheran Outpost Hospital—where patients started to die with alarming regularity. A police investigation was launched and Swango fled to neighboring Zambia, and finally back to America. He was arrested the moment he landed at Chicago's O'Hare Airport in June 1997. He was finally charged with four counts of murder, pleaded guilty and, in July 2000, was sentenced to life imprisonment without parole.

Although only ever convicted of four murders, Swango is suspected of many more, estimates ranging from 35 to 60 in the United States—and perhaps hundreds overseas. A statement issued at the time by the mass poisoner's *alma mater*, Southern Illinois University, read: 'If Swango is legally connected to all the suspicious deaths of patients under his care since he began his residency with Ohio State University's medical program in 1983, it would make him the most prolific serial killer in history'.

ABOVE: Justice finally caught up with Joseph Swango in July 2000 when he pleaded guilty to four murders.

Johann Unterweger

The most extraordinary thing about Johann 'Jack' Unterweger was that anyone believed him. When he was arrested for the murder of a teenaged girl, he seemed to be just another one-off killer. By the time he had reinvented himself as a 'reformed' celebrity ex-criminal, he had killed at least 11.

The Killer Who Became A TV Celebrity

Unterweger was born in Styria, southeastern Austria, in 1951 to a local prostitute and an American soldier he never knew. He was raised in the company of streetwalkers, their pimps and assorted petty thieves. He spent most of his late teens and early 20s in prison. By the age of 25, he had notched up 15 convictions, including burglary, rape, and pimping. So when, in 1975, he was convicted of strangling an 18-year-old girl with her own bra, the life sentence he received should have removed him from public harm forever.

While inside, however, he wrote poetry, a novel, and an autobiography titled *Fegefeuer* (Purgatory), which became a bestseller. His writing was unexpectedly proficient, and he achieved celebrity status, with a clutch of literary awards. Suddenly infamy turned to fame, and a petition organized by influential Austrians in the literary world helped him gain early release from prison in October 1990.

Unterweger was feted at glitterati events and on TV chat shows. He became a journalist, presenting himself as a reformed character and explaining away his violent past and rehabilitated future: 'I was no longer a youth. I was a beast, a devil, a child grown old before his time who enjoyed being evil. But that life is now over. Let's get on with the new.'

But Unterweger had fooled an entire nation. Within months of his release, he started killing again. During his first year of freedom, he is reckoned to have strangled at least six prostitutes. As more bodies turned up, it was only natural for the media to seek an expert on the subject— and, bizarrely, Unterweger found himself being asked for his opinions and advice on the latest deaths for which he alone was responsible. The killer basked in the spotlight while watching his books rise up the bestsellers list.

The only people not fooled were the police. They were suspicious of the publicity-seeking ex-jailbird and began linking the new slayings to Unterweger's movements. The killing spree spread across the Austrian countryside and into neighboring Czechoslovakia. Unterweger killed six women in the spring of 1991, the bodies of four victims who had vanished from the streets of Vienna being found during April and May alone.

The killings stopped in Austria shortly afterward— and began in Los Angeles. That was because Unterweger had been commissioned by a Vienna magazine to write an article on crime in Southern California. There, while asking the LA police to assist him with his research, he committed three murders in June and July, all of prostitutes whom he strangled with their own bras, afterward violating their battered bodies with sticks and other objects.

Unterweger was arrested in February 1992 in Florida, where he was traveling with his 18-year-old girlfriend. After a legal battle over whether he should be tried in the United States or Europe, he was extradited to Austria where he finally stood trial in April 1994. A psychologist described him in court as: 'A sexually sadistic psychopath with narcissistic and histrionic tendencies, prone to fits of rage and anger. He is an incorrigible perpetrator.'

Accused of 11 murder charges, including the three American cases, Unterweger was convicted of nine of them, two bodies being too decomposed for cause of death to be determined. On June 29, 1994, he was sentenced to life without parole and was taken to Graz prison where, just 12 hours later, he hanged himself in his cell using his own clothes as a noose—exactly as he had killed most of his victims.

Waltraud Wagner and colleagues

A doctor was having a quiet after-work drink in a Vienna bar in February 1989 when he overheard parts of a conversation from an adjoining table. The bar was close to the city's Lainz General Hospital, and the table was occupied by a group of nursing aides who were employed there. The women were giggling over the death of an elderly patient—who had been treated to something they called the 'water cure' for refusing medication and calling one of the nurses, Waltraud Wagner, 'a common slut'.

'Water Cure' By The Angels Of Death

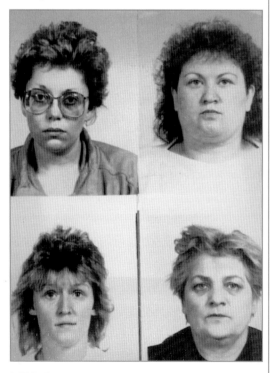

ABOVE: The 'Angels of Death', clockwise from top left: Waltraud Wagner, Maria Gruber, Stefanie Mayer, and Irene Leidolf.

The doctor seated nearby could pick up only snatches of the conversation but they were enough to shock him. He went to the police, who launched a six-week investigation that led to the arrest of Wagner and three other nurses. Together, they comprised one of the most unusual crime teams in 20th century Europe, and were subsequently proven to have murdered scores of patients in their care.

The ringleader, Wagner, had been 23 when she claimed her first victim in 1983. Disposing of a patient with an overdose of morphine, she discovered the thrill of wielding the power of life and death over her charges. She recruited Maria Gruber, 19, Irene Leidolf, 21, and the senior member of the group, 43-year-old Stephanija Mayer.

For the next six years, the evil foursome gave death a helping hand at Lainz hospital, which specialized in geriatric cases. Officially, the body count would stand at 42, but many put the final tally at between 200 and 300 victims.

Since lethal injections failed to provide sufficient excitement, the 'Angels of Death' devised their own murder method. Usually working on the night shift, one would hold the victim's head and nose, while another would pour water into the victim's mouth, causing drowning. Since elderly patients were frequently found to have fluid in their lungs, it seemed an unprovable crime.

When arrested after their loose-tongued drinking session in 1989, Wagner was first to crack, confessing to 39 killings. She said: 'The ones who got on my nerves were dispatched to a free bed with the good Lord. They sometimes resisted but we were stronger. We could decide whether the old fools lived or died. Their ticket to God was long overdue anyway.'

Although she later reduced her confession to only 10 cases of 'mercy killing', a court in March 1991 sentenced her to life for 15 murders and 17 attempted

ABOVE: Defendant Irene Leidolf testifies during her trial on March 4, 1991. She was convicted of five murders.

murders. Irene Leidolf also got a life sentence for five murders, Stephanija Mayer 15 years for manslaughter and seven attempted murders, and Maria Gruber 15 years for two attempted murders.

Austrian Chancellor Franz Vranitzky labeled the Lainz murder spree 'the most brutal and gruesome crime in our nation's history'.

Frederick and Rose West

In October 1996, Gloucester City Council demolished 25 Cromwell Street, crushing every brick so that no souvenirs could be taken of Britain's most infamous 'House of Horrors'. The house had been the site of such unspeakable depravity, cruelty, and torture that there could be no other course of action. Two years earlier, the mutilated bodies of nine of the victims of Frederick and Rosemary West had been discovered buried in the cellar or under the patio, ending a killing spree which had lasted for more than two decades, and resulted in Fred being charged with 12 murders, and Rose convicted of 10.

'House Of Horrors' Couple Killed Their Own Kids

Frederick and Rosemary met in 1969 when Rosemary was just 15 years old and already dabbling in prostitution. She was living with her mother Daisy and two younger brothers. They had escaped her violent and incestuous father, although Rosemary moved back in with him after becoming intimate with West and it is said that she still had sex with her father, with West's consent, even after their marriage.

In this respect, Frederick's childhood was very similar to Rose's. He was his mother's favorite of three sisters and two younger brothers and it is rumored that he was just 12 when she seduced him. His father treated his children as sexual playthings and Frederick grew up believing it natural to behave in this way. Indeed, when questioned by police in 1961 accused of child abuse by impregnating a 13-year-old, he commented: 'Doesn't everyone do it?'

By the time West became acquainted with Rose, he had already murdered at least once if not more. He was married at the time to Rena Costello, reputedly a prostitute, who already had a baby daughter, Charmaine. The couple soon had a child of their own, Anne-Marie, and a friend of Rena's, Ann McFall, moved in to help with childcare.

ABOVE: Evil Fred West grew up thinking that incest and rape was normal behavior. He committed suicide while awaiting trial in 1995.

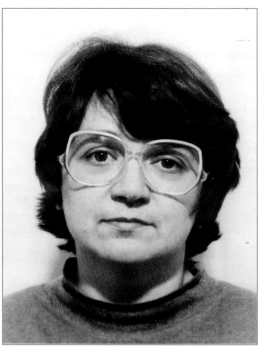

ABOVE: Rosemary West was convicted on 10 counts of murder, including those of her own children.

Ann became infatuated with Frederick, willingly taking part in his sadistic sex games, so Rena moved out, leaving the girls with their father. Ann, now heavily pregnant with West's baby, constantly urged West to divorce Rena but, unwilling to do so, he murdered Ann instead, removing her fingers and toes—later to become his signature mutilation—and burying her in a field in Kempley, Gloucestershire, along with the body of her unborn baby.

On moving in with West in 1969, Rose took the role of surrogate mother to Charmaine and Anne-Marie, and in October 1970 gave birth to her own daughter, Heather, thought to be her father's incestuous child.

ABOVE: Fred and Rose look the epitome of a normal loving couple in this photograph…yet they were anything but.

ABOVE: Heather West was murdered by her parents in June 1987 and her body buried under the patio.

Poor little Charmaine had a pitiful existence, abused by the couple and subjected to regular beatings. It is believed that Rose murdered Charmaine during a savage attack while Fred was serving a short prison sentence for burglary in 1971, hiding her body until his release, when he removed her toes and fingers and buried her at 25 Midland Road, Gloucester, their home at the time. When Rena came to visit her daughter, West also murdered her and buried her in the field in Kempley.

Fred and Rose married in 1972 and had their second daughter, Mae, in June that year. They moved into the much larger 25 Cromwell Street, enabling them to take in boarders to help with the bills. Fred fitted the cellar out as a torture chamber to enable him to engage in his sexual fantasies involving young girls, and Rose, still operating as a part-time prostitute, had a red light outside her bedroom so that the children knew not to enter when mummy was busy. Eight-year-old Anne-Marie became a regular victim of their sadistic games, held down by Rose while Fred violently raped her and threatened with more violence if she told anyone.

Rose was often pregnant, and gave birth to Tara in 1977, Louise in 1978, Barry in 1980, Rosemary Junior in 1982, and Lucyanna in 1983. Tara, Rosemary, and Lucyanna were not Fred's children. During this

ABOVE: West buried the body of his first known victim, Ann McFall, in a field in Gloucestershire...minus her finger and toes.

period, as the family expanded, so too did the Wests' insatiable perversions.

In the space of five years, the couple's appetites for violence and sex games resulted in the brutal murders of eight young women, lured by the couple into their home either as boarders or picked-up hitch-hiking or at bus-stops and taken home to be used as sexual playthings. They all suffered horrendous torture and rape. Sometimes West would wrap their heads tightly in brown tape and insert breathing tubes into their nostrils while he subjected them to his sexual deviations involving whips and chains, rape,

ABOVE: Fred West turned the cellar at his 25 Cromwell Street home into a torture chamber.

and bestiality. Once dead, they would be mutilated and buried under floorboards, in the cellar or under the patio.

One willing participant to their games was 18-year-old Shirley Robinson, who engaged in three-in-a-bed sex sessions with the couple. However, she fell in love with Fred and became pregnant with his child. Rose became jealous, despite the fact that she was pregnant at the time by a West Indian visitor. She put pressure on Fred, and Shirley vanished in May 1978. Her body was discovered in the garden on 25 Cromwell Street, along with that of her unborn child.

Their next victim was 16-year-old Alison Chambers, who moved in to become their nanny. She was last seen in August 1979 and was found underneath the lawn.

Fred's sexual interest in his own daughters did not wane and, after Anne-Marie moved out to live with a boyfriend, he switched his attentions to Heather and Mae. Despite violence and threats, Heather managed to resist his incestuous acts, confiding in a friend. She disappeared in June 1987. Her parents pretended she had run away. In fact, she was buried under the patio—a fate promised to the Wests' other children and joked about by them when later interviewed by police.

The Wests were arrested in 1992 following allegations of child abuse, and their five children under 16 were taken into care. The police found evidence of child abuse, including rape and buggery, but the case against them collapsed when two key witnesses refused to testify. However, Detective-Constable Hazel Savage of Gloucestershire Police was convinced something terrible was going on at 25 Cromwell Street. Investigating further and coaxing information from the West children, she persisted, despite the skepticism of senior officers, and obtained a search warrant in February 1994. The following day, the digging began—and Fred and Rosemary were arrested.

Fred escaped trial for the 12 murders, as he hung himself in his cell on New Year's Day 1995. Rosemary was brought to trial in October 1995 and found guilty of 10 murders, including those of her own children. She was sentenced to life, with the judge's recommendation that she should never be released.

Police believe that they may have murdered many more young girls, as there was an eight-year gap between the murder of Alison Chambers in 1979 and that of Heather in 1987. Without their bodies, the true number of their victims will never be known.

Wayne Williams

When Wayne Bertram Williams was arrested in 1981 as chief suspect in the 'Atlanta Child Murders', the killings that had caused two years of terror throughout the Georgia capital suddenly ended. And after his conviction the following year, Atlanta police declared 25 of the 30 murders solved.

Riddle Of Pudgy Geek And The 30 Child Murders

On February 27, 1982, Wayne Williams was led to the cells, tear-stained and still protesting his innocence, to serve a double sentence of life imprisonment. However, it did not end the debate over whether Williams should have borne the blame for the entire string of Georgian slayings.

Many black citizens, including some families of the victims, believed the state had manufactured much of the evidence to bring the case to a close. For although the crimes were labeled 'child murders', Williams was convicted of only two of the 30 homicides investigated—and those two murders were of adults.

The series of killings loosely (perhaps too loosely) tagged the 'Atlanta Child Murders' began in July 1979

ABOVE: Wayne Williams was convicted of double homicide, but it is believed he was responsible for 24 other murders.

public were baying for justice. But months after the slaughter of the innocents started, Atlanta Police could find no pattern beyond the fact that the victims were mainly young black males. They had been stabbed, shot or strangled and their bodies were found dumped throughout the city in creeks, woods vacant lots, under floors, and in the Chattahoochee River.

On the night of May 22, 1981 teams of officers were monitoring cars using main routes around Atlanta. A police recruit on the Jackson Parkway bridge over the Chattahoochee heard a splash—and shortly afterward Williams's car was stopped as it crossed the bridge. Along with many other drivers, he was questioned, his name taken and was allowed to go.

Two days after that face-to-face encounter with a killer, the body of a 27-year-old petty thief was fished out of the river, followed two days later by the body of a 21-year-old. Both had been strangled. Police reviewed the names taken on the bridge earlier and came up with that of Wayne Bertram Williams.

A surveillance team put a watch on the podgy 23-year-old, who lived with his parents, both teachers,

ABOVE: The prosecution in Williams's trial matched 19 different sources of fibers from around his home to a number of the victims.

when the bodies of two black children, 13-year-old Alfred Evans and 14-year-old Edward Smith, were found in undergrowth. They had been strangled. Further young victims were discovered in September and November. The first female victim, a 12-year-old, was found tied to a tree with someone else's panties forced down her throat. She had been sexually abused before being strangled.

Within a year of the first attacks, victims were turning up at the rate of one per month. The dead were aged between seven and 14, and all but two were boys. When the number of unsolved deaths reached 26, the

ABOVE: Williams vehemently protested his innocence after his arrest in May 1981.

in the Atlanta suburb of Dixie Hills, from where many of the victims came. A solitary figure, he was known as a 'scanner freak' because he spent hours tuned into short-wave radio to monitor police and ambulance activity. When an incident occurred, he would rush to the scene, photograph the action and try to sell the images to local newspapers and television stations.

Williams was arrested, still vehemently protesting his innocence. During his two-month trial, which began in January 1982, the prosecution matched 19 different sources of fibers from around his home to a number of the victims. Most significantly, dog hairs taken from

the clothes of the thief found in the river on May 24 matched those in Williams's car. There was also eyewitness testimony placing Williams with different victims.

Williams was only ever charged with the murders of the two adults fished out of the Chattahoochee. But a crucial ruling by the judge allowed the prosecution to introduce evidence which linked him with other victims even though he was not accused of their murders. The prosecution, whose case had previously hung literally by a hair, were now able to paint Williams as a predatory homosexual, who they argued was guilty of all the murders.

On February 27, the jury deliberated for 10 hours before finding him guilty and he was sentenced to two consecutive terms of life imprisonment. Appeals for a retrial have consistently been rejected.

Steve Wright

The winter of 2006 saw Britain's biggest manhunt since the search for the Yorkshire Ripper (see page 197). It began with the discovery of the bodies of five murdered women in scattered locations near Ipswich, in Suffolk. All had been working as prostitutes in the town's red light district. Police immediately warned women off the streets and appealed for clues to the killer. More than 500 officers were drafted in to work on the case, and the number of calls received to the public information line reached 10,000.

The Killer Hooked On Hookers

The murders took place during November and December 2006. The bodies of the five women, aged between 19 and 29, were discovered naked but with no signs of sexual assault. Two of the victims had been asphyxiated but cause of death for the other three was not established. In a macabre twist, two of the women's bodies had been carefully arranged in a crucifix shape.

On December 19, police arrested a local man, Steve Wright, who lived within the red light district itself and whom they knew as a habitual user of prostitutes. Wright, born in the Norfolk village of Erpingham in 1958, had joined the merchant navy after leaving school, and followed that with jobs as a docker, a steward on the liner *QE2*, a lorry driver, a barman, and finally a fork-lift truck driver. He had two children, one from a nine-year marriage that ended in 1987, another out of wedlock in 1992. Wright was an inveterate gambler with large debts and had recently been declared bankrupt. He had twice tried to commit suicide, the last attempt in 2000 with an overdose of pills.

RIGHT: Fork-lift truck driver, Steve Wright, was a known user of prostitutes and lived in Ipswich's red light district.

ABOVE: Top row left: Anneli Alderton, 24, was in the early stages of pregnancy when she disappeared on December 3. Top row right: The forensic evidence linking Wright to the murder of Annette Nichols—including tracksuit bottoms, gloves, fluorescent jacket, and samples found in his Ford Mondeo car. Bottom row left: Paula Clennell disappeared shortly after midnight on December 10. She worked as a prostitute to fund her drug addiction. Bottom row right: The body of 25-year-old Gemma Adams was found on December 2, in a river at Hintlesham.

At his trial, which began at Ipswich Crown Court in December 2007, Wright admitted hiring the girls for sex but denied any connection with their deaths. The prosecution produced DNA and fiber evidence that linked him to the victims. In a surprise move, it was also suggested that Wright may not have acted alone, as the remains of one girl was found some distance from the road but with no sign of her body being dragged

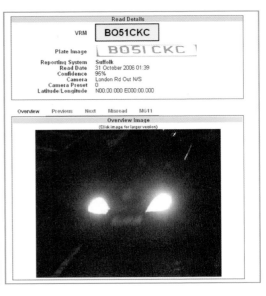

ABOVE: The jury in Steve Wright's trial visit Coddock Mill, Suffolk, where Tania Nicol's body was found.

ABOVE RIGHT: An artist's impression of Steve Wright, appearing at Ipswich Crown Court on January 14, 2008.

RIGHT: Wright's car license plate captured on camera on a road near where one of the bodies was discovered.

there by a single person.

In February 2008, Wright was found guilty of all five murders and was jailed for life, with the recommendation that he should never be considered for parole. Mr Justice Gross told him: 'Drugs and prostitution meant (the girls) were at risk, but neither drugs nor prostitution killed them. You did. You killed them, stripped them and left them... Why you did it may never be known.' The judge added: 'It is right you should spend your whole life in prison. This was a targeted campaign of murder (which entailed) a substantial degree of pre-meditation and planning.'

In view of the judge's wish that he should die behind bars, a suicide watch was put on Wright from the moment he entered Britain's highest security prison, Belmarsh, in southeast London. Meanwhile, police kept open the possibility that the 49-year-old killer may have been involved in other cases, including one of Britain's most notorious unsolved mysteries: the disappearance of estate agent Suzy Lamplugh in 1986. It emerged that Wright knew Miss Lamplugh after they worked together on the *QE2*.

RIGHT: Detective Superintendent Stewart Gull makes a statement to the media following Wright's conviction on February 21, 2008.

Aileen Wuornos

In the end, Aileen Wuornos chose death over Death Row. She effectively volunteered for her own execution. After dropping all appeals and dismissing the lawyers who were pleading her insanity, she petitioned the state for an early execution. She was described as being 'in a good mood' during her last hours. And at 9.47am on October 9, 2002, she got her wish when, at the age of 46, she was pronounced dead by lethal injection in Florida State Prison, near Starke.

Why I Hate Human Life, By The 'Damsel Of Death'

Confessing to seven murders, Wuornos was America's 'first female serial killer'—in the sense that she was the first female ever to fit the FBI profile of that normally exclusively male breed. Given her early upbringing, it would have been a miracle if her life had been anything but disturbed. Aileen was born in a Detroit suburb in 1956 to a mother who had married two years before at the age of 14 and a father she never met because he was in jail for raping a seven-year-old girl. When she was four, she was abandoned by her

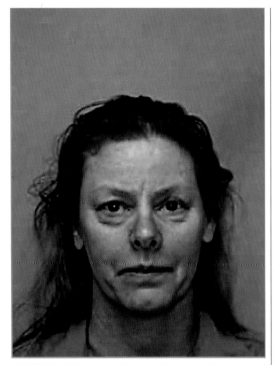

ABOVE: Aileen Wuornos was described by her own defense counsel as being 'the most disturbed individual I have ever represented'.

lesbian relationship with a woman named Tyria Moore, surviving on the proceeds of Wuornos's prostitution.

Wuornos did not embark on her brief killing spree until November 1989, when she packed a pistol in her purse and flagged down a store owner near Daytona Beach. She robbed him and shot him dead. In May 1990, she shot a construction worker who stopped his pickup truck at a roadside near Gainesville. In June, another body turned up, this time near Tampa—naked and with nine bullet holes in it. The same month, a 65-year-old missionary was murdered near Jupiter. In August, a delivery driver was shot twice in the Ocala Forest. In September, a retired police chief was shot seven times and dumped in a vacant lot in Ocala. That same month, a truck driver was found shot through the head near Cross City.

The victims of Wuornos's two-year murder rampage were all middle-aged white men who had made the mistake of picking up the gun-toting hooker on the road. In each murder, Wuornos had followed the same pattern of flagging down men who were driving alone on or near Interstate 75.

Police finally caught up with Wuornos in a biker bar in January 1991. She confessed to the seven murders, claiming the men had tried to rape her and that she had killed them in self-defense. Now tagged the 'Damsel of Death', she was tried at Daytona Beach in January 1992 for only her first murder, of the store owner. Wuornos, who was distraught when her ex-lover Tyria Moore appeared as a witness for the prosecution, nevertheless showed no remorse as she was found guilty, with a jury recommendation for the death penalty. Her counsel afterward described her as 'the most disturbed individual I have represented'.

As other indictments were added, Wuornos told the Florida Supreme Court: 'I'm one who seriously hates human life and would kill again.' However, during her 10 years on Death Row, she became a born-again Christian and said she would welcome paying the ultimate penalty. Despite concerns about the execution of potentially mentally ill prisoners, Florida Governor Jeb Bush finally lifted his stay of execution after three state-appointed psychiatrists concluded that Wuornos was 'lucid and cognisant' and ready to die.

mother and was raised by her grandparents.

She endured a childhood of physical abuse at the hands of her grandfather and of sexual abuse by neighborhood boys. At 14, she was raped and became pregnant. At 15, her grandmother died and her grandfather threw her out of the house, calling her 'a whore'. She gave her son up for adoption at birth and began a life of petty crime and prostitution.

In 1976, Wuornos was picked up while hitch-hiking by a millionaire 50 years her senior and they married soon afterward. When her husband refused to give her money to fund her wild nights on the town, she beat him up. He successfully filed for divorce. Thus, at the age of 20, Aileen Wuornos was back on the road: a drunk, a drifter, a petty thief, and fraudster. She ended up in Florida where she had a longstanding

ABOVE: The hearse carrying Wuornos's body leaves the Florida State Prison following her execution by lethal injection on October 9, 2002.

Graham Young

Even as a schoolboy, Graham Young demonstrated a sinister bent. He developed a passion for poisons, reading up on infamous villains like the wife killer Dr William Palmer (see page 155). Young's father Fred inadvertently encouraged him by buying him a chemistry set.

Danger Signs Ignored Over 'Teacup Poisoner'

Even at the age of 13, Young's comprehensive knowledge of toxicology enabled him to convince a local pharmacist in St Albans, Hertfordshire, that he was 17, and he procured a dangerous quantity of the poisons antimony, digitalis, and arsenic and the heavy metal, thallium, for 'study' purposes. He began carrying a phial of the poison around with him at all times, referring to it as 'my little friend'.

Eager to put his knowledge to the test, his first victim, a school pal, became seriously ill after his sandwiches were laced with antimony but survived. In 1961, his elder sister was found to have been poisoned by belladonna but also survived. The following year, his stepmother was found by her husband writhing in agony in the back garden of their home, with Young looking on in fascination. She died in hospital and her body was cremated. Fred Young was next to suffer attacks of vomiting and excruciating cramps, and he was admitted to hospital where he was diagnosed with antimony poisoning.

It was Young's chemistry teacher who, suspecting his pupil's murderous intent, tipped off the police. Sessions with a police psychiatrist confirmed that he was a serial killer in the making but no murder charges could be brought against him because his stepmother's cremation had destroyed the evidence. Still only 15, he was committed to Broadmoor maximum-security hospital, the youngest inmate since 1885, for a minimum period of 15 years.

Within weeks, a fellow inmate died of poisoning by

ABOVE: John Tilson, one of the surviving victims of serial poisoner Graham Young, outside St Albans Crown Court in June 1972.

ABOVE: Graham Young's fascination with causing pain and death through the administering of poison began in childhood.

cyanide, which Young claimed to have extracted from laurel bush leaves. The killer was not taken seriously and the death was recorded as 'suicide'. Another record on his file shows that in 1970, when recommended for early release, he told a psychiatric nurse that he planned to kill one person for every year he had been in Broadmoor.

Amazingly, he was still freed after nine years' incarceration and obtained a job with a company manufacturing photographic instruments. Within weeks, staff began to be struck down with a mystery disease. Of the 70 people affected, three died in four months. During a company investigation, Young could not resist revealing his knowledge of chemicals and Scotland Yard were contacted.

Young was accused of two murders, two attempted murders and two cases of administering poison.

The case was clear-cut, and a single entry in his diary, relating to the death of one of his work colleagues, would have sealed his fate: 'I have administered a fatal dose of the special compound to F. and anticipate a report on his progress on Monday. I gave him three separate doses.'

He pleaded not guilty, relishing his moment of notoriety in the dock—although he was unhappy that the press had labeled him the 'Teacup Poisoner',

believing that 'World Poisoner' would better fit his infamy. On June 29, 1972, the jury at St Albans Crown Court took less than an hour to find him guilty, and he was given four life sentences. In August 1990, warders at Parkhurst Prison found 42-year-old Young dead of a heart attack on the floor of his cell.

Zodiac Killer

Random and motiveless, they are the most difficult serial murder cases to solve. San Francisco endured a brief reign of terror in 1968 and 1969, during which time a ruthless killer slew five people and wounded two more. The killings were followed by detailed descriptions of the atrocities in letters to newspapers, signed by a cross placed on a circle: the symbol of the Zodiac.

Motiveless Crimes Grip San Francisco

The first murders firmly attributed to the 'Zodiac Killer' were of a student couple, aged 16 and 17, who were shot in a quiet lane near Vallejo, near San Francisco, in December 1968. The pair had apparently been fleeing from their car when gunned down, but there was no obvious motive for the crime.

BELOW: One of the Zodiac Killer's coded messages which contained the hidden script: 'I like killing people'.

LEFT: One of the letters sent to a San Francisco newspaper by the Zodiac Killer, featuring his trademark signature.

ABOVE: Three of the Zodiac's victims. Left to right: cab driver Paul Stine, Cecilia Shepard, and Bryan Hartnell, who survived.
BELOW: Two homicide detectives inspect the clothes of a murder victim at a San Francisco morgue in March 1974.

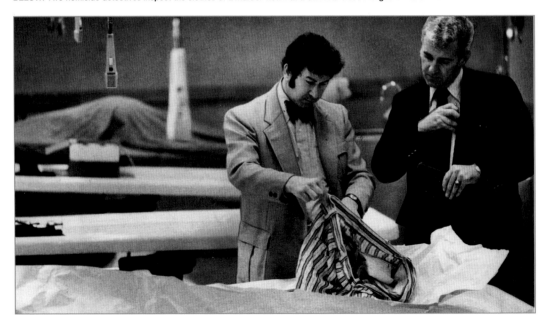

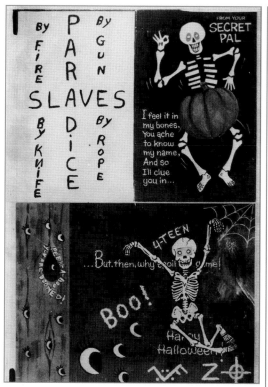

By FIRE
By P
By GUN
A
R
SLAVES
By KNIFE
By D
i
C
E
By ROPE

I feel it in
my bones,
You ache
to know
my name,
And so
I'll clue
you in...

...But then, why spoil the game!

4-TEEN

BOO!

Happy
Halloween!

ABOVE: A card sent by the Zodiac Killer to Paul Avery, a reporter on the San Francisco Chronicle.

A similar double shooting followed the next July. The gunman had driven up alongside a car and opened fire without warning, killing a 22-year-old girl and seriously injuring her 19-year-old boyfriend. Police were alerted to the crime by a call from a man, described as having a 'gruff voice', who boasted: 'I also killed those kids last year.'

Following this attack, three newspapers received coded notes which, when matched and decoded, provided a weird message from 'Zodiac' in which he said, 'I like killing people' and added that 'when I die I will be reborn in paradise and those I have killed will become my slaves'.

'Zodiac' fell silent again until September 1969 when the gruff voice at the end of the phone line directed police to the shore of Lake Berryessa, in the Napa Valley, where two students, a girl of 22 and her boyfriend aged 20, had been killed in a frenzied attack. The assailant had daubed the zodiac sign on the side of the couple's white car, along with the dates of the previous murders. The girl, who had been stabbed with a foot-long bayonet 24 times, died in hospital two days later; her boyfriend, with bayonet wounds in the back, survived. He described the attacker as wearing a black hood with slits for his mouth and eyes.

'Zodiac' moved onto the streets of San Francisco itself to strike again two weeks later, shooting a

ABOVE: Police arrest Heriberto Seda, a copycat killer from 1990. Seda planned to kill one person from each of the 12 astrological signs.

29-year-old student and part-time taxi driver as he sat in a cab. The gunman, described by witnesses as short, in his 40s, with thick horn-rimmed glasses and crew-cut brown hair, fled into side-streets pursued by two patrolmen and escaped in the wooded military reservation known as The Presidio. The shooting was followed by letters to newspapers, this time enclosing a shred of bloodstained shirt torn from the victim—and claiming, not the five slayings attributed to him, but eight murders so far.

The 'Zodiac Killer' next struck in March 1970 when a 23-year-old woman was traveling toward Petaluma, northwest of San Francisco, when another driver flagged her down, told her that one of her rear wheels was wobbling and offered her a ride. Once in his car, he warned her: 'You know you're going to die—you know I'm going to kill you.' As he slowed, she leapt out and flagged down another car. Her description exactly fitted the taxi driver's killer.

Again, 'Zodiac' wrote to newspapers, acknowledging the kidnap attempt and upping his claimed victims to 37. The last letter was sent in April 1974. Since then, nothing…and the identity of the 'Zodiac Killer' has remained one of the greatest unsolved mysteries of modern crime.

Hans Van Zom

Hans Van Zon was a wastrel, a fantasist, a liar, and a cheat. But he had one asset that compensated for these deficiencies: he was absolutely charming. It won him admirers and lovers among both men and women, some of whom paid for this trust with their lives.

Fantasist Who Couldn't Take Failure

Johannes Marinus (Hans) van Zon was born of working-class parents in Utrecht, Holland, in April 1942. He was intelligent but there was no cash to advance his education and, at the age of 16, he turned to crime, first as a minor confidence trickster, then as a burglar.

Van Zon realized that he had homosexual tendencies but tried to hide them. In 1964 he dated Elly Hager-Segor but, after his first failed attempt at lovemaking, she called off the affair. Spurned, he strangled her before slitting her throat with a bread knife. His next love affair was with a homosexual movie director, Claude Berkeley, whom he met in Amsterdam in 1965. That relationship also failed and the man was similarly dispatched by his lover.

Shortly after the slaying, Van Zon married a chambermaid, Italian-born Caroline Gigli, 47, who supported both of them on her meager wages. After an attempt to kill her, his wife went to the police, who put him in jail for a month. But it was not his wife who was to be his next victim; Van Zon was keeping a 37-year-old mistress, Coby van der Voort—and was making money on the side by selling pornographic photographs of both his wife and girlfriend.

When Coby tried to end their affair in April 1967, Van Zon fed her barbiturates, pretending they were aphrodisiac pills, before smashing her skull with a lead pipe and finishing her off by slashing her throat with the familiar bread knife. He tried to fool police by making the murder look like a bungled burglary, stealing items of Coby's jewelry and handing them to Caroline.

Van Zon was now living in a total fantasy world. He claimed to be, variously, a fashion designer, private detective, movie star business tycoon, and a CIA spy. He could not help boasting about his killings to an ex-convict, Arnoldus Rietbergen, nicknamed 'Old Nol', who used the information to 'persuade' Van Zon to commit other murders for profit. Those known about are the death of a girl in May 1967 and of a farmer that same August.

Van Zon and Rietbergen were caught in December when blows from the lead piping failed to kill their final victim, an elderly lady. In March 1970, a Utrecht court sentenced Van Zon to life, with a minimum of 20 years, and his accomplice to seven years.

Anna Zwanziger

Poor Anna Schoenleben, born in Nuremberg, Germany, in 1760, did not have much going for her. A contemporary report described her as 'ugly, stunted, without attraction of face, figure, speech; a misshapen woman whom some people likened to a toad'. It would seem that she was lucky to have ever found a husband, but the marriage ended in misery. Herr Zwanziger, a successful lawyer, was a violent bully who spent her inheritance on drink.

Poisonous 'Toad' Dies By The Sword

Anna was forced into prostitution to support herself and two children, although she insisted to her friends that she only ever slept with 'gentlemen'. Upon the death of her husband through alcoholism, she advertised herself as a housekeeper and cook to the Bavarian judiciary and, from their elevated ranks, set about finding a new husband.

There was one flaw in her plan: each of the judges she went to work for was already married or engaged. Anna's solution was simple; she set about ridding herself of all rivals to her affections by poisoning two of the women, along with one of the judges, his guests, several servants, and a baby.

The widow's first potential husband was a judge named Glaser who, although separated, was still married. Anna engineered a reconciliation between the couple and, once the wife had returned to the marital home, fed her arsenic in her tea until she died. In the process, Anna also poisoned several of the judge's guests, although they survived.

Her next victim was another judge, named Grohmann, whom Anna killed when she discovered that he had wedding plans which did not involve her.

He died an agonizing death after being served a bowl of soup. Anna also put arsenic in the drink of three servants who had upset her, although they survived.

Her third employer, Judge Gebhard, refused to believe his sickly wife's claims that food tasted strange since the arrival of their new housekeeper. It was only when he himself found a white sediment in his brandy glass that he became suspicious. It was too late. His wife died in convulsions. So did their baby after Anna fed the infant a biscuit dipped in arsenic-laced milk. Again, the servants were also poisoned but survived. Judge Gebhard had their food analyzed and traces of arsenic were found. By now, Anna had fled—but not before lacing every salt and sugar shaker in the house with arsenic.

Anna Zwanziger was arrested in October 1809 after police exhumed her victims' bodies and discovered traces of the poison. The poisoner had foolishly led them to her by writing letters to the Gebhard family asking if she could have her old job back. She eventually confessed, admitting: 'Yes, I killed them all and would have killed more if I had the chance.' She referred to arsenic as 'my truest friend' and said she 'trembled with pleasure' when handling it.

Before being beheaded by the sword in July 1811, she told her prison warders: 'It is perhaps better for the community that I should die, as it would be impossible for me to give up the practice of poisoning people.'

Picture Credits

To Katie, Leonie and Mike
Who, in the interests of research, braved more gore and guts than any homicide detective would experience in a lifetime. My sincere thanks to them.